MW01036054

BLACK WOMEN AND ENERGIES OF RESISTANCE IN NINETEENTH-CENTURY HAITIAN AND AMERICAN LITERATURE

Black Women and Energies of Resistance in Nineteenth-Century Haitian and American Literature intervenes in traditional narratives of nineteenth-century American modernity by situating Black women at the center of an increasingly connected world. While traditional accounts of modernity have emphasized advancements in communication technologies, animal and fossil fuel extraction, and the rise of urban centers, Mary Grace Albanese proposes that women of African descent combated these often violent regimes through diasporic spiritual beliefs and practices, including spiritual possession, rootwork, midwifery, mesmerism, prophecy, and wandering. It shows how these energetic acts of resistance were carried out on scales large and small: from the constrained corners of the garden plot to the expansive circuits of global migration. By unyoking the concept of energy from narratives of technological progress, capital accrual, and global expansion, this book uncovers new stories that center Black women at the heart of a pulsating, revolutionary world.

MARY GRACE ALBANESE is Associate Professor of English at SUNY Binghamton. She was a 2019–20 Fellow at the Cornell Society for the Humanities and received her PhD from Columbia University in 2017.

CAMBRIDGE STUDIES IN AMERICAN LITERATURE AND CULTURE

Recent books in this series

193. MARY GRACE ALBANESE
Black Women and Energies of Resistance in Nineteenth-Century Haitian and American Literature
192. JUSTIN PARKS
Poetry and the Limits of Modernity in Depression America
191. OWEN CLAYTON
Vagabonds, Tramps, and Hobos: The Literature and Culture of U.S. Transiency 1890–1940
190. JOLENE HUBBS
Class, Whiteness, and Southern Literature
189. RYAN M. BROOKS
Liberalism and American Literature in the Clinton Era
188. JULIANA CHOW
Nineteenth-Century American Literature and the Discourse of Natural History
187. JESSICA E. TEAGUE
Sound Recording Technology and American Literature
186. BRYAN M. SANTIN
Postwar American Fiction and the Rise of Modern Conservatism: A Literary History, 1945–2008

(*Continued after the Index*)

BLACK WOMEN AND ENERGIES OF RESISTANCE IN NINETEENTH-CENTURY HAITIAN AND AMERICAN LITERATURE

MARY GRACE ALBANESE

SUNY Binghamton

Shaftesbury Road, Cambridge CB2 8EA, United Kingdom

One Liberty Plaza, 20th Floor, New York, NY 10006, USA

477 Williamstown Road, Port Melbourne, VIC 3207, Australia

314–321, 3rd Floor, Plot 3, Splendor Forum, Jasola District Centre, New Delhi – 110025, India

103 Penang Road, #05-06/07, Visioncrest Commercial, Singapore 238467

Cambridge University Press is part of Cambridge University Press & Assessment, a department of the University of Cambridge.

We share the University's mission to contribute to society through the pursuit of education, learning and research at the highest international levels of excellence.

www.cambridge.org
Information on this title: www.cambridge.org/9781009314244

DOI: 10.1017/9781009314268

First published 2024

A catalogue record for this publication is available from the British Library.

Library of Congress Cataloging-in-Publication Data
NAMES: Albanese, Mary Grace, 1986– author.
TITLE: Black women and energies of resistance in nineteenth-century Haitian and American literature / Mary Grace Albanese.
DESCRIPTION: Cambridge, United Kingdom ; New York, NY : Cambridge University Press, 2023. | Series: Cambridge studies in American literature and culture | Includes bibliographical references and index.
IDENTIFIERS: LCCN 2023019024 (print) | LCCN 2023019025 (ebook) | ISBN 9781009314244 (hardback) | ISBN 9781009314213 (paperback) | ISBN 9781009314268 (epub)
SUBJECTS: LCSH: American literature–Black authors–History and criticism. | American literature–Women authors–History and criticism. | American literature–Haitian American authors–History and criticism. | American literature–19th century–History and criticism. | Force and energy in literature. | Women, Black, in literature. | Spirituality in literature. | LCGFT: Literary criticism.
CLASSIFICATION: LCC PS153.B53 A43 2023 (print) | LCC PS153.B53 (ebook) | DDC 810.9/928708996–dc23/eng/20230712
LC record available at https://lccn.loc.gov/2023019024
LC ebook record available at https://lccn.loc.gov/2023019025

ISBN 978-1-009-31424-4 Hardback

Contents

Figures

Acknowledgments

This book has been nourished by the support and labor of so many people. First, I extend my deepest gratitude to my dissertation advisors: Branka Arsić, Brent Edwards, and Saidiya Hartman. Their support and intellectual generosity saw this project through many different guises. I am thankful for their brilliant feedback, productive dialogue, and consistent mentorship over the years. I would also like to extend my thanks to Ross Posnock, Kaiama Glover, and Cristobal Silva, who served as generous mentors and interlocutors at early stages of this project.

At Cambridge University Press, I would like to thank my editor Leonard Cassuto for his thoughtful engagement and early support. I am also deeply thankful to Ray Ryan, Edgar Mendez, Hemalatha Subramanian, and Liz Davey for their help shaping this book into what you are now reading. Finally, I thank the anonymous readers at Cambridge University Press, whose rigorous feedback has been invaluable. I am also grateful to Betsey Duquette, Stacey Margolis, Johanna Heloise Abtahi and the anonymous readers at *J19* and *ESQ*.

At SUNY Binghamton, I would like to thank my colleagues, especially Tina Chang, Praseeda Gopinath, Libby Tucker, Lisa Yun, John Havard, Surya Parekh, Jessie Reeder, John Kuhn, David Sterling Brown, Joseph Keith, Susan Strehle, Warren Harding, Jean-Pierre Mileur, and Monika Mehta. Thanks to Donna Berg, Colleen Burke and Toni Roberts, for keeping us all afloat. I would like to extend particular gratitude to Thomas Glave, Ali Moore, Birgit Brander Rasmussen, Jenny Stoever, and Carole Boyce Davies who provided robust and brilliant commentary on the full manuscript. Their encouragement and support helped my thinking enormously and I am profoundly indebted to them. Thanks also to Pap Ndiaye and Emmanuelle Loyer who hosted me as a doctoral student at the Centre d'Histoire, Sciences Po and provided thoughtful feedback on early versions of this book.

I am grateful to the intellectual community at the Cornell Society for the Humanities. I thank my colleagues Yu-Fang Cho, Willie Hiatt, Dana

Powell, Ariel Ron, Catherine Appert, Lori Khatchadourian, Athena Kirk, Rachel Prentice, James Redfield, Alexandra Delferro, Samantha Wesner, Hannah LeBlanc, Jon Ander Mendia, Joan Lubin, Amy Chun Kim, and Paul Fleming, as well as the incredibly supportive staff: Kina Viola, Tyler Lurie-Spicer, and Emily Parsons. Much love in particular to Alena Williams and Erin Soros for their friendship, phone calls, and company on long hilly walks. I am deeply grateful to friends, colleagues, and neighbors at Cornell who helped connect me to the Ithaca community, especially Durba Ghosh, Masha Raskolnikov, Mukoma Wa Ngugi, Emily Fridlund, and Nick Admussen. And extra thanks to Shirley Samuels and other members of the New York Humanities Corridor for fostering a stimulating intellectual community upstate.

I am indebted to audiences at the Warren Center at Harvard University, Université Paris Diderot VII, the McNeil Center for Early American Studies at the University of Pennsylvania, the Columbia University Faculty House, Sciences Po, SUNY Albany, Rice University, the Futures Institute at Dartmouth (especially Elizabeth Maddock Dillon and Duncan Faherty), and the French Colonial Historical Society. This book benefited from the financial support of the Georges Lurcy Charitable and Educational Trust, the Alliance Fellowship, the Partnership for Doctoral Mobility, Cornell University's Society for the Humanities, the Center for Civic Engagement, the Citizenship, Rights and Cultural Belonging Transdisciplinary Area of Excellence Working Group, and the New York Council for the Humanities. I gratefully acknowledge the financial assistance provided for this publication through donors to the Harpur College Advocacy Council Faculty Development Endowment – an endowed fund that invests in the research, creative activities, and professional development of Harpur College of Arts and Sciences faculty at Binghamton University.

This book would have been impossible without the expertise of the staff at the Bibliothèque nationale d'Haïti, the Bibliothèque nationale de France, the Archives nationales d'outre-mer, the Digital Library of the Caribbean, the John Carter Brown Library, the Louisiana Historical Center, the Historic New Orleans Center, the New Orleans Public Library, the Ulster County Historical Society, the Nantucket Historical Association, the Delpher Open Newspaper Archive, and the Dutch Nationaal Archief. Extra thanks to Martijn Buijs, for his help translating from the Dutch, and my extraordinary TAs and students, including Maddie Gottlieb, Debarati Roy, Khadijah Boxill, Suzanne Richardson, Jenn Powers, Kayla Hardy-Butler, Shruti Jain, Patrick Saint Ange, Juliette

Schmidt, Samantha Pascal, Kelsey Jennings-Roggensack, and Celine Dorsainvil.

Shirley Bruno's work has been an enormous inspiration: thank you for your time, conversation, and intellectual generosity. I also would like to thank Grace Lynne Haynes for generously allowing us to reprint her Sojourner Truth mural in Newark. If you find yourself in Jersey, go check it out! Finally, I owe an enormous debt to André Eugène and Romel Jean Pierre, who provided the cover image – a sculpture of the lwa Ezili Dantò – for this book, as well as Leah Gordon.

This project benefited from critique and feedback from many friends and colleagues who read drafts, shared books, participated in accountability groups, or simply provided friendship and conversation: Wes Alcenat, Wendy Muñiz, Cristina Pérez Jiménez, Omaris Zamora, Sarah Quesada, Ana Schwartz, Clare Callahan, Dominique Jean-Louis, Michael Jonik, Don James McLaughlin, Nicole Hassoun, Claudel Casseus, Amelia Spooner, Hannah Shaw, Robbie Kubala, Evan Jewell, Bridget Behrmann, Sean Mark, Beatrice Volonté, Eva Dell'Armi, Vittorio Parisi, Antonin Camarassa, Michael Wookey, Haroun Hayward, Izaak Hayward, Jordan Londe, Caroline Hayes, and Andy Crow. Extra love to Emma Bérat for her wisdom, warmth, and tolerance for messages sent at 3 A.M., as well as Vesna Kuiken, whose brilliance is only matched by her generosity.

I have had the good fortune to collaborate with multiple communities, who have – in indirect but profound ways – influenced this project. I am especially grateful to the staff at the Advocacy Center of Ithaca and the Ithaca Doulas collective, especially Kate Dimpfl. I am also grateful to Tsedale Forbes, Kathleen Shohfi and Chiara Miller-Out for providing the rare and exceedingly valuable gift of childcare in a global pandemic.

I now turn to family: thanks to my aunt and uncle Sara and Michael Chaney for their early encouragement and ongoing support. To Mary, Faith, Zia, Dan, Ennio, and my grandmothers Sara and Maria, as well as the memory of my grandfathers. To Lance and especially Raffat, whose grace can be found in every page of this book. I began writing under your roof and will always be thankful for your wisdom, generosity, and unconditional acceptance. Thanks also to my parents, my brother, and especially to my sister, Katie. Finally, Greg for his love, his brilliant mind, and his steadfast support: you are my favorite interlocutor, my heart, and my home. And Aster, my little star: you kicked your way through the writing of a good deal of this book and, in that way (as well as so many others) can take some credit for its final shape.

Introduction
Modulating Modernity

In July 2019, in the midst of a record-breaking heat wave, Brooklyn went dark. In 90-degree temperatures, over 55,000 customers in Canarsie, Flatlands, Mill Basin, Bergen Beach, and Georgetown lost electricity in one of the largest power outages in New York's history. Con Edison, the city's power company, admitted that it deliberately disconnected these neighborhoods in order to prevent a widespread loss of power that would affect wealthier, whiter areas of the city. Although Black neighborhoods earn the highest scores in New York City's heat vulnerability index (a ranking system that takes into account the proportion of green space to developed space, access to air conditioning, and the percentage of people living below poverty levels), they are the first on the line when the city's infrastructure fails.[1] What the index does not take into account, however, are the social and political risks to which these neighborhoods are also exposed during a blackout. After the lights went out, 200 police officers flooded Brooklyn, with the nebulous mandate to preserve order. A week earlier, the US Department of Justice had announced that it would not press charges against Daniel Pantaleo, the white police officer who killed Eric Garner on Staten Island in 2014. Now law enforcement roamed the streets of Canarsie, policing Black children for splashing water in 90-degree heat.

Some residents in the affected areas may have found these conditions familiar: outside of Florida, Brooklyn is home to the largest community of Haitian Americans in the United States. As in the United States, power outages in Haiti are as much a sign of mechanical failure as they are of political failure. Due to an electric grid weakened by natural disasters, an overdependence on fossil fuels, and predatory international markets, Haiti often experiences blackouts. In 2018, Haiti's energy vulnerability was exacerbated by the collapse of Petrocaribe, the Venezuelan aid program

[1] Bao, Li, and Yu, "The Construction and Validation of the Heat Vulnerability Index, a Review."

which had once provided heavily subsidized oil to Central America and the Caribbean. The results of Petrocaribe's withdrawal from the area have been catastrophic: only 25 percent of the population in Haiti has access to electricity, and those that do frequently experience power outages. As the gas shortage worsened, hospitals, businesses, and schools closed; public transportation halted; and Haitians took to the streets to demand government accountability. The July 2021 assassination of President Jovenel Moïse, accused of misappropriating over two billion dollars in Petrocaribe funds, has only exacerbated the crisis.

But the Petrocaribe scandal also reaches into a deeper history of power outages in Haiti, what is called in Kreyòl *blakawout*. As Greg Beckett has argued, the *blakawout* is a loss not just of electric but of *political* power.[2] Darkness limns the contours of state violence and foreign intervention, most notably during the US-backed Duvalier regimes. During the *blakawouts* of the 1960s and 1970s, the paramilitary (known as the Tonton Macoutes) cut power to certain neighborhoods before conducting raids. Under the cover of darkness, the Tonton Macoutes carried out massacres, sexual assaults, and targeted assassinations on a vast scale. As Jean-Frantz Gation recalls in his childhood memoir of growing up in Port-au-Prince: "During the presidency of François Duvalier, the black-out every night was one of those inconveniences which one had to expect . . . the dictator kept Port-au-Prince in the dark in order to give his death troops free rein."[3]

The interconnected history of US imperialism, state violence, and the politics of energy emphasizes how the *blakawout* spreads far beyond the electric grid. Those diasporic Haitians who, in 2019, experienced the Brooklyn blackout understood all too well the power relationship between energy and violence. Yet, the *blakawout* can also be a condition for community formation. Edwidge Danticat, for example, recalls the blackouts of her childhood:

> I was born under Haiti's dictatorial Duvalier regime. When I was four, my parents left Haiti to seek a better life in the United States. I must admit that their motives were more economic that political. But as anyone who knows Haiti will tell you, economics and politics are very intrinsically related in Haiti. Who is in power determines to a great extent whether or not people will eat . . . My most vivid memories of Haiti involve incidents that represent the general situation there. In Haiti, there are a lot of "blackouts,"

[2] Beckett, *There Is No More Haiti.*

[3] Gation, *Un pays Oublié*. The original reads: "Au cours de la présidence de François Duvalier, le black-out de chaque nuit était l'un des inconvénients auquel il fallait s'y attendre... le dictateur maintenait Port-au-Prince dans le noir afin de donner toute liberté à ses escadrons de la mort," 68.

> sudden power failures. At those times, you can't read or study or watch TV, so you sit around a candle and listen to stories from the elders in the house.[4]

Danticat's recollection of her childhood counterpoises the abuses of state power against intergenerational community building. Listening to stories from her elders, she converts the manipulated and misappropriated energies of the Duvalier regime into a space of collective memory-making and historical transmission. The darkness, she implies, does not efface the lives and experiences of those without power. Instead, she looks to other forms of power that emerge when she and her family "sit around a candle and listen to stories from the elders in the house." This power enables the transmission of kinship, ancestral knowledge, and community history through human – not electrical – conduits.

The 2019 blackouts in Brooklyn and Haiti, two darkened nodes in a diasporic network, point toward the mutual constitution of energy and state violence under conditions of precarious life. Yet, as we saw in Danticat's memoir, they *also* point toward somewhere unexpectedly subversive. This subversion can be traced on scales both small and large, domestic and transhistorical. In that respect, it is important to recall that the 2019 blackouts occurred just two weeks before the anniversary of Bwa Kayiman, the Vodou ceremony which purportedly launched the Haitian Revolution. Since 1996, Brooklyn's Haitian population has commemorated Bwa Kayiman each August at the southeastern lakeside in Prospect Park. Celebrants engage in dance and drumming; they sing and share stories, and they ignore the police, who often surveil the proceedings. Although accounts of the ceremony differ, most Haitians agree on the general contours of the story: one night, in August 1791, a group of enslaved people secretly gathered in the darkness near Le Cap. The group engaged in a mutual possession by the lwa or god Ezili Dantò and planned a revolt of the Northern Plain, sparking the thirteen-year struggle which would culminate in Haitian independence. The annual Brooklyn celebration of Bwa Kayiman speaks to the communal strength of diasporic memory and the power of intergenerational relationality on scales both hemispheric and local. But when framed against the 2019 blackouts, it tells another story of energy, too. Although power has been used and abused in Haiti and the United States in order to monitor, manipulate, and exploit Black life, Bwa Kayman reminds us that energy moves at other frequencies and vibrations.

[4] Danticat, "We Are Ugly But We Are Here."

In its simplest iteration, Bwa Kayiman is the story of a *blakawout*: the obfuscatory conditions of darkness turned against the violence of plantation economies and instead directed toward emancipatory political ends. Bwa Kayiman is therefore an energy story and, moreover, a particularly *gendered* energy story. It is the tale of a Vodou possession in which enslaved Haitians channeled the energy of the female lwa Ezili Dantò, sparking a divine charge across a network of interconnected revolutionary fighters. While masculinist figures of the Haitian Revolution such as Toussaint Louverture have come to emblematize twentieth-century celebrations of Atlantic modernity, these romantic notions of male heroes obscure a wider network of people who lived, fought, and conducted cultural and spiritual power in Haiti.[5] Critics such as Jasmine Claude-Narcisse, Marlene Daut, Omise'eke Natasha Tinsley, Colin Dayan, Arlette Gautier, and Nicole Willson have excavated these networks, which include the histories of female soldiers who dressed as men, revolutionary men who dressed as women (such as Romaine-la-Prophétesse, the military leader who claimed to be the nephew of the Virgin Mary, dressed as a woman, and claimed the name "Prophetess"), and the Vodou pantheon, which includes lwa (imperfectly translated as gods or spirits) who were believed to have inspired the revolution. And more broadly, this network includes the stories of unnamed people in Haiti who channeled spiritual and folk power in the Black Americas, including the cultivation and dissemination of plants, the circuitous labors of birthwork, the eccentric circuits of marronage, and the future-oriented conduits of prophecy.

Bwa Kayiman illustrates a history very different from the raids of Duvalier, the Petrocaribe scandal, or the violence of the NYPD. It draws attention away from natural gas, electric grids, and hydroelectric generators and instead toward alternative energy systems sustained by social and spiritual connections. I open this book with a triangulation of the blackouts in Brooklyn, the Petrocaribe scandal in Haiti, and the Black feminist history of the Haitian Revolution because this triad collectively decenters familiar narratives of power, energy, gender, and modernity. Without underestimating the very real challenges the contemporary fuel crisis presents to Black civic and social life throughout the diaspora, this book asks what can energy tell us – and not tell us – about the rise of modernity? What energy systems exist outside familiar narratives of industrial

[5] On the masculinist iconographies of the Haitian Revolution, see Bernier, *Characters of Blood*; Clavin, *Toussaint Louverture and the American Civil War*; Pierrot, *The Black Avenger in Atlantic Culture*; Scott, *Conscripts of Modernity*; Wilder, *Freedom Time*.

development and the dehumanization of human capital? What is lost when critics reduce the history of energy to a narrative arc of development, consumption, and quantifiable power? And what happens when we attune ourselves to the vibrations of other forms of energy that exceed the electric grid? In asking these questions, I follow Gina Athena Ulysse's injunction to forge "new narratives" for Haiti, a country which has been "rhetorically and symbolically incarcerated" by centuries of misrepresentation by global northern powers.[6] In looking past the clichéd prison-house of developmentalist narrative, other energy stories emerge, stories which pulse with divine, prophetic, and collective power. Taking these practices as a point of departure, this book argues that Black political and spiritual life has long theorized and practiced energy not as an extractable commodity coerced from human stockpiles but instead as a force through which to reclaim one's own body, organize political labor, and work toward emancipatory political futures.

Although the revolutionary nature of Black politics and spirituality have been extensively researched, fewer studies have situated these practices within a broader history of energy. This is understandable, given the relative novelty of what are now called the energy humanities.[7] In a groundbreaking special issue of *PMLA*, Patricia Yaeger first coupled energy consumption with literary production, arguing that "energy is already embedded in older and stranger histories than our own." By recalibrating literary periodization around different modes of energy production, including tallow, wood, coal, oil, and human labor, Yaeger emphasized the co-constitutive roles of the human and nonhuman in cultural understandings of modernity. The body of scholarship inaugurated by Yaeger has developed over the past decade, drawing from literary study, political science, anthropology, history, sociology, and climate science. Anthologies such as Imre Szeman and Dominic Boyer's *Energy Humanities* and Sheena Wilson, Adam Carlson, and Szeman's *Petrocultures* have helped to institutionalize the energy humanities as an academic subfield, while recent monographs from literary scholars, historians, and political scientists have expanded the remit of the energy humanities to include a wide range of

[6] Ulysse, *Why Haiti Needs New Narratives*, xii.

[7] Yaeger, "Editor's Column." On the the coinage of the term "energy humanities," see Szeman and Boyer, *Energy Humanities*, 326. Further reading includes Barnett and Worden, *Oil Culture*; Boyer, *Energopolitics;* Diamanti and Bellamy, "Energy Humanities"; Ghosh, *The Great Derangement*; Hughes, *Energy without Conscience*; Johnson, *Carbon Nation;* LeMenager, *Living Oil*; Mitchell, *Carbon Democracy;* Schneider-Mayerson, *Peak Oil*; Wenzel and Yaeger, *Fueling Culture;* Wilson, Carlson, and Szeman, *Petrocultures.*

methodological approaches. In many ways, the development of the energy humanities has been extremely timely; it has given a central place to environmental and energy justice in both scholarship and pedagogy; it has called for unique collaborative methodologies, with its injunction, in the words of Dipesh Chakrabarty, to "rise above ... disciplinary prejudices"; and it has even provided a framework for scholars such as Jennifer Wenzel to critique the cult of productivity in academia.[8]

And yet, as scholars have increasingly attended to the concept of energy in order to address the consequences of extraction, consumption, climate crisis, and the capitolocene/anthropocene, many have reproduced developmentalist narratives of energy that remain limited to capitalist ideologies of fossil fuel. Such limitations are in part due to energy's naturalization in wealthy global northern lifestyles, rendering it, in Jamie L. Jones's words, "both everywhere and hard to see."[9] This outsized interest in fossil fuels and global northern narratives of development overlook different strategies of living with, through, and against energy currents that cannot necessarily be channeled into the conduits of modern capitalist production.[10] While fossil fuels are certainly important in understanding contemporary energy infrastructures, climate crisis, and anthropogenic violence, they have also yoked the energy humanities to narratives of capitalist consumption which, as Shouhei Tanaka has argued, "enact the material conditions of dispossession, precarity, and violence for racialized bodies that in turn sustain the energy freedoms and uses of contemporary life for others."[11] Indeed, studies in the energy humanities often universalize these privileged others into a nebulously defined third-person plural. Consider, for example, Dominic Boyer and Imre Szeman's argument in their introduction to the recent *Energy Humanities: An Anthology*: "We are citizens and subjects of fossil fuels through and through, whether we know it or not."[12]

Yet, I would like to put pressure on how Szeman and Boyer construct this collective form of belonging. Who, after all, is this "we" with seemingly unfettered (or at least naturalized) access to energy sources, who "takes for granted" their right to consume and enjoy the fruits of the "modern"? Citizenship is, after all, commonly defined as a set of exclusionary practices, and so I would like to ask: what stories are abandoned at

8 Chakrabarty, "The Climate of History," 215; Wenzel, "Taking Stock of Energy Humanities," 31.
9 Jones, "Beyond Oil," 156.
10 On the over-insistence on petrol in the energy humanities, see Jones, "Petromyopia."
11 Tanaka, "Fossil Fuel Fiction and the Geologies of Race," 37.
12 Boyer and Szeman, *Energy Humanities*, 1.

the borders of this global state of fossil fuels? In asking this question, *Energies of Resistance* not only complicates the notion of citizenship as an analytic category but also turns its attention away from carbon-intensive practices which have come to overdetermine the energy humanities. I here take my cues from Cara New Dagget, who argues, "there are other ways of knowing and living energy ... other energy epistemologies, ways of knowing and living with fuel."[13] Following Dagget – as well as calls by scholars, activists, and artists including Kent Linthicum, Mikaela Relford, Julia C. Johnson, and the Black Quantum Futurism Collective, especially Rasheedah Phillips – I argue that traditional epistemologies of energy foreclose other relationships humans have developed with energy sources.[14] Specifically, such epistemologies exclude energy practices traditionally gendered as feminine (including rootwork, spiritual practices, birthwork, and carework), thus eliding the role of Black women and gender-variant people in the rise of modernity.

This elision leads to my project's second contribution to the energy humanities. While studies of modern energy often center on cis-men, this book emphasizes the importance of Black diasporic women and gender-variant people within eighteenth- and nineteenth-century Haiti and the US. These revolutionary subjects served as conduits and conductors of collective power, including spiritual, plant, magnetic, electrical, and kinetic energy. While these energy practices were embraced by people of all gender identities (perhaps most famously, François Makandal, the *houngan*, botanist, and insurgent against French colonists), they were traditionally gendered as feminine. Cis-sexist and racist understandings of modern energy typically dismiss such practices as folkish. Yet, as Black feminist scholars – including Jennifer Morgan, Hazel Carby, Carole Boyce Davies, and Saidiya Hartman – have reminded us, the erasure of women from modernity impoverishes our understanding of Black diasporic cultures.[15]

[13] Dagget, *The Birth of Energy,* 11–12. Although I find Dagget's post-work critique of energy extremely compelling, I will use the term "labor" somewhat differently in this book. Unlike Dagget, who is primarily interested in the work ethic of Victorian Britain (defined in her project as an ideology shaped by "employment, wages, and productivity"), this project understands labor more capaciously, as a practice that can be erotic, (re)productive, non-productive, spiritual, non-quantifiable, and non-exchangeable, a form of living that exceeds the expectations of the market and resists alienation. I am committed to the notion of labor as a form of energy, albeit one that troubles the industrial demands of global northern markets, and can also include forms of labor such as community building, worship, self care, and even (somewhat paradoxically) pleasure.

[14] Drew and Worthem, *Black Futures*; Linthicum, Relford, and Johnson, "Defining Energy," esp. 372–390; Phillips, *Black Quantum Futurism*, and *Space-Time Collapse II.*

[15] Boyce Davies, *Left of Karl Marx,* "Sisters Outside"; Carby, *Reconstructing Womanhood, Race Men;* Hartman, "The Belly of the World"; Morgan, *Laboring Women.*

Drawing from Audre Lorde, Boyce Davies deploys the "'sisters outside'" framework to call for the inclusion of women and especially Black women of the Caribbean in genealogies of Black radicalism, arguing that "Black women have become sisters outside the Black radical intellectual tradition; Caribbean women, sisters outside the Caribbean radical tradition and US African American civil rights discourse and sisters outside Pan-Africanist discourse."[16] This "sisters outside" methodology calls attention to the radically modern labor of women in the US and the Caribbean, pointing toward energetic practices seldom incorporated into the Black radical tradition or studies of modernity. Following Boyce Davies, this book asks what it would mean to place diasporic women in a Black radical tradition and how might their inclusion change the contours of critical conversations around energy? What would it mean to think of practices often dismissed as feminine, queer, or "primitive" as modern forms of energy? How can scholars denaturalize national boundaries so that one might see a Haitian Revolutionary warrior, such as Marie Jeanne Lamartinière, fighting alongside the Black women of 1820s New York print culture? Or to read the wandering energy of Sojourner Truth within a lineage of Black female maroons throughout the Americas? Or to understand Pauline Hopkins as a chronicler of not only US Reconstruction but also the revolutionary Caribbean?

In asking these questions, this book forges a place for people of African descent within both the energy humanities and theories of modernity. This book also includes figures in the United States not generally taken to be part of a Haitian Revolutionary tradition but who were deeply shaped by the energetic practices of Afro-Caribbean resistance. Finally, this project takes into account many nameless figures: the gardeners, nurses, hairdressers, cooks, midwives, and priestesses who channeled diasporic energy throughout the Americas in unique and subversive ways. Through these "silenced" – to invoke Michel-Rolph Trouillot's famous paradigm – genealogies, this book traces routes of power, which spread beyond the Haitian Revolution and illuminated the map of what we might now consider the modern Americas. While traditional accounts of energy have emphasized a limited understanding of modernity – one which reduces the modern to advancements in communication technologies, animal and fossil fuel extraction, and the rise of urban centers – I argue that people of African descent combated these violent regimes through an energetic counterdiscourse that centered survival, love, and care.

[16] Boyce Davies, "Sisters Outside," 218.

A historicized and multilingual understanding of "energy" will help to scaffold this counterdiscourse. In physics, "energy" and "power" are two distinct but interrelated concepts: while power is defined as the time rate of doing work, energy is the *capacity* of doing work or making change happen from one entity to another. In the context of social or political philosophy, power may be defined as the ideological structures which make possible (or impossible) the conditions for political change; disciplinary techniques in the service of producing compliant subjects; and strategies of management, punishment, and subjugation usually understood along the axes of class, gender, or racial/ethnic exploitation. This book revises more familiar Marxist or Foucauldian understandings of power as a disciplinary formation by instead restoring the conceptualization of power to the domain of energy. Etymologically, "energy" derives from the Greek ἐνέργεια or *enérgeia* to signify activity or labor but also supernatural and/or cosmic forces. For Aristotle, activity (*enérgeia*) is defined by its potentiality (*dunamis*). Energy is thus not merely an entity's power to produce a change but rather its *potential* or *capacity* to be in an alternate state. In Haitian Kreyòl, these alternate potential states are apparent in everyday uses of both the terms *pouvwa* and *enèji* to describe the movements and desires of the lwa or gods (for example, in colloquial descriptions of the *Gede* lwa – a family of spirits that channel energies of death and fertility – as a *Fòs pouvwa* (force of power) or *akimilasyon enèji* (accumulation of energy)). In this respect, Haitian terminology is not unlike the original Greek understanding of energy: not only the product of labor but also spiritual and cosmic *potential.* In this book, "power" and "energy" are resources whose internal logics operate both within and outside of external structures of domination. Moreover, they are both ways of imagining potential futures that tendril into the spiritual world. Energy and power are thus not interchangeable but mutually constituted, spiritually sanctioned, and oriented toward futurity.

In analyzing this complex entanglement of energy and power, I do not reduce the lived experiences of Afro-diasporic subjects to their energetic output. Nor do I believe enslavement is analogous to contemporary forms of fossil fuel extraction, as critics such as Jean-François Mouhot and Marc Davidson have recently argued.[17] Such readings efface the lived experiences of enslaved people and their descendants and often have recourse to

[17] Mouhot, *Des esclaves énergétiques* and "Past Connections and Present Similarities." See also Davidson, "Parallels in Reactionary Argumentation."

troubling assumptions about Black life and labor.[18] Similarly, I emphatically reject the widespread use of the expression "energy slave," a term coined by the engineer Buckminster Fuller to denote the unit of energy which nonhuman infrastructure requires in lieu of an equivalent unit of human labor. For Fuller, "mechanization ... is man's answer to slavery."[19] I object to this term, which is still widely used in environmental studies, because enslavement is not a useful heuristic, a stable point of comparison, or a clever analogic tool. The term, which reproduces the quantificatory violence of enslavement, effaces the lived experiences of enslaved people and overlooks historical differences across systems of enslavement. It is both unethical and ahistorical.

In turning away from the traditional paths of inquiry in the energy humanities, with their vexed and often racist legacies, this project recalls Amitav Ghosh's argument that global northern manipulation of fossil fuels "reinforces Western power with the result that other variants of modernity came to be suppressed, incorporated, and appropriated into what is now a single dominant model."[20] Following Ghosh, I delineate the energetic practices of people of African descent in order to construct a counter-discourse against global northern narratives that privilege the rise of fossil fuel extraction, externalized labor, anthropogenic climate crisis, and practices of consumption, exploitation, and unevenly distributed pleasure. Instead, forms of Afro-Caribbean spirituality, protest, and politics helped forge diasporic philosophies of energy and power, albeit philosophies that are not often considered profitable, valuable, quantifiable, easily extractible, or otherwise convenient within the calculus of white supremacy. Enslaved and formally free people, I argue, found ways to redirect and redefine their power, diverting their labor into spiritual and political energy systems with liberatory ends. Ultimately, Black energy did not keep the machine of white supremacy running smoothly. Instead, the spiritual, energetic, and communal experiences of people of African descent snagged and caught at the cogs of racial capitalism, leading (in the case of Haiti) to the creation of the first Black republic and the rejection of plantation and post-plantation ideologies.

It is precisely in this nexus of racial capitalism and the energy humanities where this project contributes to established histories of gender and power in the Americas. This book rethinks narratives of the modern, not

[18] Mouhot, "Past Connections and Present Similarities," especially 209–12.
[19] Johnson, *Mineral Rites*.
[20] Ghosh, *The Great Derangement*, 108; see also Scott, *Conscripts of Modernity*.

only excavating what has been historicized as capitalist modernity (and by what mechanisms of institutional policing they have come to be included in "modernity") but also asking why critics still invest in a term which has spurred reckless consumption, climate crisis, the destruction of traditional belief systems and kinship networks, and the exploitation of life, both human and nonhuman, across the globe. While contemporary political policy has attempted to address the crisis of anthropogenic climate change with alternative fuel strategies (solar, battery, lithium, etc.), this book instead explores the violent histories of energy from alternative perspectives. What would it mean to shift our understanding of energy – and with it, modernity – away from capitalist values of consumption, supply, demand, and ideologies of individualism? What would it mean to inhabit energy through collective action, spiritual communion, and practices of care? By unyoking imperialist conquest from narratives of energy and modernity – and with it, histories of biocapitalism and coerced labor – this book imagines alternative theorizations of power and new ways of inhabiting and understanding energy that reject the teleological insistence on modernity's anthropogenic violence. In the face of racist structures of capitalist power, the subjects of this book safeguarded and rechanneled their energy and labor toward projects of community building and independence. This is not to deny the violence of institutional power, structured by modes of capital accumulation and the commodification of human beings. But it is to question the kinds of stories we tell about energy, from whose perspective, and why they matter. While traditional archival forms may disproportionately privilege tales of abjection (if recounted at all), this study expands our archive of hemispheric modernity to include the energetic pulses of Black lives.[21]

Histories of colonial energy tend to emphasize the development of the steam engine, the rise of electric power, or the beginnings of industrial agriculture, through the rise of cash crops such as indigo, cotton, sugar, and tobacco. Chapter 1, "Powering the Soul: Queer Energies in Haitian Vodou," argues that any history of colonial energy production must also recognize that nonhuman forms of power were dependent on the human energy of enslaved labor, particularly reproductive labor. Yet, far from considering enslaved labor as the flexible, malleable unit of energy desired

[21] On the violence of archival power in relation to Black women's cultural production, see Berry and Harris, *Sexuality and Slavery*; Fuentes, *Dispossessed Lives*; Hartman, "Venus in Two Acts" and *Wayward Lives, Beautiful Experiments*.

by capitalist production, this chapter instead argues that Vodou radically disrupted the logics of the plantation. Vodou personhood is antithetical to the calculus of racial capitalism, and its porosity, I argue, helped reconfigure the plantation's structures of power to resist imperialist extraction. Through an archive that ranges from colonial treatises to Vodou practices and epistemologies, this chapter highlights the ways in which Haitians expanded the category of gender and reimagined the energies of labor and birthwork under conditions of biocapitalist violence.

Chapter 2, "Marie Laveau's Generational Arts: Healing and Midwifery in New Orleans," turns from Saint-Domingue to Haitian diasporic, Afro-Caribbean and Creole communities of New Orleans. Through an excavation of the myth and legacy of New Orleans "voodoo queen" Marie Laveau, I argue that Laveau renegotiated her body as capital, resisting social, cultural, and legal forces that sought to commodify, exoticize, or criminalize her. Instead, she became a community leader, a healer, and possibly a midwife. Situating Laveau within a longer genealogy of Black women's birthwork and midwifery, this chapter argues for alternative ways of imagining reproduction, kinship, and energy economies. Ultimately, it puts pressure on the myriad myths surrounding Laveau's dynastic legacy, drawing attention away from white heteropatriarchal logics of touristic consumption, and instead allowing for bodily autonomy, love among women, and the notion of gestation and labor as an autoregenerating, independent economy.

Turning from Louisiana to New York City, Chapter 3, "Freedom's Conduit: Spiritual Justice in 'Theresa, A Haytien Tale,'" examines early African-American print culture, particularly the first African-American short story, the anonymously authored "Theresa, A Haytien Tale" (1828). While Haitian Revolutionary histories in the US have often centered on Toussaint Louverture, "Theresa" follows the travails of a young woman and her all-female family in their struggle for Haitian independence. A cross-dressing spy against the French, Theresa frequently experiences visitations, possessions, and visions from God. Theresa's political and spiritual labor forms a complex network of spiritual cosmologies and Haitian Revolutionary iconographies that help expand colonized understandings of gender and sexuality. In doing so, the tale reroutes the energy systems of both colonial plantation violence and early African-American domesticity by imagining a prophetic form of female futurity tied to Haitian independence, not biological reproduction. Ultimately, I argue, "Theresa" transforms the cult of Mary, showing how the female body serves as an instrument of divine energies in which the final product is not a child but instead political sovereignty.

Chapter 4, "'A Wandering Maniac': Sojourner Truth's Demonic Marronage" turns to a prophet seldom associated with the Caribbean. Yet, Sojourner Truth, who was born in 1797 in the predominantly Dutch Ulster County (New York), grew up in a world shaped by Atlantic empires; steeped in African, Native American, Caribbean, Spanish, Dutch, and French histories; and shaking with the tremors of the Haitian Revolution. Her first language was Dutch, her early spiritual beliefs were African, and her community was influenced by transatlantic and Caribbean channels of trade, labor, and revolution. This chapter examines the energy practices of Truth's creolized milieu within a broader discourse on Truth's celebrated mobility, historicizing her fugitivity within a transnational history of female marronage throughout the Americas. This hemispheric history of wandering evokes what Sylvia Wynter has understood as the "demonic grounds" of Black women's liberation. Suturing the demonic (an energy force that emerges from Wynter's critique of nineteenth-century physics) with Caribbean practices of marronage (a kinetic practice of flight against the immobilizing energy demands of chattel slavery), Truth, I argue, is not only an Atlantic subject but also expands critical understandings of twentieth- and twenty-first-century Caribbean philosophy.

The final chapter, "Mesmeric Revolution. Hopkins's Matrilineal Haiti", extends the coordinates of Hopkins's global commitments, charting an alternative geography beneath the Africa-oriented *Of One Blood.* By turning to the Caribbean, Hopkins reveals how Haiti emerges at key moments of energetic resistance. Moreover, she explicitly genders these moments of resistance as feminine. Focusing on the matrilineage of Hannah, Mira, and Dianthe, I argue that women in the novel carry specifically Haitian valences: from colonial Saint-Dominguan mesmerism, to the poison of Makandal, to the legacy of marronage. This muted Caribbean geography recenters women at the heart of the narrative, adumbrates Hopkins's anti-imperialist politics, and subverts the dehumanizing energy politics of plantation genealogies.

Before concluding, I would like to offer a few brief notes on terminology, orthography, and the political stakes of this project. While this book is largely centered on the experiences of people whom we might now call "women," it is also invested in destabilizing the cis-normativity of European imperialist projects. Enslaved people, as we shall see, found powerful ways to resist the violently gendered and ungendered logics of plantation economies. Although contemporary terminology is imperfect, what we might in a global northern idiom call cis-women, trans women, and gender-variant people all contributed to freedom projects throughout the Americas and redefined energy through their spiritual and political labor. I will sometimes use the term "women" to describe these individuals, especially when they described themselves as such (most famously in the case of Sojourner Truth). However, I would like to emphasize that not all the subjects of this book may have identified as "women" or understood the category of "woman" in ways identical to the way that terminology is deployed within a global northern contemporary framework.

With a few exceptions (most notably, the name Haiti itself), I will also cite Haitian terms in Kreyòl rather than French. This is an effort to respect the centrality of Kreyòl in Haitian history and recenter the experiences of the laboring classes, or what Michel-Rolph Trouillot might distinguish as the Haitian "nation" rather than the Haitian state.[22] Indeed, while this book is deeply invested in Haiti – as both a metaphor for diasporic freedom struggles and a real, material place – it is not particularly invested in the politics of statehood or institutional histories, which have traditionally overlooked women and gender-variant people. Rather, this book tells the story of people caught within multiple and sometimes imbricating scales of power and modes of belonging, which do not always include state politics.

It is also necessary to address the size and scope of these scales. The geographical and temporal framework of this book is admittedly large, drawing a complex network from Haiti to Louisiana to New York to Boston to Maryland over a period that stretches from 1791 to 1903. Yet, this vastness also has its limits: this book tells a story about the Haitian Revolution and its energetic reverberations in the continental United States. As such it contributes to scholarship on African-American and Haitian cultural histories, but it also recognizes that there are many diasporic energy stories which lie beyond the scope of this project. This is not to reinforce any notion of US or Haitian exceptionalism but instead to insist on the *exemplarity* of the Haitian Revolution, and particularly on its (often overlooked) significance to the histories and cultures of Black women and gender-variant people of the United States. Following influential scholars of Haiti and the United States, such as Marlene Daut, Brandon Byrd, J. Michael Dash, Elizabeth Maddock Dillon, and Michael Drexler, this study expands the parameters of African-American literature to include transnational, hemispheric, and multilingual scales of

[22] Trouillot, *Haiti, State Against Nation.*

relationality, which allowed people of African descent to build alliances across national lines.[23] As such, this book will discuss several different systems of enslavement and (formal) freedom that cut across British, French, Dutch, and US imperial lines, each with its own unique jurisprudence, customs, and racist hierarchies. While carefully attending to the differences between geographically and temporally contingent class and racial markers, I am also concerned with finding common ground that would bring together revolutionaries in Haiti, *gens de couleur* of New Orleans, free communities of color in 1820s New York City, Black Dutch prophets of upstate New York, enslaved mothers of Maryland, and free Bostonian women only a generation removed from slavery.

I must also be clear about the ethical commitments of this project. The white supremacist mechanisms that perpetuated slavery continue to sustain themselves through violent and limited understandings of reproduction, property, and energy – or, as Saidiya Hartman argues, "gestational language has been key to describing the world-making and world-breaking capacities of racial slavery."[24] In the United States, these violent biocapitalist histories reverberate in more insidious forms of reproductive injustice, medical racism, police brutality, and public policy hostile to Black life. In a country where African-Americans are three times as likely to die in labor as white people, where they are twice as likely to experience difficulty conceiving and sustaining a pregnancy and less likely to receive assistance, where doctors consistently overlook Black pain, where cross-racial gestational surrogacy produces white babies from nonwhite bodies at higher rates than ever before, and where post-Roe, Black people are disproportionately likely to be forced to carry unwanted pregnancies to term, we see the detritus of these biocapitalist histories, the remnants of the Code Noir, and the ever resonant threat of *partus* living and breathing in contemporary doctor's offices, hospitals, and homes. While recognizing the continuing violence of these histories, I also want to foreground the unique, creative, and loving ways Black women and gender-variant people have challenged these ideologies of extraction and consumption across borders and forged alternative ways of living not under but *against* traditional understandings of energy.

[23] Byrd, *The Black Republic;* Daut, *Tropics of Haiti;* Dillon and Drexler, *The Haitian Revolution and the Early United States;* Drexler and White, "The Constitution of Toussaint."

[24] Hartman, "The Belly of the World," 166.

CHAPTER 1

Powering the Soul
Queer Energies in Haitian Vodou

In Haitian Vodou, energy is more than a metaphor. Although certain aspects of Vodou may lend themselves to figurative language, the power that animates Haitian spiritual life can be quite literal. For believers (known as *Vodouwizans*, or more properly *sèvitè*, the servants of the gods), all life is governed by interconnected but differently modulated flows of energy, a unified force that radiates from the divine creator, *Bondye*. In the words of *houngan* (Vodou priest) and chemist Max Beauvoir, the world is constituted by "the dynamism of a life concept named 'energy,' a force that has no mass but has 'potentialities.' Divinity is seen as the source of life, thus of all energies."[1] Within this dynamic conception of the world, all beings amplify and attenuate, fluctuate and waver, ultimately striving for equilibrium between the invisible and the visible realms. Such an understanding of energy may seem far removed from developmentalist narratives concerning Haitian power, narratives which emphasize the nation's weak electric grid; overdependence on charcoal; the Petrocaribe corruption scandal; or the "power vacuum" following the assassination of President Jovenel Moïse. The cosmic flow of Vodou may also seem irrelevant to historical understandings of colonial energy production, which tend to focus on industrialized sugar, coffee, indigo, cacao, and cotton production. Yet, as this chapter will argue, Vodou's spiritual and political dynamism was forged both within and against the grain of systems of energy now seen as constitutive of modernity. Moreover, this dynamism offers its practitioners diverse and expanded ways of thinking about gender, sexuality, and modes of reproduction that make possible alternative understandings of futurity.

Vodou is often defined as a syncretic faith forged from the creolization of Roman Catholicism and African religions, particularly those practiced by Dahomean, Kongolese, and Yoruban ethnic groups. Yet culturally,

[1] Beauvoir, "Herbs and Energy," 114.

Vodou has come to signify much more, pervading, in the words of Celucien L. Joseph and Nixon S. Cleophat, "every aspect of the Haitian experience . . . Haitian cosmology, and the Haitian life and worldview of the diaspora."[2] At once an ideological battleground in Haitian politics; an anti-imperialist set of strategies; a repository of Haitian history and culture; a space for non-normative sexualities and gender identities; and rich grounds for Haitian aesthetic movements including Indigénisme, Noirisme, and Spiralism, Vodou is a faith, an archive, a remedy, and a home: a set of powerful and pervasive practices central to understanding Haitian history and culture. Given the mutability of Vodou's political and spiritual uses, it is significant that in Haitian Kreyòl, practitioners do not objectify the religion as such. Instead of practicing or worshiping "Vodou," it is more common to say that one "sèvi lwa," or that one serves the spirits. Worship orients its practitioners toward neither the individual nor a stable deity but instead the collective.[3] In this respect, Vodou is better understood as a verb rather than as a noun, rooted in interpersonal practices rather than institutional structures. This collective dynamism is constitutive of what Colin Dayan calls "the transformative and adaptive processes of vodou," the syncretism of language, cultures, and belief systems within multiple scales of global, local, diasporic, and cosmic relationality.[4]

While this syncretism has been extensively studied by scholars, the relationship between Afro-Caribbean spiritual beliefs and energy politics is often neglected in conventional criticism of Haitian modernity. In this chapter, I will excavate the ways in which Vodou's syncretic dynamism subverts conventional understandings of energy. In analyzing Vodou as both a spiritual structure and a source of power, I expand contemporary understandings of what constitutes modernity, energy, and anthropogenic activity. I argue that by refusing a deterministic telos of technological utopianism, while nuancing more familiar accounts of environmental exploitation and capitolocenic accumulation, Vodou creates alternative paradigms of energy, futurity, and modernity in the Americas. While theorists of the modern and scholars of the energy humanities have focused on the rise of the anthropocene/capitalocene through the eighteenth- and nineteenth-century industrialization of fossil fuels, electricity utilities, and coerced reproduction, Vodouwizans developed alternative understandings of human relationships to energy systems. Although contemporary right-wing detractors from David Brooks to Pat Robertson have derided Vodou

[2] Joseph and Cleophat, *Vodou in the Haitian Experience*, 1.
[3] Michel, "Vodou in Haiti," 30.
[4] Dayan, *Haiti, History, and the Gods*, 104.

as primitive, backward, and "progress-resistant," Afro-Caribbean spiritual practices are constituted by and "conscripted" into – to use David Scott's influential turn of phrase – Atlantic modernity.[5]

In what follows, I argue that Vodou cultivates an understanding of personhood distinct from the exploitative energy systems of the plantation. For people of African descent, whose energy was understood by the plantation system as quantifiable, extractable, and compliant, Vodou allowed for unruly expressions of power that refused to be channeled into the profit-driven mechanisms of white capitalist ideologies. This refusal is particularly salient in the context of Vodou understandings of gender and sexuality; while Saint-Dominguan planters relied on an extremely limited understanding of gender, one that emphasized reproductive labor and/or the construction of the "creole" family, Vodou practitioners rejected these logics. Instead, Vodou opens up expansive understandings of gender and sexuality, interrupting the profit-driven futurity of reproduction, and instead allowing for energetic paths outside of the colonial calculus of extraction, profit, and regulation.

1.1 Fugitive Reproductions

While Caribbean plantations powered themselves through many different energy systems – from electricity to water to steam to wind – the human energy costs of the plantation are often overlooked in environmental histories of the colonial period.[6] By human energy costs, I mean the fundamental mechanisms by which the plantation channeled human energy not only into economic profit but also into the surplus value of racial capital, or the ideologies of whiteness that accrued around slaveholding economies and continue to accumulate interest well into the present day. However, to understand enslaved labor as a form of energy is not to reduce the lived experiences of enslaved people into joules, therms, horsepower, or any kind of quantifiable unit of energy (a logic that would reproduce the assumptions of chattel slavery). The violence of slavery exceeds the quantification and theft of human labor output; to enslave was to attempt to destroy Black family systems, historical memory, private interiority, personal grief, and all other subjective and collective experiences. The consequences of this violence cannot be understood within or quantified by a labor theory of value.

[5] Brooks, "The Underlying Tragedy"; Scott, *Conscripts of Modernity*.

[6] Davis, *The Rise of Atlantic Economies*; Malm, *Fossil Capital*; Tann, "Steam and Sugar."

One of the most powerful forms of human labor on the plantation was reproductive labor. Although, due to its high mortality rate, colonial Saint-Domingue was not economically reliant on coerced reproduction in ways comparable to US plantation economies, the raw material of African labor as well as white supremacist ideologies of family and inheritance coalesced around certain assumptions about the Black body, whether enslaved or formally free. But Afro-Caribbean belief systems both in Haiti and throughout the Americas helped create expansive gender identities and expressions outside the normative bounds of reproductive heteropatriarchy. Vodou reappropriated and rearranged the discursive structures of energy systems frequently associated with European and US modernity, redirecting practices of consumption and exploitation into a subversive space of liberatory cosmologies. By interrupting the reproductive, profit-oriented, and heteronormative mandates of plantation economies, Vodou subverted modes of capital accumulation and social-sexual reproduction with alternative models of living. These alternative forms of relation refused to adhere to Western cis-heteronormative structures of gender and sexuality or their attendant reliance on energy extraction and reproductive violence.

Prior to the Revolution, Saint-Domingue was the French empire's most lucrative colony. Known as the "*perle des Antilles*," it was the world's foremost producer of sugar and coffee and among the top producers of indigo, cacao, and cotton export crops.[7] As Keith Tinker notes, by the 1780s, Saint-Domingue produced 40 percent of all sugar and 60 percent of all coffee consumed in Europe, easily eclipsing the output of both Spanish and British empires.[8] This unprecedented wealth depended on the labor and commodification of nearly half a million enslaved people. What Walter Johnson has influentially termed the "chattel principle" of slavery established a dual property regime, in which enslaved men and women both produced commodities for the market and were commodities themselves who stocked, exchanged, and compounded capital gains within their very bodies.[9] The presumed convertibility of the commodified enslaved person and the fact that enslaved peoples themselves provided surplus value separate them as distinct from what would emerge as the European proletariat.[10] To put a finer point on it, systems of enslavement amalgamated

[7] On the wealth of Saint-Domingue, see Dubois, *Avengers of the New World*; Geggus, *Haitian Revolutionary Studies*; Sepinwall, *Haitian History*.

[8] Tinker, *The African Diaspora to the Bahamas*, 16.

[9] Johnson, *Soul by Soul*.

[10] The scholarship on the relationship between enslaved New World labor and the European proletariat is vast. See in particular Berlin and Morgan, *The Slaves' Economy*; Mintz, "Was the

the human with the nonhuman (the commodity, the vessel, the unit of capital) in ways that lay the groundwork for twenty-first-century extractive economies now viewed as emblematic of modernity.

Yet, Johnson's notion of convertibility might translate across scholarly discourses to its cognate "fungibility," opening an aperture onto the *gendered* experiences of human commodification and the elastic exchange value of women, in particular. This exchanged and exchangeable vessel not only loses its individuality under the regime of the "chattel principle" but, following Hortense Spillers' groundbreaking work,

> the captive female body locates precisely a moment of converging political and social vectors that mark the flesh as a prime commodity of exchange. While this proposition is open to further exploration, suffice it to say now that this open exchange of female bodies in the raw offers a kind of Ur-text to the dynamics of signification and representation that the gendered female would unravel.[11]

For Spillers, the violent quantification necessitated by economies of human exchange forecloses categories of gender. Instead, ungendered flesh, malleable and liquid, registers the circulation of commodified bodies, placing Black women outside the hegemonic universalism of (white) womanhood. This violent calculus of blood, bodies, sugar, and cotton created conditions under which the commodity form became metonymized in the Black woman's body. Yet, even as plantation economies violently excluded Black women from gender as an analytic category, they also reduced sex differentiation to the injunction *partus sequitur ventrem*, the legal doctrine that determined the status of the child based on the condition of the mother. This extractive and exploitative regime structures Spillers' "American grammar," a system based on the simultaneous denial of gender and overdetermination of sex and hypervaluation of reproductive anatomy.

Saint-Domingue's Code Noir emphasizes the ways in which colonists imagined Black women as a contested site of social and capital reproduction. Designed to consolidate French sovereignty in the colonies and formally define the status of enslaved peoples, the Code was first passed by Louis XIV in 1685. It detailed strict regulations concerning marriage, religious practice, attire, subsistence, discipline, and manumission of

Plantation Slave a Proletarian?" and "The Question of Caribbean Peasantries," 31–4; Turner, *Chattel Slaves to Wage Slaves*.

11 Spillers, "Mama's Baby, Papa's Maybe."

enslaved people.[12] Versions of the Code would remain in force throughout the nineteenth century, and many of the document's articles were incorporated into US slave codes, particularly in Louisiana, where French colonial influence remained a pillar of local jurisprudence.[13] In its attempt to control enslaved life, the Code took particular interest in the social and reproductive roles of Black women. Following the doctrine of *partus*, the Code established a heteronormative family structure premised on the sexual assault of Black women by white men: Article VIII states, "if the father is free and the mother a slave, the children shall also be slaves."[14] But perhaps more surprising to scholars accustomed to Anglo-American slaveholding systems is Article IX, which explicitly encourages the intermarriage of enslaved women and enslavers in specific cases where an unmarried man's sexual assault of an enslaved woman produces a child. As the Code states,

> Article IX. [If unmarried men should have a child] during his concubinage with this slave .... he should then marry according to the accepted rites of the Church. In this way she shall then be freed, the children becoming free and legitimate.[15]

Although, like much of the Code, Article IX was not rigorously enforced, it helped establish the triadic caste system – *noirs*, *blancs*, and *gens de couleur* – that would become a unique structure of French circum-Caribbean societies from Saint-Domingue to New Orleans. The Code Noir thus established two distinct forms of racial capital organized around white supremacist heteropatriarchal violence. First, in formalizing *partus*, the Code Noir reduced enslaved women to vessels, sources of reproductive labor and capital accrual. Second, the Code Noir allowed for specific instances of marriage in which the formerly enslaved woman was legally "freed" by what, under the conditions of slavery, could only be sexual assault. Such acts of manumission and unfreedom incorporated the formerly enslaved woman into the fiction of a heteronormative body politic, one that attempted to efface forms of Black kinship by writing Black womanhood into white, Catholic family structures. In doing so, whiteness consolidated its identity through a violent erasure of Black relationality within the formal name of freedom. The particular violence of the Saint-Dominguan plantation system, then, is not only the violence of *partus* but

[12] See Peabody, *There Are No Slaves in France*; Sala-Molins, *Dark Side of the Light*.

[13] Aubert, "'To Establish One Law and Definite Rules'"; Palmer, "The Origins and Authors of the Code Noir."

[14] Code Noir. [15] Ibid.

also how plantation systems marked some Black women as convertible (i.e., "free" wives) and others as providers of labor. In doing so, the Code created a rigid white kinship structure, in which some violated Black women could be assimilated into a seemingly universal gender (and yet, still marked by colonial structures as distinct from white women), while other Black women were, following Spillers' influential paradigm, ungendered.[16]

Although, as Carolyn Fick has argued, colonial society in Saint-Domingue "did not reproduce itself," Black women's bodies were central to the mythmaking power of white supremacist structures.[17] This centrality becomes clear in the pseudoscientific racist theories of French colonists, including jurist Médéric-Louis-Élie Moreau de Saint-Méry, whose *Description topographique, physique, civile, politique et historique de la partie française de l'isle Saint-Domingue* (published in Philadelphia, 1797–8) remains one of the most comprehensive accounts of white colonial jurisprudence and pseudoscientific theories of race in Saint-Domingue. In it, he constructs an elaborate taxonomy of "racial" categories in which the figure of the mixed-race woman embodies a threat to colonial order:

> Recall that I mentioned mulatto women as the most precocious Creoles. This quality, their natural disposition, the seductions of their fellow men, the effect of a reputation that attaches to the entire class, are so many causes that destine them, early on, for incontinence. You would be sorry to learn to what extent this disorder has increased, and that sometimes the period that separates childhood from puberty and that belongs, so to speak, equally to both, is hardly respected. From that follows all evils, of which the inability to reproduce is not the least, or the coming of offspring who are feeble and weak.[18]

Moreau de Saint-Méry not only insists upon the purported "precocity" of mixed-race women and girls – thus naturalizing their vulnerability to sexual assault – but also forecloses the possibility of Black futurity by

[16] Spillers, "Mama's Baby, Papa's Maybe." [17] Fick, *The Making of Haiti*, 34.

[18] Moreau de Saint-Méry, *Description topographique, physique, civile, politique et historique*, 104–5. Translation provided by Garraway, "Race, Reproduction and Family Romance," 236. The original reads:

> On se rappelle que j'ai cité les Mulâtresses comme les Créoles les plus précoces. Cette particularité, leurs dispositions naturelles, les séductions de leurs semblables, l'effet d'une reputation qui appartient à toute la classe, sont autant de causes qui les vouent de bonne heure à l'incontinence. On serait affligé de voir jusqu'à quel point ce désordre s'est accru et quelquefois le terme qui sépare l'enfance de la puberté et qui appartient, pour ainsi dire, également aux deux, est à peine respecté. De là tous les maux dont le moindre n'est pas d'empêcher la reproduction, ou de n'en faire résulter que des êtres faibles et débiles.

accusing mixed-race women of sterility due to their (again purported) promiscuity. Doris Garraway analyzes the particularly racist and cis-sexist dimensions of Saint-Méry's claim, arguing that he "constructs a fantasy of white male paternity over the entire class of mulattoes, thus effectively denying them any significant role in the biological reproduction of colonial society."[19] This denial of reproductive agency not only consolidates white supremacist and misogynistic pseudoscience around the contested figure of the mixed-race woman but also, as Marlene Daut has argued, obscures what kinds of revolutionary action might be legible to historians of Haiti: "[i]n their writings, the colonists' obsession with the sexuality of women of color has often served to cover up an anxiety about the possibilities, real or imagined, for these women to transgress colonial authority and contribute to anti-slavery efforts."[20] Moreau de Saint-Méry's pseudoscientific claim of sterility reveals that, although not named as such, Black women's bodily autonomy was one of many transgressions that stirred white colonial anxieties. As we will see in Chapter 2, many eighteenth- and nineteenth-century Black women had sophisticated knowledge of abortifacients and contraceptives, which helped them preserve their freedom; rather than attribute "sterility" to libertinage or pseudo-scientific racist hierarchies, perhaps Moreau de Saint-Méry might have looked toward the scientific and spiritual knowledge structures Black people practiced, cultivated, and transmitted under his nose. Instead, his observations only reveal the ways in which white heteropatriarchy both overdetermined and negated the colonial category of gender. In producing dehumanizing fictions of Black womanhood – or what Daut has called the trope of the "tropical temptress" – French colonists attempted to invalidate the possibility of Black futures, while misreading cultural practices that allowed for alternative understandings of gender, sexuality, and futurity beyond the colonial system.

In neglecting Black women's scientific knowledge, Moreau de Saint-Méry also underestimated the spiritual structures that expanded the conditions of what constituted a Black "woman" in Saint-Domingue: Vodou. Elsewhere in his compendium, he warns his reader that "nothing is more dangerous, in all its relations, than this cult of Vaudoux [sic]."[21] The purported danger of Vodou emerges from its very ability to elide classification, hence collapsing those distinctions so important to Enlightenment

[19] See Gaffield, "Complexities of Imagining Haiti"; Garraway, "Race, Reproduction and Family Romance."

[20] Daut, *Tropics of Haiti*, 205.

[21] Moreau de Saint-Méry, *Description topographique, physique, civile, politique et historique*, 51. The original reads: "rien n'est plus dangereux sous tous les rapports que ce culte du Vaudoux."

ideologies of race. Unlike Moreau de Saint-Méry's clearly delineated racial taxonomies, Vodou muddles classificatory structures central to the Enlightenment project of epistemic capture and instead syncretizes practices "borrowed from Africa, and to which creole customs have added several variants and traits which reveal European ideas."[22] Vodou's syncretism, which dilates the scope of both diasporic and gender identity, ultimately unravels the logics of heteropatriarchal reproduction legislated by the French. As such, Vodou creates a fugitive and unruly space for alternative forms of gender identity and sexual expression. In this respect, Vodou usefully aligns with C. Riley Snorton's argument that "the ungendering of blackness is also the context for imagining gender as subject to rearrangement .... To suppose that one can identify fugitive moments in the hollow of fungibility's embrace is to focus on modes of escape, of wander, of flight that exist within violent conditions of exchange."[23] What Snorton calls the "transitive and transversal" properties of Blackness – misread and derided by French colonists like Saint-Méry – accrue around Afro-Caribbean spiritual beliefs, which reject European gender binaries that upheld the reproduction of white supremacy.[24]

As scholars such as Omise'eke Natasha Tinsley, M. Jacqui Alexander, Roberto Strongman, Kantara Souffrant, and Elizabeth Pérez have argued, Afro-Caribbean spirituality resists the violatory disciplining and cataloguing of Black life and instead allows for modes of gender identification which refuse to be reduced to heteronormative demands of capitalist reproduction or white ideologies of family.[25] In Haiti, this refusal established an alternative energy economy, replacing a tropological and material landscape of electricity, steam engines, sexual assault, and coerced reproduction with the erotic and spiritual energy flows of gods and ancestors. This does not necessarily mean that the people discussed in this book were LGBTQ-identified, nor that they should be read along the grain of global northern categories that might catalogue them as lesbian or transgender. Before continuing, I would like to qualify what a "queer" reading of Haitian Vodou might entail and offer a brief critical genealogy to better elucidate my usage of the term in this project. Scholars have frequently cautioned against too hastily translating terminologies of gender and

[22] Ibid., 46. The original reads: "empruntés de l'Afrique, & auxquels les moeurs creoles ont ajouté plusiers variantes, & des traits qui décèlent des idées européennes."

[23] Snorton, *Black on Both Sides*, 57. [24] Ibid.

[25] Alexander, *Pedagogies of Crossing*; Pérez, *Religion in the Kitchen*; Souffrant, "Vodou Aesthetics, Feminism, and Queer Art in the Second-Generation Haitian Dyaspora"; Tinsley, *Ezili's Mirrors* and "Songs for Ezili."

sexuality across cultures, especially those cultures marked by racial and ethnic difference, yet they have not always agreed upon the best ways to construct a shared vocabulary across different experiences. In Haiti, this language has been particularly fraught. As a case study, consider the term *masisi*. Popularized for global northern audiences with Anne Lescot's and Laurence Magloire's 2002 documentary *Des hommes et des dieux* (*Of Men and Gods*), the term *masisi* is a sometimes derogatory, sometimes reclaimed slur that is often translated as a gay man/men or queer man/men. Yet, as Roberto Strongman cautions, Haitian sexual epistemologies resist translation into "First World terminologies."[26] Criticizing the filmmakers' choice to subtitle culturally embedded terms like *masisi*, *madivinez*, and *en kachet* with "gay," "lesbian," and "closeted," respectively, Strongman makes a compelling case for greater linguistic precision in articulating difference across cultures. Tinsley has expanded Strongman's critique by attending to global northern critics' use of the gendered pronouns "he" and "his" when describing Haitian Vodou, thus obscuring the ungendered third-person Kreyòl pronoun *li*, or the fact that *masisi* also often call themselves *fi* and *fanm-girl* (loosely translated as women).[27] Tinsley implores us to "take seriously not only that *masisi* does not 'mean' gay man but that it also may not mean any kind of man," reminding critics to "resist global Northern terminology, certainly, but also queer readings that privilege the language of nonnormative sexualities while remaining curiously without language around nonnormative genders."[28] Or, as Thomas Glave argues in his introduction to *Our Caribbean*, one of the first anthologies of gay and lesbian Caribbean literature, "Contrary to the opinion of some, we are not – cannot possibly be – all the same."[29]

While critical of the ways in which global northern critics have deployed Western-centric terminologies to elide diverse experiences of gender and sexuality, I will cautiously use the term "queer" in this project. In this respect, I follow critics Dasha Chapman, Erin Durban-Albrecht, and Mario LaMothe, who have qualified their terminology with a reminder that "[a]ny warning to carefully mobilize the concept 'queer' in relation to Haiti contains a reminder to diminish rather than increase the gaps that scholarly analyses of the Haitian experience have generated."[30] In this spirit, "queerness," as I here deploy it, identifies spaces for nonnormative expressions of gender and sexuality without forcing gender and sexuality

[26] Strongman, "The Afro-Diasporic Body in Haitian Vodou," 19. [27] Tinsley, "Songs for Ezili."
[28] Ibid., 432. [29] Glave, *Our Caribbean*, x.
[30] Chapman, Durban-Albrecht, and LaMothe, "*Nou Mache Ansanm* (We Walk Together)," 284.

to align with the political commitments or expectations of global northern academics and activists. It gestures toward beliefs and practices that are indexed to historical, cultural, and religious contexts which, especially in the eighteenth and nineteenth centuries, resist taxonomic identification or other forms of epistemic violence. As we will see in the following section, an understanding of "queerness" requires attending not only to cultural contingencies like place, space, periodization, and language but also to philosophies of personhood that do not adhere to global northern assumptions of the self.

1.2 Spiritual Reserves: Vodou and Personhood

Epistemologies of gender and sexuality in Haiti cannot be understood outside the context of Afro-Caribbean spiritual traditions and their attendant philosophies of personal identity. For this reason, it is important to situate what I mean by "queerness" within a broader framework of Vodou understandings of the self. If classical Enlightenment personhood insists on the self-same subject, defined by an uninterrupted consciousness that is consistent across time and space, Vodou unravels the seat of selfhood into a porous, transtemporal, trans-spatial, and complexly gendered reassemblage of parts. This is firmly at odds with the self-governing Lockean subject, whose personal identity indexes a consistent and linear conception of time:

> In [consciousness] alone consists *personal Identity, i.e.* the sameness of rational Being: And as far as this consciousness can be extended backwards to any past Action or Thought, so far reaches the Identity of that *Person*; it is the same *self* now it was then; and 'tis by the same *self* with this present one that now reflects on it, that that Action was done.[31]

Personal identity in Lockean philosophy is characterized by a single unified consciousness, which is temporally stable, linear, and consistent. While there are certainly competing models of personhood in the European Enlightenment tradition (for example, Hume's bundle theory of the self), Locke's understanding of personhood and property profoundly shaped political consciousness, jurisprudence, civic life, and institutional structures in the United States and still inflects contemporary legislation and jurisprudence. In contrast, Haitian Vodou theorizes personhood as a collective of overlapping parts, each with different relationships to time, space, the material world, and consciousness. In Vodou, the person is

[31] Locke, *An Essay Concerning Human Understanding*, 9.

subject to amalgamation with the ancestors and lwa: parts of a person may wander – for example, in dreaming – through Montréal, New York, Port-au-Prince, Porto-Novo, Accra, or other nodes in the diaspora; a person may be possessed by a lwa whose gender identity is not consistent with their own and thus may be temporarily regendered; an ancestor may speak to an individual, pulling them into a spiraling past or propelling them into a prophetic future. The violent commodification of human life which sustains racial capitalism loses its hegemonic grip when confronted with such practices: how do you quantify a person who refuses to be stable, singular, and fixed? How do you count a soul that does not adhere to the base unit of the one self-same individual?

Although there are great variations in how Vodou is practiced, understandings of personhood almost always include a triadic relationship among

1. the *ti bonanj* (translated into English as "the small guardian angel" and often figured as a person's fuel, source of energy, or what Karen McCarthy Brown has called the "spiritual reserve tank");
2. the *gwo bonanj* ("the big guardian angel," or the psyche, soul, store of memory and dreams); and
3. the *mèt tèt* ("master of the head") the vodou lwa (spirit) that guides the devotee.[32]

In addition to these three major components of personhood, Vodou practitioners often include other spiritual forces such as the *namn* or soul, what Beauvoir calls the "vital energy in a person whose forces are localized in each cell of the anatomical structure," or the *zetwal* or "star" of a person, which resides outside the body and guides one's spiritual advancement. (Shooting star, for example, might indicate the death of someone or a change in their spiritual condition.) Other components of the person may include the lwa *rasin* or lwa *eritaj*, which connects the individual to their ancestors, and the *wonyison*, a group of spirits that accompany and can modify the vibrations and frequencies of the mèt tèt.[33] I have called this combination of forces "personal identity" or "the person," but neither term fully encompasses Vodou's understanding of the self. There is no generic term in Kreyòl that accounts for all these parts. Much like the practice of sevi lwa, personhood is better understood as a verb than a noun: a dynamic set of processes that are porous, multiple, and amalgamated with the energies of the collective.

Unity of body and consciousness is therefore inconsistent with Haitian understandings of the self. Instead, the concept of transcorporeality – or, in

[32] McCarthy Brown, *Mama Lola*, 9. [33] Beauvoir, "Herbs and Energy," 126–8.

the words of Strongman, the belief in the person as "multiple, removable, and external to the body that functions as its receptacle" – powers Vodou's dynamic conception of personal identity.[34] Consciousness, or the gwo bonanj, for example, is detachable from the body it inhabits. In dream states, or states of possession, the gwo bonanj departs the body, wanders, and visits loved ones in dreams, other lands, or beyond the grave. In contrast, the ti bonanj, or little angel, is intimately tied to the body. In an interview with an urban *manbo* (priestess), McCarthy Brown solicits the following definition of the ti bonanj: "When you are walking a long way or carrying something very heavy and feel so tired that you know you are not going to make it, it is the ti bonanj that takes over so you can do what you have to do."[35] The ti bonanj is the energy or life force, the engine which powers the body but is separate from its constitutive parts. Finally, the engine of the body is driven by an archetypal mèt tet, or master of the head, a dominant lwa whom each person is said to serve and who may influence one's personality. (For example, a calm person may serve a peaceful lwa.)[36] These parts exist both within and outside the body in a delicate set of energy relations, which are forged in a network of transtemporal and intergenerational labor, modulating the frequencies, amplitudes, vibrations, and electromagnetic forces of what Beauvoir calls a "continuous state of energy equilibration."[37]

Vodou's understanding of divine energy as a force that powers all human and nonhuman actions reappropriates the exploitative logics of the plantation engine, diverting human energy production away from capital accumulation. This intimate ecology of the soul, and its relation to energy and labor, radically transforms the power relations of chattel slavery. Take, for example, the Vodou ritual of "mounting" or "riding," in which the mèt tet harnesses the fuel of the ti bonanj in an act often translated as "possession." Yet, to be possessed – or more precisely to have your "horse ridden" (*monte chwal*) by a god – does not imply domination, appropriation, or property ownership, as European ideologies of personal identity might suggest. Describing the difficulty of translating the concept of "mounting" into English, Dayan argues that being mounted does not reproduce the power structures of enslavement but instead destroys "the cunning imperial dichotomy of master and slave . . . the surest way back to

[34] Strongman, *Queering Black Atlantic Religions*, 1.

[35] McCarthy Brown, "Afro-Caribbean Spirituality," 9.

[36] McCarthy Brown, *Mama Lola*, 112–13. See also Strongman, *Queering Black Atlantic Religions*, 12–14.

[37] Beauvoir, "Herbs and Energy," 126.

the self, to an identity lost, submerged, and denigrated."[38] Mounting therefore encourages an active and collaborative relationship between the devotee and the possessing mèt tet. Patrick Bellegarde-Smith and Claudine Michel also prioritize the collaborative nature of mounting: "Vodou metaphysics differs somewhat from Western definitions in its earnest communal grounding, which always considers men and women's personhood as entailed in an entity larger than themselves... Vodouists probe the finality of existence within a framework of collectivity, ancestors, and wholeness of being."[39] To serve as the engine, or fuel, for a governing lwa radically subverts the hierarchical structure of plantation economies and instead connects the individual person to an energetic network of communal relationality.

The relationality engendered by "mounting" has consequences for Haitian political and cultural life. Possession is central to one of the most celebrated of Haiti's foundational myths: the ceremony of Bwa Kayiman. Bwa Kayiman took place in mid-August 1791, when a group of enslaved people gathered secretly in the woods near Le Cap. The group engaged in spiritual practices (including, according to different sources, songs, dance, mounting, and animal sacrifice) and planned a revolt on the Northern Plain. The ensuing revolt sparked the thirteen-year struggle that would culminate in Haitian independence.[40] While many narratives of Bwa Kayiman identify the ceremony's leader as the houngan Boukman Dutty, some early Haitian historians identify a woman known as Manbo Marinette Bwa Chèch at the proceedings. Other accounts identify a manbo named Cécile Fatiman, which suggests possible Islamic influences on the Revolution. In his 1824 *Voyage dans le nord d'Hayti*, the Haitian poet Hérard Dumesle draws attention to a "young virgin" who reportedly killed a pig and divined messages from its entrails.[41] While it would be easy to dismiss Dumesle's account as the kind of lurid exoticism so often used to denigrate Haiti, his attention to the pig suggests a powerful spiritual presence at the ceremony: as Tinsley and Krista White have argued, the significance of the black pig indicates that the presiding spirit of Bwa Kayiman was the lwa Ezili Dantò, the powerful Queen of

[38] Dayan, *Haiti, History and the Gods*, 72–4.

[39] Bellegarde-Smith and Michel, "Danbala/Ayida as Cosmic Prism," 458–9.

[40] Dalmas, *Histoire de la révolution de Saint-Domingue* is generally acknowledged to be the first account of the ceremony. For the historiographical debate on Bwa Kayiman, see Hoffmann's "Histoire, mythe et idéologie." See also Fick, *The Making of Haiti*, 29–30; Geggus, "The Bois Caïman Ceremony"; Ramsey, *The Spirits and the Law*, 42–4.

[41] Dumesle, *Voyage dans le Nord d'Hayti*, 89.

the Petwo Nation, who often demands black, or Creole, pigs, as a sacrifice.[42]

Within the Ezili pantheon, Dantò is the greatest warrior. Unlike her sister, Ezili Freda, a capricious, flirtatious, and stereotypically effeminate, even camp lwa who presides over love and beauty, Ezili Dantò is a powerful fighter, a protective mother, and a queer icon particularly worshipped by lesbian Vodouwizan. Syncretized with the Black Madonna of Częstochowa, or the Black Virgin of Poland, she is, according to McCarthy Brown, "above all else the mother" and yet her maternity, unlike the cult of the Virgin, is strictly matrilineal: she carries in her arms not a son or savior but a daughter sometimes called Anayiz or Ti-Gungun.[43] Furthermore, her maternity resists sentimentalization: she is unmarried, stern, and sometimes furious, a "prism focusing light on the single mother and head of household."[44]

Tinsley has expanded on McCarthy Brown's work to push against the essentialistic borders of maternity embodied in the Ezili pantheon. As Tinsley argues of Dantò: "what if womanness doesn't mean being expected to be a docile worker until five o'clock, then everyone's caretaker after? What if it doesn't mean bearing children or being able to bear children or taking care of lovers who act as children?"[45] Following Tinsley, I would like to suggest that Dantò embodies a way of mothering that is unbound to sentimentality, heterosexual assumptions, or reproductive capacity. Instead, she channels the energy of carework into forms that can be angry, violent, or revolutionary.[46] If Haiti's most famous heroes, such as Toussaint Louverture and Jean-Jacques Dessalines, have traditionally been portrayed in this light – that is to say, as fierce warriors and bearers of justice – Dantò collapses distinctions that would separate nationalist male warriors from

[42] Haitian lwa belong to several "nations," the most visible of which are the Rada and Petwo (but also including Ibo, Kongo, and up to seventeen others). Rada lwa are generally considered older and gentler, and are associated with Dahomey, whereas Petwo lwa emerge from New World conditions of slavery and as such are often figured as powerful, volatile and "hot." A pantheon of lwa will offer variations on a spirit, each inflected by her relationship to nation. For example, the Ezili pantheon includes: Ezili Dantò (Petwo), Ezili Freda (Rada), as well as Gran Ezili, Ezili Je Wouj, Ezil Taureau, and Lasirenn. See Demangles, "The Faces of the Gods."

[43] McCarthy Brown, *Mama Lola*, 228. On the representation of Anayiz, see McAlister, "The Madonna of 115th Street Revisited." On the influence of the Polish Black Madonna on representations of Ezili, see Kingsbury and Chestnut, "In Her Own Image."

[44] McCarthy Brown, *Mama Lola*, 255–6.

[45] Tinsley, *Ezili's Mirrors*, 52.

[46] Strongman suggests that Dantò does not bear children herself but instead welcomes and mothers the children born of Ezili Freda's heterosexual relations: "In order for Freda to remain sexually available, she must remain childless, but what to do with the offspring of such copious copulation? Freda hands over her little girl, Anais, to her maternal sister, Dantòr, who cares for her as if the child were her own." Strongman, *Queering Black Atlantic Religions*, 43.

sentimental female keepers of the hearth and home. In doing so, she allows us to read care as revolutionary, the domestic as worldly, and gender as fluid and relational.

While Dumesle does not dwell on the implications of Ezili's presence at Bwa Kayiman, he does discuss at length the ceremony's practice of collective possession. Claiming to reproduce the conspirators' pledge, he cites several lines of verse in Kreyòl, which he offers as a footnote in his otherwise French chronicle. Carolyn Fick has identified the sources of this pledge in a compilation of letters written by the nuns of the Communauté des Religieuses Filles de Notre Dame du Cap-Français, an interracial convent for the education of young girls. A former pupil, a mixed-race woman named the Princesse Améthyste, had, according to Fick, practiced Vodou, headed a "company of Amazons," and frequently led other students off the grounds to dance, chant, and invoke the lwa.[47] While Dumesle elides the testimonies of these nuns – and thus fails to understand the ways women may have participated in Bwa Kayiman – he reproduces the chant they claimed to overhear. Since historicized as "Boukman's prayer," this pledge has been celebrated in some of the most famous accounts of the Haitian Revolution, including C. L. R. James's *Black Jacobins*.[48] But few critics have noted that this famous text's source was, perhaps, a group of young girls:

Bondié qui fait soleil, qui clairé nous enhaut
Qui soulevé la mer, qui fait grondé l'orage,
Bon dié la, zot tandé
Caché dans youn nuage
Et la li gadé nous, li vouai tout ça blancs faits!
Bon dié blancs mandé crime, et part nous vlé bienfets
Mais dié là qui si bon, ordonnin nous vengeance;
Li va conduit bras nous, la ba nous assistance,
Jetté portrait dié blancs qui soif dlo dans gié nous
Couté la liberté li pale coeurs nous tous.[49]

[This God who made the sun, who brings light from above
Who raises the sea, and who makes the storm rage
That God is there, do you understand,
Hiding in a cloud,
S/He/They watches us, sees all that the whites do!
The God of the whites asks for crime and wants nothing good for us
But this god who is so good demands vengeance

[47] Fick, *The Making of Haiti*, 104. [48] James, *The Black Jacobins*, 86–8.
[49] Dumesle, *Voyage dans le Nord d'Hayti*, 88.

S/He/They will conduct our arms, we are strengthened by his aid
Topple the portrait of the god of the whites who is thirsty for the tears in our eyes,
Listen to the liberty which speaks in all our hearts.]

By insisting on corporeal infiltration, Boukman's prayer recalls the Vodou practice of mounting typically attributed to the revolutionaries of Bwa Kayiman. Yet, this encounter does not reproduce the logics of chattel slavery: as Dayan has argued, it liberates the subject within a communal context, allowing for an experience of "abandon consecrated most often by the community."[50] Dumesle's God embodies the relational potential of mounting by metaphorically and literally linking a network of Haitian revolutionaries: "Li va conduit bras nous, la ba nous assistance" ["S/He/They will conduct our arms, we are strengthened by his/her/their aid"]. This ambiguously gendered divine authority collapses the distinctions between the political and the spiritual, inviting the gods into a secular call to listen to liberty, or "couté la liberté."

Kreyòl, unlike French, does not have gender pronouns, and the "Bondye" or God represented by *li* can designate male, female, or non-binary subjects; moreover, when a subject is possessed in Haitian Vodou, they temporarily assume the gender identity of the lwa occupying their mèt tèt. The temporary regendering facilitated by Vodou's transcorporeal beliefs opens up forms of queer subjectivity that do not fall along the axes of global northern understandings of identity, desires, or theories of the Lockean individual.[51] Moreover, Vodou is particularly aligned with queer women's desire. As Roberto Strongman argues, the horse and rider metaphor invites a gendered reading in which "the concavity of the saddle, the vessel-like quality of the horse, and the synergy between the horse and its rider evoke a repectacularity that is distinctly female and laden with sexual connotations that present trances as a mystical union."[52] Vodou thus inscribes the body with spiritual and mystical power while dislocating the global northern assumption that the body is synonymous with or determinative of gender identity. In Haitian Vodou, men, women, and gender-variant people are equally saddled, ridden, and filled with the divine.

While many feminist reassessments of the Bwa Kayiman ceremony have focused on female spiritual leadership – for example, the presence of Mambo Marinette or Cécile Fatiman – it is important to follow that leadership to its logical conclusion: Women were not only key participants in Bwa Kayiman, but the devotees were possessed, or ridden, by a queer or

[50] Dayan, *Haiti, History and the Gods*, 138. [51] Strongman, *Queering Black Atlantic Religions*, 48.
[52] Ibid., 45.

madivinez woman: Ezili Dantò. In accordance with Strongman's theorization of transcorporeality, these famed early revolutionaries presumably experienced cross-gender identifications that allowed for a more flexible understanding of gendered subjectivity than is typical in global northern epistemologies. As Tinsley asks of Ezili's political significance: "What would it mean ... if we took seriously that the Haitian Revolution was launched not by a man or even a woman but by the spirit of women who love women?"[53] Indeed, if we are to accept Ezili as the governing lwa of Bwa Kayiman, it follows not only that the Revolution was launched by a woman-loving spirit but, given the cross-gender identifications inherent in mounting, that Haiti's foundational revolutionaries were *all*, at least temporarily, queer women.

1.3 "Dantò pase, ou di se loray-o"

Scholars have often cautioned against too hastily ascribing political import to Bwa Kayiman. Laurent Dubois, for example, argues, "though religious practices facilitated and spurred on insurrection, it was only their combination with careful political organization that made the 1791 uprising successful."[54] But I would like to ask why critics distinguish between "religious practices" and "careful political organization." Indeed, as Haitian Vodou proves the spiritual is political. The critical injunction to distinguish between the political (coded as secular, rational, and masculine) and the spiritual (coded as unreasonable, unruly, and feminine) is perhaps understandable, especially given the ways in which Haitian Vodou has been exoticized and vilified by the global north. However, this distinction reinforces a binary which Bwa Kayiman – and particulary Ezili Dantò – insists on collapsing. The spiritual spark of Ezili's mass possession on the northern plains in 1791 demands that religious practice be understood not only as a political instrument but also as a form of a particularly modern power: a collective engine of revolutionary worshippers, providing the fuel to drive events which would eventually lead to Haitian independence.

Bwa Kayiman's intersection with energy systems is apparent in the role of electricity in traditional accounts of the ceremony. It is not for nothing that canonical accounts of Bwa Kayiman emphasize the tempestuous conditions of the possession. Dumesle, for example, describes the oath at Bwa Kayiman as a collective utterance which "electrisa les coeurs par un transport nouveau" ("electrified their hearts with renewed

[53] Tinsley, *Ezili Mirrors*, 11. [54] Dubois, *Avengers of the New World*, 101.

transport").[55] The Haitian statesman Dantès Bellegarde emphasizes how "as the storm raged and lighting broke across the sky, a negress of tall stature brusquely appeared," and the historian Horace Pauleus Sannon highlights "the flashing glow of lightning."[56] In Haiti, thunder and lightning are particularly linked to Dantò: a Vodou song, recorded by McCarthy Brown, praises the spirit's wild bluster: "*Lè ou wè Dantò pase, ou di se loray-o*" ("When you see Dantò pass by, you say it is a thunderstorm").[57]

Like other environmental phenomena, including earthquakes, storms, the wind, and the depths of the ocean, electricity is a sacred natural principle, associated with several Haitian spirits, or lwa including Maman Brijit, consort of Bawon Samedi and caretaker of the dead; Sobo and Badè, two militaristic brothers whose spirits mingle with lightning, thunder, and windstorms; and Agawou Tonné, lwa of thunder and lightning.[58] As a natural phenomenon channeled through, and made visible by, human conduits, electricity is situated between the living and dead, arrivals and departures, the nonhuman and the human. Just as the water god, Agwè Tawoyo, both honors the natural world of the sea and its historical echoes of the Middle Passage, electricity in Vodou cosmologies draws from the organic forces of the natural world while simultaneously channeling that natural power into human actors and political histories.

This rhetorical investment in lightning, thunder, and stormy conditions developed in tandem with the development of European and white settler Enlightenment understandings of electricity. The notion of electricity in the eighteenth century, as James Delbourgo has argued, heightened the paradoxes of Enlightenment classificatory schema. For Delbourgo, "electricity defied the logic of Cartesian dualism, according to which mind and body were separate entities, by putting mind and body into startlingly direct communication. The centrality of the body as an experimental instrument meant that in no other branch of enlightened science were the act of cognition and the experience of passion more intensely related:

55 Dumesle, *Voyage dans le Nord d'Hayti*, 88.

56 Bellegarde, *Histoire du people haitien*. The original reads: "tandis que l'orage grondait et que les éclairs sillonnaient le ciel, une négresse de haute stature apparut brusquement." Sannon, cited in Joseph, *Thinking in Public Faith, Secular Humanism, and Development in Jacques Roumain*, 414. The original reads "la lueur fulgurante des éclairs."

57 McCarthy Brown, *Mama Lola*, 231.

58 J. Michael Dash, *Culture and Customs of Haiti* (Westport, CT: Greenwood Press, 2001) 70; *Secrets of Vodou*, eds. Milo Rigaud, Robert B. Cross, and Odette Mennesson-Rigaud (New York: City Lights Publish, 1985); Gerdès Fleurant *Dancing Spirits: Rhythms and Rituals of Haitian Vodun, the Rada Rite* (Westport, CT: Greenwood Press, 1996) 85–86.

to know was to feel and to feel was to know."[59] In emphasizing the tactile over the optic register, experiments in electricity challenged Enlightenment epistemologies that privileged the visual as an objective way of registering, understanding, and mastering the world. Instead, as David Parisi argues, "vision proved an inadequate register; seeing signifiers of electricity's presence – sparks leaping between bodies, bodies convulsing as electrical charged moved between them – only served to fuel the desire for an embodied tactile encounter with electricity."[60] Electricity accommodated both ideologies of rational disembodied progress and decentralized corporeal ecstasy and for this reason was often tied to radical politics as well.[61] At once academic and popular, empiricist and romantic, individual and collective, electrical demonstrations flashed and darkened through the *Siècle des Lumières.*

While colonial imagery of electricity grappled with Enlightenment and Romantic contradictions of "progress," management and ecstatic transport, Dantò helps us understand electricity from another perspective. Eschewing the binaries of the rational/irrational which haunted eighteenth-century debates on electricity, she shows us how the spiritual, the unseen, or the sensory experience of possession are mutually constituted with political organization, careful planning, and "reasonable" demands for sovereignty. In doing so, she taps into a notion of futurity that is not tied to European technologies of management, linear modes of capital accumulation, or the expectation that women be reproductive vessels or traditional mothers. Instead, her presence at Bwa Kayiman fuels a network of interlinked and queered revolutionary actors, electrified with the power of divine justice. This possessed and spiritually ecstatic orientation toward the future replaces the profits of colonization with prophets of liberation. Contextualized with Vodou epistemologies of personhood, reproduction, futurity, and freedom, figures such as Dantò reveal new ways of understanding colonial energy systems.

[59] Delbourgo, *A Most Amazing Scene of Wonders,* 8–9. [60] Parisi, *Archaeologies of Touch,* 68.

[61] Benjamin Franklin's experiments with electricity, as well as his celebrated correspondence with Joseph Priestley, rhetorically intertwined with his republicanism to the extent that John Adams could complain to Benjamin Rush, in a letter dated April 4, 1790, "The History of our Revolution... will be that Dr Franklins electrical Rod, Smote the Earth and out Spring General Washington." John Adams to Benjamin Rush, April 4, 1790, in *Letters of Benjamin Rush,* ed. Lyman H. Butterfield, vol. 2 (Princeton, NJ: Princeton University Press, 1951) 1207. On electricity and radicalism, see Farclough, *Literature, Electricity and Politics 1740–1840*; O'Rourke, *Art, Science, and the Body in Early Romanticism.* On electricity as a disciplinary technique, see Wesner, "Revolutionary Electricity in 1790."

The following chapters of this book will continue to follow the complex ways Black futurity was linked to energetic practices of spirituality, tracing how Haitian culture spread beyond the first Black republic and came to shape freedom struggles in the contemporary United States from Louisiana to New York to Boston. Energy does not, as we will see, respect national borders but instead pulsates through the lives and lived experiences of people throughout the diaspora. These energy systems animated local US civil rights struggles within a wider framework of diasporic history and dislocated global northern assumptions about energy reproduction and futurity. People of African descent reclaimed the energetic harnessing of their bodies, converting corporeal profits into kinetic and prophetic glimpses of emancipated futures.

CHAPTER 2

Marie Laveau's Generational Arts
Healing and Midwifery in New Orleans

Marie Laveau's life and legend span more than a century, from European colonial empires to the Haitian Revolution to the US Civil War, Reconstruction, Jim Crow, and the concomitant rise of US imperialism in Latin America and the Caribbean. In many ways, Laveau's story forms a parallel to the story of Haiti. She began her career in early nineteenth-century New Orleans as a community leader in a trans-Caribbean space deeply influenced by an influx of Haitian émigrés.[1] She began her life *as legend* in the early twentieth century, at a time when white US Americans spun their prejudice into tales of snake worship, zombification, and savagery in order to justify imperialism in Haiti. Laveau creates a mirror to the long nineteenth century, her myths and afterlives revealing not only the contested grounds on which Black Caribbean identity took its many forms but also the energy politics of diasporic cultural practices, including healing, birthwork, botany, and intergenerational care.

Overdetermined by myth, Laveau's life is notoriously difficult to narrate. Of the proliferating and often contradictory tales that confound her biographers, the legend of her daughter remains one of the most puzzling. Many twentieth-century accounts claim that a daughter, referred to as Marie II, inherited Laveau's Vodou dynasty after her mother's death in 1881.[2] While some scholars give credence to this myth, others, including

[1] Between 1791 and 1804, New Orleans received several waves of Saint Dominguan émigrés (including white planters, enslaved Black people and free people of color or "gens de couleur"). In 1809, New Orleans' population doubled after around 10,000 Haitians (including 3,100 gens de couleur) arrived by way of Cuba after being expelled by the Spanish. On the demographic influences of Haiti in New Orleans, see Dudley, *Building Antebellum New Orleans*.

[2] Although many sources refer to Louisiana Vodou as "Voodoo," I have chosen to favor the Haitian spelling of *Vodou* when referring to New Orleanian spiritual practices. This is not to collapse the distinction between Haitian and New Orleanian Vodou, but instead to reject the usual pejorative associations with "Voodoo." The Haitian spelling of Vodou is also more faithful to the etymological root of the term, the Dahomean word "*vodu*" or "*vodun,*" which means "spirit." These practices are distinct from but share many cultural roots with what is often referred to as "hoodoo," a folk religion practiced throughout the southern USA but unlike Vodou, not distinct to New Orleans or in service

Carolyn Marrow Long, express greater skepticism around the existence of a successor.[3] Indeed, the daughter most often credited with assuming the mantle of Laveau II, Euchariste Heloïse Glapion, reportedly died in 1862. My aim here is not to prove a distinction between Marie I and Marie II but instead to explore the temporal logics of energy reproduction generated by Marie Laveau's legend. The suggestion of Laveau II, even if only mythical, gestures to a form of social and cultural reproduction that exceeds the energy calculus of cis-heterosexual futurity. Some accounts claim that Laveau II was the first Marie's rival; others claim that she was her daughter; many believe that Marie Laveau I and II are the same person, a single life stretched over a century. The legacy of Laveau's afterlives operates within a broader network of spiritual practitioners, some of whom were captured by archival and policing technologies, but many of whom eluded traditional means of historical production. The myths surrounding Laveau's dynastic legacy powerfully metamorphose white heterosexual reproductive logics, allowing for bodily autonomy, self-love, and the notion of gestation and labor as a collective economy of birthing energy, which we will see anticipate Audre Lorde's injunction that Black women "must learn to mother ourselves."[4]

We cannot know if the woman who claimed to be Laveau II was a direct biological descendant of Marie Laveau I. The archival mechanisms that have constructed this narrative of dynastic inheritance are too flawed to establish a traditional genealogy. However, Laveau's mythos of (self) mothering is a starting point for imagining alternative forms of relation, birthing, and futurity that matrilineal succession might have signified in nineteenth- and early twentieth-century New Orleans. I will thus situate Laveau within an energy economy of midwifery, rootwork, and healing practices, both working along and against the archival grain, to use the influential language of Ann Laura Stoler.[5] On one hand, reading Laveau as mother, healer, and possible birthworker reminds us that archival capture has predominantly reduced Black women's experiences to a precise accounting of reproductive life. As Jennifer Morgan has influentially argued, the relationship between birthing and racial capitalism reveals how

of the lwa. However, like Vodou, it is a syncretic spiritual practice that draws from herbs, minerals, animals, and other elements of the natural world to care for practitioners and their communities.

[3] Long, *A New Orleans Vodou Priestess*; Ward, *Voodoo Queen.*

[4] Lorde, "Eye to Eye," 173 and "Black Women, Hatred and Anger."

[5] Stoler, *Along the Archival Grain.*

> [r]eproduction (and thus enslavability) was tethered to enslavement in a way that foreclosed the possibility that kinship might destabilize capital. To be enslaved meant to be locked into a productive relationship whereby all that your body could do was harnessed to accumulate capital for another.[6]

And yet midwifery and other healing arts, as practiced by Black women (both free and enslaved) of New Orleans and the Americas more broadly, subvert these linear genealogies of capital accumulation and biological reproduction. Instead, Black midwives and healers created new structures of possibility and ways of practicing care, constructing kinship, tending to (and, when it suited them, foreclosing) genealogical lines of descent, and redirecting their energy toward practices unassimilable into the capitalist market. This chapter will contextualize Laveau's healing practices and community leadership within a framework of Black midwifery in the US South and the Caribbean. Although Laveau is seldom explicitly described as a midwife, her role as an herbalist, mother, and community leader leads us to questions of reproductive freedom. As birthwork in the nineteenth-century US became increasingly medicalized and profit-driven, Laveau created a countereconomy of healing practices, relationality among Black women, and energy reclamation. This countereconomy allows us to read the legacy of Laveau II outside the logics of touristic legend and supernatural cliché and instead asks us to take seriously the queer potential of mothering, midwifing, and healing adumbrated by dynastic matrilineage.

2.1 Midwifing Laveau

Despite or perhaps because of her archival paucity, Marie Laveau has powerfully shaped pop cultural contours, appearing in countless novels, operas, TV shows, films, whiskey commercials, country songs, and even Marvel comic books, where her fictional avatar frequently fights heroes such as Dr. Strange and Blade. Her myth is intensely local, as any tourist to New Orleans, with its Laveau-themed ghost tours, tarot readings, and myriad forms of tat, could tell you. Yet, her life also radiates throughout the Americas: Derek Walcott's 1979 musical *Marie LaVeau,* directed by J. R. Smith, reclaims the "Voodoo Queen" as a uniquely Caribbean figure, while Isabel Allende's pulpy *El Zorro: Comienza la leyenda* (2005) deploys Laveau to imbue Zorro's Californian *criollo* iconicity with French

6 Morgan, *Reckoning with Slavery*, 5.

Caribbean *créolité*.[7] In the United States, Laveau re-emerged in public consciousness in the 1970s, likely due to a revival of interest in Zora Neale Hurston, who wrote scrupulously of Laveau and her "hoodoo" milieu in 1935's *Mules and Men*.[8] At the confluence of second-wave feminism and the Black Arts movement, Laveau became a contested figure. White feminists, such as Francine Prose in her 1977 novel *Marie Laveau*, highlighted Laveau's perceived social, economic, and sexual power.[9] However, such interpretations of Laveau were controversial. Ishmael Reed, for example, honored the influence of Laveau in his "Neo-Hoodoo aesthetic" while satirizing white feminist celebrations of the "Queen of Business" in novels such as *The Last Days of Louisiana Red* and *Mumbo-Jumbo*.[10] A generation later, Jewell Parker Rhodes's 1994 *Voodoo Dreams* and 2005 *Voodoo Season* reclaim Marie from both white feminist appropriations of the 1970s and white masculinist pseudoanthropological optics popularized by "all the . . . white males who had written about Marie Laveau."[11]

The "white males" (and females) to whom Rhodes refers form a lineage longer than Laveau's purported dynastic reign. The first wave of Laveau's mythologization occurred at the end of Reconstruction, when white writers flooded local and national print culture with lurid narratives of New Orleans "voodoo," in an attempt to consolidate white political power. Fabricated accounts of devilry, snake worship, and orgies on the shores of Lake Pontchartrain painted a portrait of savagery, forming a rhetorical denial of Black personhood that neatly imbricated with the legal erosion of Black rights, including segregation statutes, poll taxes, literacy tests, the Grandfather Clause, and the 1896 ruling *Plessy v. Ferguson*, as well as extrajuridical forms of policing and terror with the rise of the Klu Klux Klan and the Crescent City White League. These racist narratives implicitly and explicitly argued that people of African descent were unfit for civic standing, illustrating, as Michelle Y. Gordon has argued, "the intertwined crises that black citizenship, Radical Reconstruction, and desegregation posed to postbellum white patriarchal supremacy."[12] Marie

[7] Allende, *El Zorro*; Walcott, *Marie Laveau and Steel*. See also Walcott's film, *Marie Laveau*, directed by J. R. Smith.

[8] Hurston, *Mules and Men*.

[9] Prose, *Marie Laveau*.

[10] Dick and Reed, "A Conversation with Ishmael Reed," 231; Reed, *Mumbo-Jumbo* and *The Last Days of Louisiana Red*.

[11] Rhodes and Ramsey, "An Interview with Jewell Parker Rhodes," 596.

[12] Michelle Y. Gordon "Midnight Scenes and Orgies": Public Narratives of Voodoo in New Orleans and Nineteenth-Century Discourses of White Supremacy, *American Quarterly* 64:4 (December 2012), 771.

Laveau, or rather some fictionalized version of her, frequently stood at the center of these crises, an embodiment of the racial ambiguity, unruly sexuality, and spiritual and political autonomy which at once threatened and titillated white audiences.

In George Washington Cable's 1881 novel *The Grandissismes*, for example, Laveau takes a thinly disguised form as the character Palmyre the Philosophe, a romantic "tragic quadroon" and regal "voodoo priestess," prone to fits of what Cable portrays as jealous violence. She is introduced as a "barbaric beauty . . . a femininity without humanity. . . a creature that one would want to find chained."[13] Rhetorically re-enslaved in "chains" and dehumanized as a "creature," Cable's Laveau sets back the clock on Black liberation in ways that recall representations of Saint-Dominguan women, as discussed in Chapter 1. Laveau's 1881 obituaries demonstrate similarly dehumanizing rhetoric. In the ironically titled "A Sainted Woman," published June 18, 1881 in the weekly *New Orleans Democrat*, Laveau is remembered as "the prime mover and soul of the indecent orgies of the ignoble Voudous."[14] Sensational versions of Laveau's life also ran in the national press, with the *New York Times* obituary of Marie emphasizing her "black arts" and "wild weird dances."[15] In these obituaries, Laveau's life was narrated in incoherent, racist, and often contradictory ways: to some white journalists, including Lafcadio Hearn, the "Queen of the Voodoos" was a saint, a healer, a consort of General Lafayette and Aaron Burr, and even a Confederate sympathizer.[16] To others, she was a master blackmailer, an evil priestess, a medium to the dead, an ugly hag, a beautiful temptress, a wicked procuress, and a lover of snakes.

Laveau's contradictory legends were revived again in the early twentieth century due to the vast public historical undertaking of the Louisiana Writers' Project (LWP). Directed by Lyle Saxon, the LWP was a regional subsidiary of the Federal Writer's Project, a New Deal program that offered employment for white writers to collect tales of "local color" extracted (without payment or formal acknowledgment) from Black Louisiana residents. Drawing from oral narratives and Louisiana archives, LWP workers transcribed and translated civil and ecclesiastic records concerning Laveau and her family; they typed copies of articles from the

[13] Cable, *The Grandissmes*, 89. [14] A Sainted Woman," New Orleans Democrat, June 18, 1881.

[15] "The Dead Voodoo Queen – Marie Laveau's Place in the History of New Orleans," *New York Times*, June 23, 1881.

[16] "Death of Marie Laveau – A Woman with a Wonderful History, Almost a Century Old, Carried to the Tomb Tuesday Morning," *Daily Picayune*, June 17, 1881, 8.

nineteenth-century press and undertook interviews with seventy Black New Orleans residents who claimed to have interacted with Laveau. The methodological missteps and ethical failings of this project are readily apparent: many of the informants spoke Louisiana Creole as their first language, or what the white interviewers dismissed as "Negro dialect." The WPA did not possess sound recording equipment, and all interviews were therefore the product of notes taken by white interviewers or simply recreated from memory. In fact, white LWP workers were known to embellish and sometimes invent testimony.[17] Thus, the LWP narratives should not be read as significantly more reliable or "authentic" than the sensational press of the 1870s–1890s. However, they do establish an archive of the fear and anxiety Marie Laveau provoked in white audiences, a fear buttressed by contemporary anxieties about Black women's reproductive freedom and New Orleans' role in the Anglo-American civic sphere.[18] Moreover, the LWP collected these narratives at the end of the US occupation of Haiti, at a time when US popular culture was eagerly spinning tales of Haitian zombies, satanic "voodoo," and Afro-Caribbean alterity in order to deny the possibility of Black sovereignty and globalize white supremacist strategies of extraction and exploitation. As Peter Hudson has argued in the context of banking internationalization of the 1930s, domestic US racism formed in a mutually constitutive relationship with imperialism in the Caribbean in which "'profits' came in the form of both shareholder dividends and the reproduction of global white supremacy."[19]

White LWP employees such as Saxon, Edward Dreyer, Catherine Dillon, and Robert Tallant all profited from this reproduction of white supremacist violence, each authoring books on "Voodoo" and Laveau.[20]

[17] Archives of the Archdiocese of New Orleans, City Archives in the Louisiana Division of the New Orleans Public Library, the Notarial Archives Research Center at the Conveyance Office, New Orleans, the Historica New Orleans Collection, the Louisiana State Museum's Historical Center at the Old Mint Building, Special Collections at Tulane and the University of New Orleans, the Louisiana Division of Archives in Baton Rouge; primary data at the Moreland-Springarn Research Center at Howard and at the National Archives and Records Administration in Washington, DC.

[18] Frailing and Harper, "The Social Construction of Deviance."

[19] Hudson, *Bankers and Empire,* 14.

[20] Edward Dreyer compiled *Gumbo Ya-Ya* (1945), a collection of Louisiana folk tales; in 1940, Catherine Dillon produced a 700-page "Voodoo" manuscript; Marcus Christian, director of the LWP's "Negro Unit" at Dillard University, compiled another manuscript, entitled "Voodooism and Mumbo-Jumbo." Dillon's manuscript and other materials related to the LWP can be found at the Cammie G. Henry Research Center at the Watson Memorial Library, Northwestern State University of Louisiana at Natchitotches. See also the Robert Tallant Papers at the New Orleans Public Library; the Lyle Saxon Papers in Special Collections at Howard-Tilton Memorial Library at Tulane and the Earl K. Long Library at the University of New Orleans.

The most influential of these was Tallant's vehemently racist *Voodoo in New Orleans* (1946), followed by the *The Voodoo Queen* (1956), which sloppily synthesized nineteenth-century print culture, including travel guides, serial articles, sensational novels, and 1930s oral histories from the LWP. Both volumes enjoyed great success, in large part because they insisted on their own authenticity. Tallant begins his 1946 book with the assertion, "[m]uch nonsense has been written about Voodoo in New Orleans," implicitly assuring the reader of his ability to correct that "nonsense" with fact, collected and condoned by the federal government. Troublingly, Tallant's account of Laveau's life (and African-American spirituality more broadly) still enjoys outsized influence in academic literature. *Voodoo in New Orleans* remains the most cited source on Laveau, and while many of these citations are critical of his project, others are not. This careless acceptance of Tallant's racist fantasies is apparent not only in popular culture and the tourism industry but also in the medical field, where *Voodoo in New Orleans* is cited in modern medical literature as an authority on African-American cultural beliefs on issues ranging from hypertension to obstetrics and gynecology to mental illness.[21]

Contemporary critics have made a greater effort to demystify the Laveau legend, rewriting her biography through careful archival tracing and verification. In the 1990s and early 2000s, scholars influenced by "history from below" methodologies began to take Laveau seriously as a cultural subject. Reappraisals include scholarship by religious studies scholar Ina Fandrich, whose 1994 dissertation, "The Mysterious Voodoo Queen Marie Laveaux: A Study of Power and Female Leadership in New Orleans," was later published as a monograph under the same name in 2005; anthropologist Martha Ward's *Voodoo Queen: The Spirited Lives of Marie Laveau*; and conservator Carolyn Morrow Long's 2006 *A New Orleans Voudou Priestess: The Legend and Reality of Marie Laveau.*[22] While Ward and Fandrich take great pains to portray Laveau within a feminist framework of spiritual power, Long's archival training foregrounds the fissures between what she calls the "Laveau Legend" and the historical figure. Through a reconstruction of Louisiana census, ecclesiastical, notary, court, police, and city director records, Long counters the

[21] See Adebimpe, "American Blacks and Psychiatry"; Baer, "Prophets and Advisors in Black Spiritual Churches"; Bailey, "Hypertension"; Crooks, "On the Psychology of Demon Possession"; Kimball, "A Case of Pseudocyesis Caused by 'Roots'"; Spector, *Cultural Diversity in Health and Illness.*

[22] Fandrich, *The Mysterious Voodoo Queen*; Morrow, *A New Orleans Voudou Priestess;* Ward, *Voodoo Queen.*

fantastic fictions of Laveau's life with a carefully sutured historical portrait that distances itself from the sensationalism of Laveau's mythologies.

Long's archival work provides an important corrective to the nineteenth- and early twentieth-century myths surrounding Laveau's life, and I will reproduce some of her findings here: the historical Marie Laveau was born around 1801, the descendant of French colonists, enslaved Africans, and *gens de couleur*. While nineteenth-century narratives insisted that Marie was the daughter of a wealthy white planter, it is now believed that she was the daughter of two *gens de couleur*: Marguerite Darcantel, an enslaved woman who gained her freedom after nursing her enslaver from illness, and Charles Trudeau Laveaux, a free man of color who owned some properties, including a grocery store in the Faubourg Marigny. If Marie Laveau was indeed a healer, as many narratives about her – both negative and positive – suggest, she may have learned her skills from her mother, Marguerite. Although Marie's parents never married, Charles Trudeau Laveaux publicly declared Marie his natural daughter and provided her with property on the Rue D'Amour. On August 4, 1819, Marie Laveau married Jacques Paris, a free man of color from Haiti. Later in the 1820s, he disappears from the archives, at which point Marie becomes known as some variation of the Widow Paris, appearing over the years as Marie Lavaud Widow Paris, Mrs. Laveau Paris, Widow Mary Paris, and Marie Paris, Widow of Christophe. She later entered into a domestic partnership with a white man of Norman descent named Louis Christophe Dominic Duminy de Glapion. Upon his death in 1855, Marie appears in the archives as Mrs. Lavant Paris, Mary Glapion, and Marie Glapion, Widow of Dominick. Although the *New York Times* and *Daily Picayune* claimed that Marie mothered fifteen children, documentation only exists for seven: Marie Heloïse Euchariste (born in 1827 and assumed by some twentieth-century writers to be Marie II), Marie Louise Caroline, Christophe Jean Baptiste, François Maurice Christophe, Marie Philomène, and Archange Edouard. She also raised at least three of her grandchildren and in 1852 sponsored a seven-year-old boy named François at the Institut Catholique des Orphelins Indigents, a school established with funds bequeathed by an African-born former slave. She died of dysentery in 1881.[23]

This is what the archives tell us of Laveau: the mundane facts which debunk exoticized narratives of the ignominious "Voodoo Queen." And yet archives do not speak: instead, as Michel-Rolph Trouillot reminds us,

[23] See Carolyn Morrow Long's magisterial *A New Orleans Voudou Priestess.*

archives are created by people embedded in uneven structures of power. An assemblage of lawmakers, judges, journalists, archivists, police officers, and government employees determine what can be considered a "historical" source, which sources are collected and assembled into the archive, which archived sources can be made into a narrative, and which narratives are finally imbued with retrospective significance.[24] Rather than passively listening to what the archive "tell us" or what "history says," Trouillot insists that we actively attend to archival silences, asking "[w]e imagine the lives under the mortar, but how do we recognize the end of a bottomless silence?"[25] Marie's life is an example of such seemingly bottomless silences: she was purportedly illiterate, signing X in lieu of a name. She left no letters, diaries, or interviews. Indeed, her archival silence is as central to her mythos as her archival presence. As her *New York Times* obituary laments, "Now her lips are closed forever and as she could neither read nor write, not a scrap is left to chronicle the events of her exciting life."[26] Whatever "scraps" might have been reconstructed into a biography never made it past Trouillot's first stage of historical production, for they were never acknowledged as historical sources in the first place.

While Laveau's archival traces, embodied in the racist imagination as a pair of silent lips, serve as an important corrective to the falsehoods of "local color" writers, the very logics of "historic evidence" reproduce the racist structure of the archive. As Marisa J. Fuentes reminds us of enslaved women's role in historical production:

> [they] appear as historical subjects through the form and content of archival documents in the manner in which they lived: spectacularly violated, objectified, disposable, hypersexualized, and silenced. The violence is transferred from the enslaved bodies to the documents that count, condemn, assess, and evoke them, and we receive them in this condition.[27]

The white supremacist mechanisms of archival violence so eloquently delineated by Fuentes structured the lives of both free and enslaved Black women in the Americas. The formal freedom enjoyed by Laveau and other *gens de couleur* escaped the slave ledger but found quantification in other forms: in arrest records, often due to vagrancy and sumptuary laws; bills of property sales; and myriad other economic and judicial attempts to quantify and regulate Black life. To limit Laveau's life to what has been publicly acknowledged as "fact" participates in the fetishization of

[24] Trouillot, *Silencing the Past*, 30. [25] Ibid., 30.
[26] "The Dead Voudou Queen" *New York Times*, June 23, 1881. [27] Fuentes, *Dispossessed Lives*, 5.

archival authority, which not only reproduces white supremacist knowledge but also effaces the network of Black actors who evaded archival capture. To quote Zora Neale Hurston's incisive 1947 review of Robert Tallant, "[t]he best efforts of the author [Tallant] were in digging out of the newspaper files the names of the bestknown Hoodoo 'doctors' of the past. No light is thrown upon those numerous others, however, who did not for one reason or another attract the notice of the press or the police."[28]

Black life, as Hurston knew, lays bare the methodological and ethical failings of traditional historiography. More recently, Black feminist scholars, including Morgan, Fuentes, Hartman, Stephanie Smallwood, and Jessica Marie Johnson have continued this tradition of archival critique, calling for alternative modes of historical redress that evade the disciplinary exposure and incarceration at the hands of Hurston's "press or ... police." The methodologies that Hartman has influentially termed "critical fabulation" offer a mode of speculative and imaginative redress that refuses to reify the lacunae of the archive into what Trouillot might consider "silences."[29] Instead, Hartman's production of an imaginative counterhistory explores the logics of the archival "grammar of violence."[30] In her groundbreaking "Venus in Two Acts," Hartman puts pressure on the possibility of narrative redress through an exploration of the subjunctive mood in historical narration:

> Is it possible to exceed or negotiate the constitutive limits of the archive? By advancing a series of speculative arguments and exploiting the capacities of the subjunctive (a grammatical mood that expresses doubts, wishes, and possibilities), in fashioning a narrative, which is based upon archival research, and by that I mean a critical reading of the archive that mimes the figurative dimensions of history, I intended both to tell an impossible story and to amplify the impossibility of its telling.[31]

Laveau's life is situated at the nexus of these "impossible" stories: to read Laveau in the subjunctive mood requires a methodology that at once depends on the structure of the archive – its legal documents, birth records, and police reports – and exists outside the archive's logics. The subjunctive, as a grammatical mood and *not* a tense (a *temps* or time), refuses chronological distinctions that neatly categorize life into past, present, and future. Instead, the subjunctive allows the past to rupture the present; it tendrils into the future, and it forecloses the linear cataloging of traditional archival technologies. In this respect, Laveau's temporal

[28] Hurston, "Reviewed Work," 438.
[29] See Hartman, "Venus in Two Acts" and *Wayward Lives*.
[30] Hartman, "Venus in Two Acts," 4.
[31] Ibid.,11.

entanglement – one further complicated by the unruly genealogy of Marie Laveau I and her purported daughter – speaks to the "beautiful experiments" Hartman later explores in 2019's *Wayward Lives*. Narrating the lives of young Black women of New York City and Philadelphia at the turn of the twentieth century, Hartman not only redefines previously criminalized and often nameless Black women as "sexual modernists, free lovers, radicals, and anarchists" but also places their unruly strategies at the center of her own methodology.[32] Building her work around these stigmatized lives that have been failed by traditional historical methods, Hartman articulates a mode of analysis that respects the fugitivity, errantry, and opacity of the women she chronicles. As she writes of her archival search through late nineteenth-century photography:

> I browsed thousands of photographs taken by social reformers and charity organizations, hoping to find them, but they failed to appear. They averted their gaze or they rushed past the photographer; they clustered at the edge of the photos, they looked out of windows, peered out of doorways, and turned their back to the camera. They refused the terms of visibility imposed on them. They eluded the frame and remained fugitives–lovely silhouettes and dark shadows impossible to force into the grid of naturalist description of the taxonomy of slum pictures.[33]

Hartman's insistence on the visual opacity and temporal fugitivity of Black women has resonated with recent critical engagements with Laveau. Critiquing the voyeuristic impulses of traditional historical methodologies, Lisa Ze Winters, for example, foregrounds the "instability of and contradictions in Laveau's archive" to argue for the centrality of "intimate, sexual lives to the (re)production of an African diaspora across Atlantic space and time."[34] Through a reading of Laveau's portraiture against representations of the Vodou lwa Lasirèn, Ezili Freda and Ezili Dantò, Ze Winters constructs an alternative archive of Laveau that vacillates between the closure of the past and the radical openness of the future, the indicative and the subjunctive, or "the tension between what happened and what could happen."[35] Omise'eke Natasha Tinsley also decenters archival authority through a speculative engagement with the Vodou pantheon, specifically with Laveau's shared kinship with Ezili Freda. Tinsley wonders: "[Marie's] description echoes that of the Ezili, lwa of the feminine and of the inner depths of creativity, mistresses of the erotic and the esoteric. During her lifetime, Marie Laveau, like Ezili Freda, was known as the

[32] Hartman, *Wayward Lives*, xv. [33] Ibid., 18. [34] Ze Winters, *The Mulatta Concubine*, 71.
[35] Ibid.,106.

bride of Danbala. Does this make the lwa Marie Laveau – or, perhaps, the pantheon of Marie Laveau – sisters to the Ezili? Cousins? Lovers, or wives? And what to make of the queer connection that the Ezili and Mademoiselle Marie share?"[36] By disrupting traditional historiographical methods with a deeper archive of queer Caribbean spirituality, these recent readings of Marie Laveau refuse to restrict Black women's lives to axes predetermined by global northern ideologies of linear time, heterosexual reproduction, and fantasies of legibility and transparency. Instead, they gesture toward an ethics of historical production that exists in intersubjective and temporally complex articulations among diasporic bodies of kin, mothers, daughters, lovers, and gods.

I take my methodological cues from Hartman, Ze Winters, and Tinsley, building on their speculative modes of redress and temporal unruliness while attending to the potential violence embedded in the speculative project. If speculation opens alternative modes – sensorial, affective, and intergenerational – of historical production, it also invokes, as Ian Baucom reminds us, exploitative histories of racial capitalism and the fungibility of Black life; voyeuristic impulses of entertainment and consumption; and the specters of a violent white supremacist history that continues to shape our present day.[37] To speculate on Laveau's life and legacy, particularly as a healer and birthworker, is also to invoke the painful legacies of the speculum, a technology of vaginal dilation developed by J. Marion Sims on unconsenting and unanesthetized Black women. The speculum transforms the vaginal canal into a cavity, into lack, into a passive instrument in the reproduction of racial capital, and into a vehicular embodiment of the narrative of medical "progress" at the cost of Black lives. In contrast, the midwives, healers, herbalists, and birthworkers delineated here do not break open compliant bodies; nor do they project their needs, desires, and prejudices onto the perceived emptiness of their subjects. Following the practice of midwifery, my methodology refuses both violent speculation and the reproduction of archival silences. Midwifing, as a common medical practice that aims to restore power to the birthing person, might in this respect point us toward alternative archival and critical paradigms. Etymologically, the midwife is *with* but does not usurp the experiences and instincts of the birthing person.[38] As a scholar, my place here is

[36] Tinsley, *Ezili's Mirrors*, 8. [37] Baucom, *Specters of the Atlantic*.

[38] The compound "midwife" formed in Middle English around 1300. "Mid" is likely a preposition meaning "with," while "wife" in its earliest history meant "woman." See Thompson and Varney Burst, *A History of Midwifery in the United States*, xxviii.

propositional and medial, proximate but marked by difference and distance. The midwife avoids the prone and bound birthing body, and instead takes her cues from the needs, desires, and knowledge of the birthing person. In doing so, midwives respect the temporally complex process of birthwork – for labor, as any birthing person will tell you, is very seldom linear. To think of the critic as a midwife and historical production as a mode of nonlinear birthing not only decenters traditional loci of medical and archival power but also situates individuals within a network of mutual care, helping tend to a historical narrative that is embodied yet not reified, essentialized, or temporally bound.

2.2 Labors of Freedom: Reproductive Justice in Nineteenth-Century Louisiana

In contrast to what Kenneth Aslakson has called the "quadroon-plaçage" myth, Black women exercised control over their own bodies and family structures.[39] A vast body of scholarship, including work by Morgan, Deborah White, Sasha Turner, and Diana Paton, attests to many ways people of African descent, both free and enslaved, sought to determine their own reproductive futures.[40] Although the biological policing of conception, gestation, birth, and childcare affected and affects all Black people, birthing people were especially vulnerable. People with the capacity to birth thus developed strategies to subvert capitalist modes of extraction and reclaim their own energy economies from their enslavers. Many of these strategies, including plant-based remedies, Cesarean births, and inoculation, were African in origin, altered by contact with other African ethnic groups and nations, and transmitted through intergenerational networks.[41] People of African descent also adapted these medical practices to new environments, often drawing from Native American knowledge systems to diversify their knowledge of regional flora and botanical

[39] Aslakson, "The 'Quadroon-Plaçage'" and *Making Race in the Courtroom.*

[40] Bush-Slimani, "Hard Labour," 157–8; Camp, *Closer to Freedom;* Owens, *Medical Bondage*; Fett, *Working Cures*; Hine and Wittenstein, "Female Slave Resistance," 123–7; Morgan, *Laboring Women*; Penningroth, *The Claims of Kinfolk*; Schwartz, *Birthing a Slave*; Turner, "The Nameless and the Forgotten"; White, *Ar'n't I a Woman?*

[41] Covey, *African American Slave Medicine*, 47.

remedies in North America and the Caribbean.[42] Through complex processes of contact, acculturation, and adaptation, birthing people asserted control over their reproductive lives through diverse methods, intervening at different stages of the processes of conception, gestation, birth, and childrearing. They practiced coitus interruptus, abstinence, and prolonged breastfeeding to avoid unwanted pregnancies; some developed, intentionally or unintentionally, secondary amenorrhea due to malnutrition or fasting; others used barrier methods; many consumed ointments and herbs to thin the uterine lining, suppress ovulation, induce menstruation, or produce premature contractions resulting in miscarriage or abortion. Although, as White cautions, it is impossible to know the extent to which Black people engaged in practices of reproductive control, it is not unreasonable to suggest that birthing people have never been reducible to passive instruments of reproductive violence.[43] There is sufficient evidence – from both white supremacist institutions (white-owned newspapers, medical journals, plantation ledgers) and enslaved people (folk tales and songs, oral histories, archeological sites) – to suggest that people of African descent practiced birth control, induced miscarriages and abortions and exercised other forms of reproductive self-determination.

The uneven accrual of historical evidence and disproportionate privileging of white supremacist sources sanctioned by archival authority renders histories of reproductive freedom extremely difficult to trace. Many critics have read these practices as a form of "passive" gynecological resistance; others have characterized these acts in the language of labor politics, interpreting the refusal to reproduce as a form of strike; others still have emphasized how enslaved women strategized "playing small."[44] Yet, the resistance paradigm runs the risk of reproducing the misogynistic and racist assumptions of white institutional knowledge structures. There is a slim margin between resistance and resilience, the latter of which, as

42 See Fett, *Working Cures*; Hazzard-Donald, *Mojo Workin'*.

43 As Deborah White cautions in *Ar'n't I a Woman*, "It is almost impossible to determine whether slave women practiced birth control and abortion. These matters were virtually exclusive to the female world of the quarters and when they arose they were attended to in secret and were intended to remain secret" (84). On anti-Blackness in statistical analysis and conventional methodologies in the sciences and social sciences, see McKittrick, "Mathematics Black Life." See also Smallwood, *Saltwater Slavery*.

44 On passive resistance, see Allain, "Infanticide as Slave Resistance"; Bauer and Bauer, "Day to Day Resistance to Slavery"; Hine and Wittenstein, "Female Slave Resistance." On the labor politics of childbirth, see Hartman, "The Belly of the World"; on the ruses of "playing small," see Bailey, *Misogynoir Transformed*.

Kaiama Glover reminds us, is predicated on degradation and condescension.[45] People of African descent were not only agents of resistance but also experienced trauma, bereavement, grief, and many other affective states that were unacknowledged by white planters, whose financial interests depended on stereotypes of resilient Black sexuality, fecundity, and inability to love. Scholars such as Paton and Turner have argued for a more nuanced consideration of gynecological resistance, highlighting the material conditions of enslaved life (such as malnutrition, physical labor, abuse) and the risk of sudden infant death syndrome (SIDS) to make sense of situations in which Black women were accused of inducing abortions or infanticide.[46] The occlusion of parental grief in favor of an uncritical resistance paradigm risks reproducing anti-Black and misogynistic colonial propaganda, which centered on the unfeeling and unnatural Black mother.

Instead, it is important to understand that people of African descent entered into or resisted birthwork within a context of diverse possibilities and limitations, including, in the words of Paton, "expectations about possible children's futures, the social and spiritual value attributed to motherhood by their peers and kin, the need for kin in later life, [and] the desire to space children in order to ensure that existing children could be cared for."[47] WPA narratives conducted in the US South in the 1930s testify to such reproductive expectations and the diversity of practices they necessitated. As discussed earlier in this chapter, these accounts are marked by racist biases that likely warped the collection and transcription of Black oral histories. Yet, given the detail with which botanical knowledge is recounted and corroborated with archaeological evidence, it is possible to assume that these narratives provide useful, if flawed, insights into the practices of Black midwives. For example, Lu Lee, a formerly enslaved midwife from Texas, described how pregnant people "unfixed" themselves by taking calomel, indigo, cotton root, and turpentine. According to Lee, turpentine manufacturers even attempted to change the formula once they learned that Black women were using the substance to provoke miscarriages.[48] Fittingly, it was often the very products of their stolen labor – indigo, cotton – that allowed enslaved people to reclaim their energy production and deny their enslavers the means of compounding human

45 Glover, "New Narratives of Haiti," 206.

46 Turner, "The Nameless and the Forgotten." See also Cowling, Paton, and West, *Motherhood, Childlessness and the Care of Children;* Paton, "Maternal Struggles and the Politics of Childlessness," 251–68; Turner, *Contested Bodies.*

47 Paton, "Maternal Struggles and the Politics of Childlessness under Pronatalist Caribbean Slavery."

48 Rawick, *The American Slave.*

capital. These WPA accounts, moreover, are supported by site-specific archaeological evidence. Laurie Wilkie, for example, recovered known contraceptives and abortifacients in the former home of Black midwife Lucrecia Perryman, including jars of senna, quinine, turpentine, camphor, vaseline, and cod liver oil.[49] While many of these substances are used to hasten childbirth in late pregnancy, they are also known to stimulate uterine contractions potent enough to cause miscarriage or abortion earlier in gestation. It is likely that a midwife would understand the uses of such substances and would have deployed them creatively and judiciously, in consultation with the birthing person.

While much scholarship on reproductive freedom and unfreedom has focused on enslaved women, free people of color, such as Marie Laveau, also struggled against policies and technologies of reproductive regulation and management. In New Orleans, free women of color in *placée* relationships with white men used strategic reproduction to gain social and economic privileges for their children. For this reason, they were especially vulnerable to sex work regulations, which in the antebellum period were often promulgated under the guise of "nuisance" and "vagrancy" laws.[50] Free women of color also frequently served as midwives and administered to birthing people of all races. While the intimate lives of sex workers and those perceived to be sex workers produced anxieties in white authorities panicked by the moral exposure of the "public woman," the intimacy of midwifery was vilified and regulated precisely for its *lack* of publicity. Behind closed doors, midwives, whether free or enslaved, evaded the white medical gaze and resisted modes of reproductive coercion rooted in the collusion of managerial plantation strategies and the burgeoning field of obstetrics.

Although scholars discuss reproductive life before the twentieth century in contemporary terms of "abortion," "miscarriage," or "conception," birthing people in the nineteenth century may not have used the same language to describe their reproductive experiences. The temporal markers and linear structure of modern understandings of pregnancy and childbirth are incompatible with the diversity of theories about life, conception, and personal identity in the eighteenth and early nineteenth centuries.

49 Wilkie, *The Archaeology of Mothering*, 162–79 and "Expelling Frogs and Binding Babies."

50 Aslakson, "The 'Quadroon-Plaçage'"; Dormon, "Louisiana's 'Creoles of Color'"; Gehman and Dennis, *The Free People of Color of New Orleans*; Gehman and Reis, *Women and New Orleans*; Gould, *Chained to the Rock of Adversity*; Lacoste, "'Quadroon Ball' Myths Are Debunked by Historian"; Martin, "*Plaçage* and the Louisiana *Gens de Couleur Libre*; Morazan, "Quadroon Balls in the Spanish Period."

For example, it is difficult to distinguish between contraceptives and abortifacients during this period: until the mid-nineteenth century, pregnancies were not confirmed until the time of "quickening" or when fetal movement became detectable to the gestating person, usually around twenty weeks into the pregnancy.[51] An abortion performed before quickening (usually by chemical means, for example, by taking herbal emmenagogues) was thus not considered a termination of pregnancy but instead a preventative measure or an induction of menstruation. The use of quickening as a legal metric to mark the beginning of pregnancy was derived from British common law and remained legally in effect in most US states until 1860.[52] Yet, as the fields of obstetrics and gynecology gained legitimacy in the nineteenth century, public perceptions of the beginning of life began to shift from the pregnant person's subjective, interior, sensory experience to external metrics, confirmable and quantifiable by white male medical practitioners. Doctors became increasingly aware of the early signs of pregnancy (enlargement and softening of the cervix, the deepening of nipple color) and, with the invention of the stethoscope in 1818, could detect a fetal heartbeat. As pregnancy became externalized and public, legislation quickly developed to limit women's reproductive autonomy and channel the energy production of birthwork into white heteropatriarchal structures of profit.

These restrictions were intimately intertwined with white supremacist ideologies of race. Doctors frequently practiced surgical techniques on enslaved women without their consent and without anesthesia, the most notorious of whom was J. Marion Sims, known as the "father of modern gynecology." Sims's inhumane experiments on enslaved women led to the invention of the modern speculum, as well as "advancements" in Cesarean sections, obstetrical fistulae repair, and ovariotomies. As Deirdre Cooper Owens has argued,

> reproductive medicine was essential to the maintenance and success of southern slavery... Doctors formed a cohort of elite white men whose work, especially their gynecological examinations of black women, affected the country's slave markets. Each slave sold was examined medically so that she could be priced. Southern doctors knew enslaved women's reproductive

[51] Brodie, *Contraception and Abortion in Nineteenth-Century America*; Klepp *Revolutionary Conceptions.*

[52] Morh, "Patterns of Abortion and the Response of American Physicians," 184. Cited in Wilkie "Expelling Frogs and Binding Babies," 275. See also Stagenborg and Skoczylas,"Battles over Abortion and Reproductive Rights," 215–16.

> labor, which ranged from the treatment of gynecological illnesses to pregnancies, helped them revolutionize professional women's medicine.[53]

Viewed by white scientists as expendable nonhuman material, Black women were no longer considered skillful subjects (midwives, healers, birthing people whose instincts were to be trusted) but instead unskilled and ungendered experimental objects.[54] Yet, some of Sims's victims – Betsy, Lucy, and Anarcha, and those whose names were not recorded – were themselves skilled medical providers, aiding Sims's experiments and learning to care for and heal each other. Their own knowledge, developed despite Sims's torture, formed a counterarchive of relational energy practices.

Sims's experiments were by no means outliers in the institutionalization of obstetric and gynecological healthcare. In 1856, a group of physicians, including Erasmus Darwin Fenner, a specialist in yellow fever, and D. Warren Brickell, a professor of obstetrics who studied and "perfected" Sims's techniques, founded the New Orleans School of Medicine.[55] The School established the first system of clinical instruction as well as one of the first departments of obstetrics in the United States. In his inaugural lecture on obstetrics, delivered in November 1857, Brickell ominously hints at the human lives and labor which made such "achievements" possible: New Orleans, he notes, enjoys a "superabundance of anatomical material, and ... liberal laws which permit the freest use of these great privileges."[56] To put it more bluntly, Brickell, like Sims, experimented on Black women without their consent and without anesthesia. Under the auspices of the New Orleans School, he practiced the removal of polyps, drained ovarian tumors, researched treatments for venereal disease (known as "diseases of women"), and experimented with "breeding" techniques on people of African descent, often fatally harming his victims.[57]

Midwives threatened such experiments. Brickell complained of midwives in an 1857 article in the *New Orleans Medical News and Hospital*

[53] Owens, *Medical Bondage*, 4.

[54] I here of course am thinking of Hortense Spiller's influential work on fungibility and gender, "Mama's Baby." See also Snorton,"Anatomically Speaking" in *Black on Both Sides*.

[55] McQueeney, "The City That Care Forgot."

[56] "Introductory Lecture Delivered by D. Warren Brickell M.D." (New Orleans: Bulletin Office, 1857).

[57] These experiments were published in the *New Orleans Medical News and Hospital Gazette*, a medical journal and the mouthpiece of the New Orleans School of Medicine. The journal was edited by Brickell and Fenner and ran from 1854–61.

Gazette as "curses of communities in which they are found."[58] While "meddlesome" women of all races delivered babies – Harriet Beecher Stowe notably practiced midwifery and experimented with mesmeric healing on postpartum women in the 1840s – it was primarily women of color who were vilified, particularly when they presided over the births of white women.[59] Although physicians were responsible for extremely high maternal and infant mortality rates, midwives of New Orleans attracted the condemnation of physicians, planters, journalists, and politicians, who accused them of negligence, ineptitude, unhygienic practices, sorcery, and homicide. An 1848 notice in the *New Orleans Daily Crescent* reports a complaint against a free woman of color named Jane, whose purported misrepresentation as a licensed "skilful midwife" [sic] led to the death of her client, a white woman.[60] Similar reports frequently appear in Louisiana print culture, reaching their peak in the 1860s. In December, a coroner's inquest condemned an "ignorant midwife" for ignoring the symptoms of lockjaw, resulting in the death of a newborn; a week later, another midwife is accused of "mismanagement and ignorance" for giving a child an overdose of gin; a notice titled "Fatal Incompetency" on December 17, 1868, accuses a Black woman named Amelia Jessop of falsely representing herself as a midwife, leading to the death of a child.[61]

Concomitant with increased panic around Black midwifery in the local New Orleans press was the increased politicization of birthwork and especially abortion at a national level in the 1860s–70s. While moral anxiety around reproductive autonomy had always operated in slaveholding societies, especially those that followed the injunction of *partus*, the regulation of midwifery in the United States follows a unique arc from Emancipation to post-Reconstruction. The campaign against Black midwives accelerated just as Black futurity and self-determination were becoming tangible political goals. While the political and civic gains of Reconstruction are frequently framed in terms of the masculinized public sphere of government, Reconstruction also saw Black women practicing midwifery for both themselves and white women, earning independent income, and helping women shape their reproductive lives. This domestic

58 Brickell, "Two Cases of Vesico Vaginal Fistula Cured," 579, cited in McQueeney, "The City That Care Forgot," 89.

59 Bannister, "Meddlesome Midwifery"; Hedrick, *Harriet Beecher Stowe*, 197, and "'Peaceable Fruits.'"

60 *New Orleans Daily Crescent*, April 26, 1848.

61 "Coroner's Inquest," *New Orleans Daily Crescent*, December 4, 1860; "Coroner's Inquest," *New Orleans Daily Crescent*, December 11, 1860; "Fatal Incompetency," *New Orleans Daily Crescent*, December 17, 1868.

force posed a more intimate challenge to white supremacy than familiar Reconstruction narratives of Black leadership in the public sphere of government. As white terrorist organizations deployed ideologies of white womanhood to uphold racist hierarchies, the perceived threat of Black midwives – and their attendant reminder of reproductive choice and Black women's energy autonomy – became a target for tactics of policing, management, and terror. Abortion was prohibited in Louisiana in 1870, and by 1880, most other states had followed suit. The 1873 Comstock Act made it illegal for doctors to advise women about birth control, and midwives came under increased pressure and regulation from the medical establishment, which sought to restrict its competitors. Just as obstetrics developed out of and in conjunction with mass-scale enslavement, US legal restrictions of abortion formed in a mutually constitutive relationship with white supremacist policing of Black futures.

The success of obstetrics as both a social regulatory mechanism and an economically lucrative enterprise thus relied on the marginalization of Black midwifery and the vilification of traditional birthing practices. In 1894, New Orleans attempted to regulate midwifery by requiring practitioners to register with the Secretary of the Board of Health.[62] Black midwives and healers, however, were forbidden from practicing birthwork or registering as midwives: "This section does not apply to the so-called midwife of rural districts and plantation practice, who, in the sense of this act, are not considered as practicing Midwifery as a profession."[63] By writing Black midwives and "plantation practices" out of the profession, Louisiana law recognized the autonomy of Black medical practices while attempting to denigrate that knowledge by segregating it from professional norms. Attempts to regulate birthwork, however, were largely unsuccessful: a 1915 review of a pamphlet on British midwifery in the *New Orleans Medical and Surgical Journal* reported that 70 percent of Louisiana births were officiated by midwives, compared to 35 percent in San Francisco and Omaha. The reviewer concludes that "[i]gnorance of midwives is deplored, but it cannot be condoned nor overlooked."[64]

Propaganda campaigns against Black midwives frequently centered around lurid tales of abortion and infanticide. In a transcript of the New Orleans Parish Medical Society's Symposium on the Control of Criminal

[62] "Practice of Medicine Surgery and Midwifery" Act 49, *Acts Passed by the General Assembly of the State of Louisiana: Baton Rouge, 1894*.

[63] Ibid.

[64] *The New Orleans Medical and Surgical Journal*, vol. 67 (Baton Rouge: Louisiana State Medical Society, 1915), 208.

Abortion, held on February 25, 1918, a physician identified as Dr. J. M. Elliott laments that "[t]he evil [of performing abortions] comes from the ignorant and immoral midwife ... We have a lot of poor midwives, colored, etc. with no education and few morals, who would possibly do anything."[65] This linkage between reproductive policing and white supremacy had a deep transnational history that extends beyond the Anglo-American coordinates of US political history. Women-led birthing practices, whether conducted independently or under the care of midwives, elders, or healers, had long been in tension with the plantation system and its afterlives in the white medical institution. Tales of unnatural and violent motherhood were particularly prevalent in colonial Saint-Domingue, where the birth rate was exceedingly low: rather than acknowledge the abuse, stress, and negligence of plantation societies, colonists instead accused midwives and enslaved women of killing children by sticking pins in the heads of newborns, thus inducing *mal de machoire* or lockjaw.[66] According to French physician Michel Étienne Descourtilz, an enslaved midwife from the Rossignol-Desdunes plantation confessed to killing over seventy children using this method in order to "save them from slavery."[67] Although it is impossible to know the circumstances under which this "confession" was obtained or interpreted, Descourtilz's anecdote highlights the threat (whether real or perceived) that Black midwives posed to the plantation system.

With the onset of the Haitian Revolution, and its concomitant mythologizing of warrior women, this imaginative linkage between Black liberation and a uniquely feminine monstrosity became even more intimate. General Leclerc, writing of his failed recapture of Saint-Domingue, reported the words of an enslaved woman and her children being led to execution. On the scaffold, the mother allegedly implored her daughters to "Rejoice that your wombs will not have to bear slave children."[68] While white colonists' accounts of gynecological and obstetric practices depended on racist assumptions about Black inhumanity and unmaternal grotesquerie, their reports may have contained, albeit in warped and manipulated

[65] *The New Orleans Medical and Surgical Journal*, 70 (Baton Rouge: Louisiana State Medical Society, 1918), 838.

[66] See Boisvert, "Colonial Hell and Female Slave Resistance in Saint-Domingue"; Weaver, *Medical Revolutionaries* and "'She Crushed the Child's Fragile Skull.'"

[67] de Vaissière, *Saint-Domingue (1629–1789)*, 252 n3; cited by Boisvert, "Colonial Hell and Female Slave Resistance in Saint-Domingue," 67.

[68] Metral, *Histoire de l'expédition des français*, 180–81. See also Eddins, "'Rejoice!'"; Fick, *The Making of Haiti*, 221; Girard, "Rebelles with a Cause," 69.

form, some understanding of reproductive choices exercised under slavery. As Angela Davis contends, "Black women have been aborting themselves since the earliest days of slavery. . .[refusing] to bring children into a world of interminable forced labor where chains and floggings and sexual abuse for women were the everyday conditions of life."[69] For some birthing people, miscarriage, abortion, and infanticide offered ways of depriving enslavers the possibility of compounding human capital; for others, they were tragic and undesired outcomes of plantation abuses. It is reasonable to assume that birthing people's experiences fell along a vast affective spectrum that could include (perhaps sometimes simultaneously) joy, relief, and pride as well as grief, mourning, and anger. Reproduction, or its foreclosure, garnered a wide range of responses dependent on the individual, their positionality, and their historical and cultural context. Much like today, conception, gestation, birth, miscarriage, and abortion meant different things to different people with unevenly distributed access to power, privilege, and choice.

While the affective dimension of reproductive autonomy might resonate with contemporary understandings of birthwork, the moral framework of reproduction was likely incompatible with contemporary US discourses of abortion and personhood. In New Orleans in particular, a unique amalgamation of spiritual views converged that was distinct from the Christian "pro-life" theological framework of the twentieth and twenty-first centuries. Prior to the mid-nineteenth century, the Catholic Church held a variety of views on abortion. Following Aristotelian theories of delayed ensoulment, theologians Aquinas and Augustine were tolerant of early term abortion, and upper-class women in eighteenth-century France publicly shared knowledge of contraception and abortifacients.[70] Similarly, Haitian Vodou accepts, if somewhat reluctantly, that abortion may be practiced under certain circumstances. According to Karen McCarthy Brown, "Vodou morality is not a morality of rule or law but a contextual one . . . Abortion 'is murder' but it is also the only choice to make in some situations."[71] The contextual nature of reproductive choice is echoed by Patrick Bellegarde-Smith:

> Abortion is not a good thing in Haitian Vodou. . . On the other hand, you've got to do what you got to do, and then you will argue your way out of it with the spirit world later. They might actually understand the

[69] Davis, "Racism, Birth Control, and Reproductive Rights," 355.
[70] Dombrowski and Deltete, *A Brief, Liberal, Catholic Defense of Abortion.*
[71] McCarthy Brown, *Mama Lola*, 241.

> conditions that led you to doing this. It's not a nice idea to have an abortion, but the person has to do what a person has to do. This applies, generally speaking, to all kinds of moral dilemmas that each and every individual faces in life.[72]

The relative permissiveness of Roman Catholicism and Haitian Vodou converged in early nineteenth-century New Orleans to shape a fairly tolerant attitude toward contraception and abortion, a tolerance which was increasingly eroded as Louisiana became incorporated into Anglo-American US culture. To Anglo-American audiences, Caribbean and Louisianian tales of abortion and infanticide were stripped of their theological contexts and instead became evidence of "creole" depravity.

White abolitionists seized on what they perceived to be this depravity, transferring their condemnation from the individual body of the mother to the institution of slavery. Yet, those condemnations of institutions, as Hartman has argued, came back to center on the (often abject, deformed, or violated) Black woman's body.[73] Anxieties around abortion frequently appeared in abolitionist Anglo-American literature, sometimes as genteel references and sometimes as melodramatic tableaux. In Harriet Jacobs's *Incidents in the Life of a Slave Girl*, for example, Jacobs explains how her enslaver and abuser Dr. Flint offered to teach her methods to avoid or abort a pregnancy:

> He intimated that if I had accepted his proposals, he, as a physician, could have saved me from exposure ... He then went on to say that he had neglected his duty; that as a physician there were certain things he ought to have explained to me. Then followed talk such as would have made the most shameless blush.[74]

Although the narrator here betrays a "shameless blush," Harriet's editor Lydia Maria Child was an advocate for contraception. She frequently attended public lectures on birth control and even commended one of the most famous lecturers on the circuit, Dr. Frederick Hollick, as a man capable of "plain, familiar conversations. . .with great modesty of language and propriety of demeanor."[75] It is clearly not contraception in principle

[72] Tippet and Bellegarde-Smith, "Speaking of Faith," 153.

[73] Hartman, *Scenes of Subjection*; see also Hendler, *Public Sentiments*; Sánchez-Eppler, *Touching Liberty*; Weheliye, *Habeas Viscus*.

[74] Jacobs, *Incidents in the Life of a Slave Girl*, 58.

[75] Lydia Maria Child "Letter XI April 7 1844" in *Letters from New York*, 11th ed. (New York: C.S. Francis, 1850); and "Letter from New York, No. 11," *United States Gazette* (May 5, 1846) Cited from April R. Haynes, *Riotous Flesh: Women, Physiology, and the Solitary Vice in Nineteenth-Century America* (Chicago: University of Chicago Press, 2015) 29.

that troubles Jacobs's white editor but rather the vulgarities of anatomical discussion, obviously designed by Dr. Flint to violate, and, in that respect, not unlike the verbal assault he inflicts on Jacobs earlier in the narrative ("stinging, scorching words; words that scathed ear and brain like fire," she laments).[76] But it is also the subject position of Jacobs that seems to trouble Child: Jacobs was an enslaved Black woman, and *not* the bourgeois white audience of married couples who enjoyed Dr. Hollick's lectures. For many wealthy white women, reproductive freedom was/is merely a question of lifestyle and consumer choice, but white abolitionists could not concede such luxuries to Black women. If white abolitionists considered that they "saved" Black women from carrying the children of their enslavers, they burdened them with the conceptual pregnancy of sentiment and sensation, the labor of bearing white abolitionist ideologies.

While Jacobs only referenced reproductive control with cautious obliquity, other abolitionist accounts of abortion and infanticide indulged in the lurid. Margaret Garner's 1856 decision to kill her two-year-old daughter rather than allow her to be re-enslaved (best known today as the inspiration for Toni Morrison's 1987 novel *Beloved*) attracted national attention from abolitionists and proslavery advocates alike. The press surrounding her capture and subsequent trial became a rallying cry for abolitionists, who used her story to prove how slavery degraded morality and maternal sentiment. As a journalist in the *Pittsburgh Visitor* wrote in February 1856, "[t]he name of Margaret Garner shall be a memento of which posterity shall be proud, and will certainly be cherished by good men and women for ages to come."[77] Although exceedingly rare, infanticide became a focal point for abolitionist culture in the 1850s and Garner a touchstone for slavery debates. Garner's criminal mythos overshadowed her lived experience: following her trial, she disappears from the archive, although rumors circulated that she settled, and eventually died, in New Orleans.

Whether or not Garner actually chose to move to New Orleans, it is significant that her myth ends in the Crescent City. Anglo-American abolitionist tales of infanticide frequently invoked New Orleans as a metonym for depravity, unnatural sexual appetites, and unmaternal grotesquerie. In Harriet Beecher Stowe's *Uncle Tom's Cabin*, written five years before the Garner case, the francophone Louisiana "quadroon" Cassy

[76] Jacobs, *Incidents in the Life of a Slave Girl*, 55.

[77] Cited from Mark Reinhardt *Who Speaks for Margaret Garner?* (Minneapolis: University of Minnesota Press, 2010) 1.

recounts the murder of her infant after seeing her two older children sold into slavery: "I would never again let a child live to grow up! I took the little fellow in my arms, when he was two weeks old, and kissed him, and cried over him; and then I gave him laudanum, and held him close to my bosom, while he slept to death."[78] Cassy carries the cultural markers of many Louisiana spiritual workers: like Marie Laveau, "she seemed to work by magic" and was "familiar with many healing arts."[79] But Cassy's revolutionary potential is ultimately hampered by Stowe's sentimentality: the unruly creole woman is ultimately reunited with her children, tamed into gentility, and absorbed, as Carolyn Berman has argued, into the Anglo-American family.[80]

While Stowe's portrait of Cassy's infanticide predates popular representations of Marie Laveau, Charles Chesnutt's 1921 *Paul Marchand, F.M.C.* references the Laveau legend more directly. Chesnutt's version of the "voodoo" queen takes the form of the "mammy" Zabet Philosophe, a direct echo of George Washington Cable's Palmyre la Philosophe. Like popular representations of Laveau, Zabet is a refugee from the Haitian Revolution, hairdresser, prophetess, midwife, healer, nurse, and surrogate mother. She is also implicitly tied to infanticide by swapping her enslaver's white daughter (who dies during the voyage from Saint-Domingue to the United States) with her own mixed-race grandchild, son of her enslaver, and her daughter. Complicating the racist logics of reproductive legibility demanded by both plantation societies and Jim Crow, Zabet reveals the racial-sexual abuse underlying slaveholding logics. Under threat of being sold or whipped, Zabet confesses that the swapped infant was "[h]is child as much as any! I brought the child with me, and when the little girl died, I brought the boy instead to Pierre Beaurepas!"[81] Through this forced confession, Zabet foregrounds the contiguity between the colonial trope of infanticide and the Reconstruction-era trope of child-swapping, the death (be it literal or civic) of the white child standing in for the stolen life of the Black "usurper." Moreover, this contiguity reverberates along the axis of the Haitian Revolution, implicitly coded here as an unnatural midwifery, a birthing of a sovereign nation to which European and North American powers conceded no birthright.

Laveau's legend developed in tandem with fictional representations of Black midwives, mothers, and healers such as Zabet and Cassy. Her

[78] Stowe, *Uncle Tom's Cabin*, 427. [79] Ibid., 412, 419. [80] Berman, *Creole Crossings*.
[81] Chesnutt, *Paul Marchand*, 96.

frequently celebrated (or feared) skills as a botanist and healer, as well as her close ties to children both biological and adopted, implicitly code her as a birthworker. Moreover, as Winters and Tinsley have argued, Laveau's affinity with the Ezili pantheon places her in the realm of childbirth and reproductive choice: the abundant Ezili Freda protects the more pleasurable aspects of reproduction (from sex to children's play), while Ezili Dantò tends to the maladies, hardships, and difficult choices associated with birth and childrearing.[82] Eziaku Nwokocha recounts her experience, discussing her reproductive freedom with the latter:

> I remain open to children, but I argued with Ezili Dantò that I was not financially, professionally, or emotionally ready to have one. Moreover, I did not have a partner to help with rearing a child and I did not want to do so alone. I told the lwa that continuing my education was very important to me and that once I finished my graduate studies and secured a steady job to provide for my family, I would be more comfortable with the idea of having children. The lwa informed me that this was permissible and that I would have all I wanted and more. Though the lwa gave me a command, it was within my power, as a non-initiate, to negotiate.[83]

Nwokocha's negotiation with Dantò spiritualizes debates around reproductive choice and freedom. Laveau, a skilled botanist, caretaker, and mother, may herself have conducted similar conversations with birthing people in New Orleans. The insistence on negotiating with the lwa in Vodou complicates the normative injunction to bear children, instead allowing parenthood and birthwork to take diverse shapes along a spectrum that is collective, relational, and intersubjective.

These nuances among the figures of the Ezili pantheon and their relationships to maternity became, when viewed by the white contemporary press, vulgarized and misconstrued into a misogynistic virgin/whore dichotomy. Nowhere is this more apparent than in conflicting reports of Laveau's healing practices. According to some contemporary accounts, her herbal knowledge renders her a saintly nurse; in others, she is a witch and sorcerer. These stark binaries resonate, more broadly, with white attitudes around Black motherhood – either a sainted and desexualized caretaker or an unnatural and alluring Jezebel. Laveau's obituary in the *Daily Picayune,* thought to be authored by Lafcadio Hearn, emphasizes how she was "skilled in the practice of medicine and was acquainted with the valuable healing qualities of indigenous herbs." He goes on to claim that she was a

[82] See Braziel, "Atis Rezistans," 29; McCarthy Brown, *Mama Lola*, 242.
[83] Nwokocha, "The 'Queerness' of Ceremony," 78–9.

nurse during the yellow fever and cholera epidemics who drew on considerable "skill and knowledge" to "minister to the fever-stricken."[84] This kindly Laveau was, in Hearn's telling, not only a talented medicine woman but also a sainted mother to fifteen children, an adoptive mother to orphans, a community leader, and a soothing caretaker.

Negative portrayals of Laveau also highlighted her botanical knowledge and maternity, although to opposite effect. In Robert Tallant's novel *The Voodoo Queen of New Orleans*, the voodoo Doctor John accuses Laveau: "You are always having babies – always babies."[85] His exasperation with Laveau's hyperfecundity is met with frequent allusions to Laveau's alleged practice of infanticide: "Had it not been said that she committed murder in secret, that she used human bones and babies' skeletons in her rites?"[86] Moreover, Tallant repeats this myth in the purportedly historical *Voodoo in New Orleans*, where he reports the testimony of a French woman who claimed to live across the street from Laveau in 1880s: "[s]he was an evil woman ... She killed babies that were not wanted by their mothers ... Oh she killed lots of children. They say her armoire was filled with skeletons ... She was awful!"[87]

Tallant's discomfort with this figure of uncontrollable maternity, Black energy politics, and reproductive autonomy is compounded by the ways in which white observers emphasized Laveau's herbal knowledge. Tallant attributes a quasi-Faustian characteristic to Laveau's "gris-gris": "all the time she was creating new charms, new gris-gris, and it seemed to her that the knowledge to do this came to her from some great inward power."[88] The diabolical construal of a Black woman's "great inward power" is more explicitly named as evil in another passage in the novel. Here, Laveau embodies the most stereotypical forms of witchcraft, crying "I must have a cat, a black one, and I must make much gris-gris to sell. I will need roots and herbs, bones and dried creatures – frogs, lizards, bats!" – a demand that impels Doctor John to call her "Witch!"[89] This accusation of witchcraft likely had its source in "local color" tourist literature of the late nineteenth and early twentieth centuries. The *Picayune Guide to New Orleans* writes of Laveau and her associates: "[like] the witches in Macbeth, they would gather from the woods and bayou frogs and crocodile and Congo snakes to throw into the boiling pot to make their famous charms or 'gris-gris.'"[90] These contradictory representations of Laveau as a

[84] "Death of Marie Laveau" *Daily Picayune* June 17, 1881, 8.
[85] Tallant, *The Voodoo Queen of New Orleans*, 138. [86] Ibid., 305. [87] Ibid., 89.
[88] Ibid., 150. [89] Ibid., 102. [90] *Picayune's Guide to New Orleans*, 65–6.

witch and saint, killer and mother, and healer and poisoner code her as a midwife, a woman with the power to simultaneously control, impede, harm, and support Black reproductive lives.

Zora Neale Hurston's account of Laveau reckons with these contradictions, but her portrayal of Laveau's association with contraception, sterility, miscarriage, and abortion offers an alternative set of possibilities for Black reproductive freedom. Roughly contemporary to the LWP project, Zora Neale Hurston explored Laveau's life and legacy, making several trips to New Orleans between 1928 and 1930, and was eventually initiated into spiritual practice by Laveau's nephew. In an August 6, 1928, letter to Langston Hughes, she famously wrote: "I have landed in the kingdom of Marie Laveau and expect to wear her crown someday."[91] The results of these trips were first published in the October–December 1931 *Journal of American Folklore as* "Hoodoo in America"; another version later appeared in 1935's *Mules and Men.*[92] The ethical and methodological differences between the LWP's and Hurston's projects are nowhere more apparent than in Hurston's scathingly rigorous review of Tallant's *Voodoo in New Orleans*:

> There is no revelation of any new facts, nor any analysis of what is already known. It is rather a collection of the popular beliefs about Hoodoo from the outside. The snake-worship, sex orgies, Greek Pythonesses, and goat sacrifices proceeding from false premises, and governed by hasty generalizations. It offers no opportunity for serious study, and should be considered for just what it is, a creative-journalistic appeal to popular fancy.[93]

While Hurston's fieldwork has its own methodological problems (contemporary poet Brenda Marie Osbey scoffs at "Zora Neale Hurston and her laughable tales of snakes and nudity and black cat bones"),[94] her integration into spiritual communities, her commitment to historicization of Hoodoo/Voodoo/Vodou in a comparative cultural context, and her keen understanding of the archival politics of Laveau's life render her accounts of New Orleanian spirituality far more reliable than those perpetuated by the LWP and mark a significant ethical and methodological turn in the field of anthropology.

In the fall of 1928, Hurston studied under Luke Turner, a "voodoo doctor" and self-declared nephew of Laveau. During her tutelage, she became initiated into New Orleanian Hoodoo and ultimately the recipient of the "crown of power," a symbol of spiritual achievement. During Hurston's apprenticeship,

[91] Hurston to Langston Hughes August 6, 1928; cited from Kaplan, *Zora Neale Hurston*, 18.
[92] Hurston, *Mules and Men* and "Hoodoo in America. [93] Hurston, "Reviewed Work," 438.
[94] Osbey, "Why We Can't Talk to You About Voodoo," 4.

Turner repeatedly invokes reproductive freedom and control. However, unlike racist white-authored accounts of Laveau's witchcraft and infanticide, these practices are never named as curses. Instead, Turner's account of contraception, and possibly abortion, remains remarkably ambivalent:

> If it be a woman, you will take the egg of a guinea fowl, and put it into the powder of the fruit of cayenne and the dust of Goofer, and you will set it on the fire in your own house and in clear water from the skies you will boil it until it shall be hard. This you will do so that there shall be no fruit from her womb.[95]

Turner's account of New Orleanian Goofer recalls descriptions by Bellegarde-Smith and McCarthy Brown of the contextual moral nature of Haitian Vodou. The practice of preventing or removing "fruit" from the womb can be construed as a curse, a form of reproductive coercion that mimics the reproductive violence of plantation societies and foreshadows the mass sterilization of African-Americans in the US in the twentieth century. Yet, Turner, as interpreted by Hurston, is ambiguous about the extent to which birthing people collaborate in this process. Sterility need not be a curse: for some, this may have been a desired outcome and means of evading sexual and reproductive violence. If one reads Turner's explication of Hoodoo within the contextual ethos of Afro-Caribbean spirituality, it is clear that the procedure's meaning is dependent on people's circumstances. Furthermore, unlike planters and doctors, whose attempts to control Black reproduction focused almost entirely on the birthing body, Hurston highlights the stakes of contraception and sterility for all people regardless of birthing ability: she reports on practices that allow "seed [to] dry up so that they shall not multiply."[96] Hurston refuses to see Laveau within the strict dichotomy of Sinner or Saint, bearer of curses or emancipatory enchantments. Nor does she reproduce the cis-sexist colonial assumptions that reproduction is the sole responsibility of a birthing person. Hurston instead presents Vodou as a multivalenced spiritual practice available to a community of people of various gender identities. In doing so, she dilates critical understandings of reproductive freedom and allows for more capacious forms of relation among people of African descent.

2.3 "Deviant Energy" and Intergenerational Mothering

Although Laveau is figured as a community mother and healer in ways that align with midwifery, very few nineteenth-century accounts mention her

[95] Hurston, *Mules and Men* 205. [96] Ibid., 245.

daughter and none recognize her descendants as Vodou "queens" or successors in any spiritual or political understanding of the term. When Laveau died in 1881, some obituaries referenced her daughter Marie Philomène Glapion (or Madame Legendre). George Washington Cable wove these obituaries into a fictional narrative when, in his 1886 "Creole Slave Songs," he described the younger Laveau as "a woman of some seventy years, and a most striking and majestic figure. In features, stature, and bearing she was regal. One had but to look on her, impute her brilliancies – too untamable and severe to be called charms or graces – to her mother."[97] An accompanying illustration by Edward W. Kemble (see Figure 2.1) portrays both women, the elder Laveau seated and hunched, the younger Laveau standing straight behind her mother, her hands gracefully clasped before her. Despite the studied differences in posture, they wear similar expressions of severity, staring at something (or someone) slightly outside the frame of the picture. While Cable falls short of naming the younger Laveau as a queen or Vodou practitioner, he sets in motion the romantic associations that would conflate the two into a dynastic singular woman.

In the twentieth century, the white journalist G. William Nott was one of the first to solidify these associations in a November 19, 1922 article in the *Times Picayune* entitled "Marie Laveau, Long High Priestess of Voudousim in New Orleans." In it, he claimed that the younger Laveau took up the mantle of the mother's business and that "with the passing of years [her] fame as a dabbler in black magic began to spread."[98] Nott's article was later reprinted in Lyle Saxon's 1928 *Fabulous New Orleans;* Saxon added his own twist to the legend, reporting that the younger was "known to the police as a worker of black magic."[99] The Louisiana Writers' Project, led by Saxon, repeats these claims: informants frequently describe Marie Laveau as a young to middle-aged woman, not the elder she would have been in the 1860s and 1870s. Drawing from these oral histories, white LWP workers would embellish Laveau family history. Catherine Dillon, in her unpublished 700-page "Voodoo" manuscript, coined the names "Marie I" and "Marie II" to differentiate between the reports of an elder and younger Laveau.[100] Robert Tallant further bolstered this myth, claiming "The truth of course is there were at least two Marie Laveaus. There may have been more. There is evidence that a

97 Cable, "Creole Slave Songs," 818.

98 Nott, "Marie Laveau, Long High Priestess of Voudouism in New Orleans." Reprinted in Saxon, *Fabulous New Orleans*, 244–6.

99 Saxon, *Fabulous New Orleans*, 243.

100 Dillon, "Voodoo."

Figure 2.1 "Marie Laveau," Edward Windsor Kemble, April 1886

dynasty was established in an attempt to pass the rule of the cult from the mother to the daughter. It seems also to have been a deliberate attempt to found a legend of immortality."[101] LWP writers repeated the myth of two Laveaux with such conviction that it has even been perpetuated in scholarship, notably in Martha Ward's 2009 biography of Marie Laveau, *Voodoo Queen*, and Shirley Thompson's study of Louisiana Creole identity, *Exiles at Home.* Yet, as Carolyn Morrow Long argues, there is little reason to believe that any of Marie's surviving daughters took up her mantle. Of the two daughters who are most frequently credited with assuming the throne, one (Marie Heloïse Euchariste Glapion) died in 1862, and the other (Marie Philomène Glapion) purportedly shunned "Voodoo." Her granddaughters, Adelai Aldina Crocker and Marie Crocker, are also thought to have died in the 1870s.

Yet, this plurality of Laveaux points to something more than racist local color. While white LWP writers perpetuated the myth of a Laveau daughter to imbue their field reports with a sheen of vampiric immortality and dynastic fantasia, they are perhaps correct in a very limited sense: Marie Laveau was not a unique and isolated figure. Instead, she was part of a network of women who drew from spiritual practices and healing traditions, including midwifery and birthwork, to subvert white supremacist and patriarchal structures of transmission premised on the linear reproduction of property, capital, race, and human energy. Nineteenth-century reports reveal many would-be Laveaux in the archives, with their names either forgotten, or never inscribed. These women raise several questions: why must a genealogy of female spiritual leadership be premised on the assumption of heteropatriarchal sexual reproduction? What would it mean to construct a genealogy of spiritual power that recognized love among women and gender-variant people, a genealogy that understood sisterhood, midwifery, and mothering beyond the confines of biological transmission? And what energy is generated in the roots – both literally and figuratively – of these practices?

To LWP writers, this spiritual power could only be understood through dynastic logics – as a linear transmission of property premised on heterosexual reproduction. But Laveau worked with and alongside a number of women, such as the free woman of color Betsey Toledano, who, when put on trial in 1850 for "interracial assembly," defended her right to practice the religion of what she called the "mother-land," arguing that "Voudouism was an African religion with its signs and symbols, that she had been

[101] Tallant, "*Reviewed Work*", 52.

educated in its precepts and mysteries by her grandmother, who came over from Africa."[102] Rosine Dominque, also tried in 1850, fought in court for a wooden statue of the Virgin, defending her right to practice her religion.[103] This is to say nothing of the women and gender-variant people who evaded court and municipal records, reported in the press simply as Laveau's "wenches" or "Africa's daughters." These women only enter the archive as criminals, sex workers, sexual deviants, and disturbers of the peace, yet they leave countertraces of spiritual practices, matrilineal knowledge, and forms of relationality that disrupt the racist policing of Black lives. As Jessica Marie Johnson has argued, women of African descent resisted encroachments on their freedom through intimate bonds, both in and outside the civic sphere. Misread by white observers as "lecherous, wicked, and monstrous," these women instead formed a spiritual sisterhood that resisted reproducing the cis-heterosexual, linear, and genealogical channels of energy production.[104]

That is to say, the legacy of Laveau's daughter is not a question of inheritance, transmission, property, or indeed propriety. Instead, Marie Laveau indexes a multiplicity of women who refused to behave according to the strictures of white supremacist ideals of respectability and whose energy refused to be harnessed. The myths surrounding Laveau's dynastic legacy transform white reproductive logics, instead allowing for bodily autonomy, self-love, and love of others outside the heterosexual nuclear family. If there is a Laveau II, we might understand her as the product of many different kinds of relationality, including lovers, flings, life partners, spiritual mothers and sisters, caretakers, students, teachers, peers, and colleagues – or indeed, as simply oneself: What if we took seriously the suggestion that Marie Laveau I and Marie Laveau II are one and the same? What would it mean to stretch a life over a century, for a woman to essentially birth herself? The reproduction of Laveau I into Laveau II subverts white masculinist assumptions about motherhood and instead suggests that gestation and labor might lead simply to mothering oneself: an independent and autoregenerating economy of self-love that rejects the logics of heteropatriarchal transmission.

[102] "The Rites of Voudou," *Daily Crescent*, July 31, 1850; "The Voudous in the First Municipality," Louisiana Courier, July 30 1850; "Unlawful Assemblies" *Daily Picayune* July 31, 1850; cited by Morrow Long, *A Vodou Priestess*; 104–6. On the quandary of interpreting Toledano's testimony, see Winters, *The Mulatta Concubine*, 82–102.

[103] *Third Municipality Guards, Mayor's Book 1838–1850*, June 27, 1850, volume 7 495, microfilm NOPOL.

[104] Johnson, *Wicked Flesh*, 14.

Laveau's legacies as a healer, community leader, and possible midwife allows an ethos of self care, and yet, this independent form of self-gestation, operates outside the individualistic boundaries of the secular liberal subject, instead drawing from a collective and intergenerational force of women. In this respect, the legacies of Laveau anticipate Audre Lorde's injunction to Black women that "we can learn to mother ourselves." First published in *Essence* in 1983 under the title "Black Women and Anger" and later reprinted in *Sister Outsider* (1984) as "Eye to Eye: Black Women, Hatred, and Anger," Lorde's essay emphasizes the labor of mothering outside biologically essentialist notions of the heteropatriarchal nuclear family. Instead, she argues:

> We can learn to mother ourselves. What does that mean for Black women? It means we must establish authority over our own definition, provide an attentive concern and expectation of growth which is the beginning of that acceptance we came to expect only from our mothers. It means that I affirm my own worth by committing myself to my own survival, in my own self and in the self of other Black women. On the other hand, it means that as I learn my worth and genuine possibility, I refuse to settle for anything less than a rigorous pursuit of the possible in myself, at the same time making a distinction between what is possible and what the outside world drives me to do in order to prove I am human. It means being able to recognize my successes, and to be tender with myself even when I fail.[105]

Lorde's queering of motherhood not only eschews the logics of white heteropatriarchal reproduction but also invokes self-love as a "rigorous" and future-oriented survival strategy. Drawing from Lorde's reflections on mothering, Alexis Pauline Gumbs has built a Black feminist critique of what she calls "queer intergenerationality" or "the experimental creation of a rival economy and temporality in which Black women and children would be generators of an alternative destiny."[106] For Gumbs, Lorde's words speak to an exercise in creating and reproducing the self, a practice that allows alternative forms of relationality often read as deviant by white heteropatriarchal optics. Much as Laveau's labor as a mother, healer, and community leader was misread by the white press, Gumbs's notion of queer intergenerationality interrupts white capitalist narratives that limit what and who a mother can be. As Gumbs argues, Lorde's notion of mothering helps establish

[105] Lorde "Eye to Eye," 173. [106] Gumbs, "We Can Learn to Mother Ourselves," 12, 200.

> a form of mothering that is a *deviant energy* for counternarrative and poetic interruptions that not only threaten the reproduction of the narrative of heteropatriarchal capitalism, but also offer something else in its place ... queerness generates an alternative intergenerational sociality through which the violent narratives of patriarchy and capitalism can be replaced by dynamic forms of community accountability, desire and transformation [italics mine].[107]

For Lorde and Gumbs, the discursive creation of labor, gestation, and nurturing do not produce a reified female identity but instead constitute a practice that offers what Gumbs elsewhere calls a, "possible action, the name for that nurturing work, that survival dance.[108] Gumbs's language of mothering as "generative" of a "deviant energy" is not simply metaphorical but refers to concrete labor and the power it generates, power that, on one hand, could be measured in an empirical capitalist calculus (how many calories need one ingest in order to produce four ounces of breastmilk? how many hours must one work to afford hospital bills, childcare, and infant supplies?). But more importantly, Gumbs's language of energy also exceeds and escapes the violence of capitalist quantification. This "survival dance" covers a vast temporal span of concrete albeit often unrecognized labor, which includes, for Gumbs, the violatory theft of Black women's milk for white children, the labor of immigrant nannies, "chosen and accidental" mentors, house mothers of ball culture, community caregivers, and radical childcare collectives who subvert quantifiable and definable metrics of mothering but nevertheless produce something – queer, transformative, and vibrating with power – that articulates an intergenerational and collective energy.[109]

Laveau, the women, and gender-variant people in her milieu, her "daughters," and the midwives of New Orleans, help excavate an alternative economy of energy and an alternative understanding of Black kinship. To white interlocutors such as the LWP writers, this economy and familial structure was limited by racist scripts of Black femininity: witchcraft, sexual deviancy, and criminality perpetuated by a villainous cast of baby killers, crones, and seductresses. Yet, viewed through Gumbs's and Lorde's theorizations of self-love and collective energy politics, Laveau's life and labor are far more radical. We might, then, read the narrative of Laveau I and Laveau II as a form of creation and reproduction of the self, a means of claiming control over one's own life and legacies, as well as an

[107] Ibid., 57. [108] Ibid.," 22. [109] Ibid., 22–3.

understanding of oneself within a network of care, midwifery, and mutual mothering. The raw energy of this care work is converted into human kinship and genealogies carefully pruned, directed, and regenerated by the knowledge of medicine women and healers. Laveau and the women around her midwifed and mothered themselves and each other, bringing into the world other forms of power, energy, and love.

CHAPTER 3

Freedom's Conduit

Spiritual Justice in "Theresa, A Haytien Tale"

Over 1000 miles away from Marie Laveau's New Orleans, Black New Yorkers also looked toward Haiti to reimagine futurity on scales both local and transnational. Much like in Louisiana, the influence of the Haitian Revolution on New York's population was concrete and demographically measurable. Thousands of white planters, fleeing Saint-Domingue, poured into New York City, bringing with them enslaved men and women. Indeed, it was in part fear of a second Saint-Domingue that led to the passage of New York's gradual abolition law in 1799.[1] But the influence of Haiti was also cultural and imaginative: the first Black republic became a beacon around which discourses of African-American rights and civil liberties coalesced. Well aware of this influence and eager to nurture transnational solidarity across Black diasporic populations, Haiti's early leaders consciously and actively sought diplomatic, political, and social ties with free Black communities in the United States. This chapter will explore the nature of these efforts, which included collaborations between the Haitian state and the African Methodist Episcopal (AME) Church; state-sponsored immigration programs, which encouraged African-Americans to settle in Haiti; and the facilitation of a Black transnational print network that connected New York with the Caribbean. This chapter will also explore the lives of Black women, who are often overlooked by these institutional histories. To that end, I turn to "Theresa, A Haytien Tale" (1828), the first known work of African-American short fiction, which appeared under the pseudonym "S" in the first African-American newspaper, *Freedom's Journal.* Published just half a year after New York State emancipation, "Theresa" shifts attention away from tropes of Black masculinity, female docility, and race futurity that were prevalent in literatures of the early nineteenth century. Instead, the tale offers a pathway for Black women's liberation that shares more with (often unarchived)

[1] Harris, *In the Shadow of Slavery,* 70.

forms of Haitian spirituality than it does with institutional histories and state politics. Ultimately, I argue, "Theresa"'s spiritual and political resistance forges prophetic pathways for women's energy, queering traditional reproductive understandings of futurity. The tale envisions emancipated and nonlinear futures untied to the sentimental cult of domesticity and, in doing so, proposes an energy economy in which women's political labor leads not to the birth of a child but instead to Black sovereignty.

At once highly patriarchal and deeply internationalist, *Freedom's Journal* runs both against and along the grain of a Black feminist reading of "Theresa." The newspaper's editors – Samuel Cornish, a pastor of the First Colored Presbyterian Church in New York City, and John Brown Russwurm, a Jamaica-born doctor and the first Black graduate of Bowdoin College – founded the paper in 1827, envisaging a periodical that would be international in scope. The newspaper circulated not only in the northern United States and parts of the US South but also in Port-au-Prince (Haiti), Liverpool (Britain), and Waterloo (Canada).[2] This international ethos was reflected in the journal, which included Caribbean history, portraits of Haitian leaders such as Toussaint Louverture and Henry Christophe, and laudatory editorials defending Haitian sovereignty.[3] Contributors frequently celebrated Haitian *manhood*, or as a particularly unsubtle May 4, 1827 editorial put it, those who "wield[ed] the sword of war or sway[ed] the rod of empire." As important interventions by critics such as Jacqueline Bacon, Frances Smith Foster, and Marlene Daut have shown, "Theresa" foregrounds the importance of women's political participation in ways that disrupted the masculinist assumptions of *Freedom's Journal*. In Foster's words, "women writers (or at least writers with feminized pseudonyms) appeared in the paper's earliest issues, and gender and women as subjects and agents were common."[4] By foregrounding the actions of women in the Haitian Revolution, the tale adumbrates what Marlene Daut has called a "radical Franco-Haitian grammar" along lines that have traditionally been gendered and often dismissed.[5] "Theresa" therefore not only complicates

[2] For a full list of agents, see Bacon, *Freedom's Journal*, 53.

[3] The newspaper's interest in Haiti indicates its internationalist and specifically pan-African ethos which looked beyond the Caribbean. It not only reported on foreign developments, but often invoked ancient Egypt and Ethiopia in its efforts to "circulate far and near". On the figuration of Haiti in *Freedom's Journal*, see Bacon, *Freedom's Journal*, 165–71 and Daut, *Tropics*, 288–328. On Haiti in early African-American culture, see Byrd, *The Black Republic*; Daut, *Tropics of Haiti;* Fanning, *Caribbean Crossing;* Levine, *Dislocating Race and Nation.*

[4] Foster, "Forgotten Manuscripts," 637.

[5] Daut, *Tropics of Haiti*, 293. See also Daut, "Before Harlem."

the spatial mapping of what has traditionally been historicized as African-American literature but also complicates critical understandings of race, gender, and sexuality.

Discussions of nineteenth-century African-American fiction often fall along a strict gender binary. On one hand is a predominantly stoical masculinist narrative exemplified in Frederick Douglass's wrestling with Covey or the assimilation of Toussaint's "Black Spartacus" myth into the African-American canon.[6] On the other is the tradition of sentiment and domesticity frequently associated with Black women writers and often filtered through the biases of white female amanuenses.[7] "Theresa," however, refuses to conform to either of these paradigms. The women of the tale have neither fathers nor husbands; they flee their homes to cross-dress as soldiers; and through heroic and unladylike deeds – including forging papers, spying, and opening their bodies to spiritual possession – they help to achieve Haitian independence. And although male figures both historical (Toussaint L'Ouverture, General Charles Leclerc, and General Joseph Balthazar Inginac) and fictional (the daughters' murdered uncle) appear in the tale, no men ever speak.

Moreover, the characters of "Theresa" do not simply reproduce the masculinist logics of aggressive valor in female form. Although they dress in male military uniforms, move freely in space, and directly contribute to the war effort, their true heroics manifest through an intimate spirituality that has traditionally been coded as private and feminine. The author emphasizes Theresa's and her family's private spiritual experiences, which include contemplation, possession, prophecies, and direct pleas to God. Although these encounters may seem personal, insignificant, or even passive, they constitute an active engagement with revolutionary energy: through its spiritual landscape, "Theresa" reimagines the forms political labor might take. Spiritual experience does not unfold in the safe realm of home and hearth. Rather, the women of the tale explore a dangerous landscape, prophesy the future, merge their bodies with gods, and conduct divine energy to emancipatory political ends. As we saw in Chapter 1, Caribbean personhood theorizes a complex negotiation of spiritual energy – a triadic structure comprising the *ti bonanj* (the objective shell or "spiritual reserve tank"), the *gwo bonanj* (soul, memory, and dreams), and the *mèt tet* (the possessing

6 See Pierrot, *The Black Avenger in Atlantic Culture*; see also Drexler and White, "The Constitution of Toussaint."

7 This is perhaps best exemplified in the frequent critical and pedagogical juxtaposition of Frederick Douglass's "manhood" against the constrained domestic spaces of Harriet Jacobs's *Incidents in the Life of a Slave Girl*. See Drake, "Rewriting the American Self"; Morgan, "Gender-Related Difference in the Slave Narratives of Harriet Jacobs and Frederick Douglass."

spirit). "Theresa" embodies this structure, channeling the "fuel" of Black women's labor away from the biocapitalist violence of colonial economies and toward the *mèt tet*, the divine spiritual driver, who reimagines and reconverts the energies of diasporic subjects into a space of liberation. While the logics of the colonial state attempted to reduce Black women to reproductive fuel, and while the logics of Catholicism imagine its most significant woman as a reproductive vessel, "Theresa" refuses these dehumanizing conversions. As I have argued elsewhere, the tale draws from a complex theological network that draws from Catholic mysticism, Protestant revivalism of the Second Great Awakening, and Vodou spirituality in order to rewrite both the cult of Mary and the plantation system's reproductive biocapitalism.[8] In doing so, the tale imagines the female body as an instrument in which the final product is not a child (whether savior or chattel) but instead political sovereignty.

Rather than cast Black women as victims or Virgins, the author of "Theresa" imagines futurity in other, queerer ways. Its eponymous character eschews traditional romance, loves her all-female family, and spends the story dressed as a man in military garb. In this respect, the anonymous author of "Theresa" understood more about Haitian history than many celebrated chroniclers of the first Black republic. Drawing from Haitian Revolutionary history, "Theresa" refuses colonial categories of gender and linear descent. Following in the footsteps of cross-dressing Haitian historical figures like Marie Jeanne Lamartinière, Sanité Belair, and Romaine-la-Prophètesse, the author of the tale expands the pantheon of revolutionary heroes to include characters outside the masculinist paradigm familiar to early African-American print culture. Rather than celebrate the linearity of cis-heterosexual futurity, "Theresa" instead constructs multiple temporal horizons, inhabiting pasts and prophesying futures unyoked to traditional understandings of Black women's reproduction. These unruly temporalities reveal a practice of reading diasporic literature ecstatically and in doing so convert the energies of Black women into political futurity.

3.1 "Fathoming the Dish Kettle": Gender and Domesticity in African-American Print Culture

Because readers are likely not familiar with "Theresa," I will give a brief summary of the tale: in the midst of the Haitian Revolution, Madame Paulina, a free woman of color, flees from Saint Nicolas with her daughters Amanda and Theresa. Hoping to escape to Vega Real (in the present-day

[8] Albanese, "Caribbean Visions."

Dominican Republic), the women forge passports and disguise themselves in military uniforms: Paulina dresses as a French captain and disguises her daughters as Haitian soldiers, ostensibly her prisoners.[9] The women briefly encounter a French official from whom Paulina "collects much valuable information" (January 25, 1828). The women then retire to "a grove of peace" (January 25, 1828), where Theresa undergoes her first spiritual experience, prophesying the role she will play in Haitian independence and supplicating God to free the Haitians. Having received her vocational call and "aroused by some internal agent" (February 8, 1828), Theresa departs from the Pimento grove to seek Toussaint and give him the information from her mother's conversation with the Haitian troops. She leaves a note for her family on the bark of a Gourd tree.

In her dreams, which she believes are "prophetic," Paulina envisages Theresa's departure and, upon waking, she and Amanda mourn their loss until they discover Theresa's note. Meanwhile, Theresa has found Toussaint's camp, disclosed important military secrets to his army, and quickly departed, keen to reunite with her family in the Pimento grove. As she returns, under the protection of a military escort, Theresa is again seized by lengthy prophetic visions ensuring the "destruction of the French" (February 8, 1828). Yet, these visions culminate in disappointment when she finds that her family is gone. Grieving violently, she reduces her military escort to tears and even briefly threatens to denounce the Haitian cause. Yet, in a final bouleversement, French troops attack, and a chaotic battle ensues, which the Haitians ultimately win. In the wake of the battle, Theresa, accompanied by the "Captain" Inginac (a real historical figure who fought in the revolution and, at the time of the tale's publication in 1828, served as secretary-general in the cabinet of Haitian President Jean-Pierre Boyer) discovers her mother and sister in an abandoned baggage cart, presumably injured but safe. As the narrative

[9] This has significant implications for literary traditions of "passing." The tale implies that Paulina is lighter skinned than her daughters, suggesting that kinship is defined by more than a perceived similarity of phenotype. This also suggests that racial markers were so indeterminate in a colonial context, where racial categories were differentiated by sartorial choice and political affiliation rather than perceived differences in skin color. Such a critique would have been particularly salient in a Haitian context in which over one hundred pseudoscientific racial categories existed, a bizarre hierarchy invented to contain and regulate Blackness. It also resonates with the 14th clause of the 1805 Constitution, which rendered all Haitians – regardless of their skin color – *noir*, thus as Julia Gaffield has argued, reconfiguring Blackness as a political rather than a biological category. Either way, the author exposes the pseudoscientific fiction of race. See Garraway, "Race, Reproduction and Family Romance"; see also Gaffield, "Complexities of Imagining Haiti" and Daut, *Tropics of Haiti*, especially 77–89.

concludes, we are told that "joy succeeds sorrow" (February 15, 1828), and the family is finally reunited.

"Theresa" is both exemplary and exceptional. The story stands out for a number of reasons: first, it embodies the internationalist commitment of early African-American print culture well documented by critics such as Daut, Bacon, Robert Levine, and Anna Brickhouse.[10] As Bacon has shown, the editors, writers, and readers of *Freedom's Journal* were "guided by a sense of the connections between Africans throughout the globe and the unique destiny of the African race," drawing from ancient historical writings and Biblical texts to write an anticolonialist narrative which established Africa as, in the words of one editorial, "the birthplace and cradle of civilization."[11] The journal's investment in ancient African civilizations was discursively tied to the contemporaneous struggle for civil rights in the United States, challenges to white supremacist ideologies, and especially contemporary colonization debates centering around Liberia and Haiti – debates that would ultimately drive the newspaper's founders apart.[12] While emigration was a controversial question in the 1820s, it gained substantial traction with the African-American community, especially compared to the more contentious debates of the 1850s. However, most African-American sympathies did not lie with the African Colonization Society (much to the dismay of the white agents who interviewed them): instead, people of African descent looked to Haiti as a powerful, sovereign, and Black-led alternative to Liberia.[13] As stated by the pseudonymous author "Africanus" in *Freedom's Journal*: "[Haiti] has now demonstrated that the descendants of Africa are capable of self-government: the plea so often urged by the adherents of slavery, 'the poor creatures, should we free them, will starve to death,' will now be but 'sounding brass' in the opinion of every reasonable man."[14]

Beginning with Haiti's 1805 Constitution, which established free soil citizenship for anyone of African descent, the nation's leaders envisaged the republic as a beacon for Black freedom struggles worldwide.[15] By the

[10] See Bacon, *Freedom's Journal*; Levine, *Dislocating* Race and Nation; Brickhouse, *Transamerican;* Daut, *Tropics of Haiti.*

[11] On Egyptology in the newspaper, see Bacon, *Freedom's Journal*, especially 148. On Egyptology in the antebellum U.S., see Trafton, *Egypt Land.* See also Hay, *Postapocalyptic Fantasies in Antebellum American Literature.*

[12] See Levine, *Dislocating Race and Nation*, 90–4; Lewis, "A Traitor to His Brethren?"

[13] Rauh Bethel, "Images of Hayti"; Dixon, *African America and Haiti;* Fanning, *Caribbean Crossing*; Polgar, *Standard-Bearers of Equality*; Power-Greene, *Against Wind and Tide.*

[14] Africanus, *Freedom's Journal* October 12, 1827.

[15] Even divided, both the Republic of the South and Kingdom of the North pursued hemispheric alliances. For example, in 1814, President Alexandre Pétion extracted a promise from Simón Bolívar

1820s, Haiti's commitment to global Black emancipation had taken on additional pragmatic urgency. Keen to re-establish a strong Haitian identity after years of division, President Jean-Pierre Boyer attempted to refashion Haiti as a righteous and exalted nation, one which would unite not just the Kingdom of the North and the Republic of the South, nor just the island of Hispaniola, but peoples of African descent throughout the globe – especially the United States.[16] In 1825, Boyer's desire for new citizens was exacerbated when French gunboats appeared on Haiti's shore demanding 150 million francs (the equivalent of 22 billion USD). What has become known as the *dette odieuse* gave Boyer further incentive to persuade a potential source of labor to settle in Haiti. In a series of letters written to Loring D. Dewey and widely circulated in the northern United States, Boyer describes Haiti's free soil politics in an appealingly literal sense: "Those who come, being children of Africa, shall be Haytien as soon as they put their feet upon the soil of Hayti: they will enjoy happiness, security, tranquillity, such as we ourselves possess, however our defamers declare to the contrary."[17] Later in the exchange, he writes:

> What joy it will give hearts like yours, to see these scions of Africa, so abased in the United States, where they vegetate with no more utility to themselves than to the soil which nourishes them, transplanted to Hayti, where they will become no less useful than estimable, because the enjoyment of civil and political rights, ennobling them in their own eyes, cannot fail to attach them to regular habits, and the acquisition of social virtues, and to render them worthy by their good conduct, to enjoy the benefits which their new country will bestow upon them! (CRE 16-17).

Boyer's discursive construction of free soil takes a surprisingly lyrical turn: the arid rights-deprived earth of the United States withers next to the lush nourishment of "civil and political rights in Haiti." Moreover, the "good conduct" and "social virtues" promised by Boyer resonate with discourses of propriety favored not only by *Freedom's Journal* but also by African-American institutions of worship, such as the African Methodist Episcopal

that exchanged military supplies and temporary political asylum for the abolition of slavery in what would become the republics of Latin America. Meanwhile, the Northern monarchy pursued a close relationship with Northern people of African descent in the United States, particularly via the writings of Baron de Vastey. See Fischer, "Bolivar in Haiti;" and Daut, *Baron de Vastey & the Origins of Black Atlantic Humanism*

16 See Trouillot, *Haiti*. See also Gonzalez, "Defiant Haiti"; Hinks, "'Perfectly Proper and Conciliating'"; Salt, "Haitian Soil for the Citizens' Soul."

17 Dewey was acting against the wishes of the ACS, which favored Liberia over Haiti. See Dewey, *Correspondence Relative to the Emigration to Hayti*, 10. The text is marked as "translated," presumably from French, but the translator is not credited.

Church. This was a canny rhetorical strategy, as Black churches in New York and Philadelphia were central organizing hubs for Haitian emigration projects, often working in close cooperation with Boyer, hosting public lectures, circulating or reprinting promotional emigration material, and organizing missionary expeditions to Haiti.[18] In 1824, AME founder Bishop Richard Allen in partnership with James Forten established the Haytien Emigration Society of Philadelphia, a direct challenge to the Liberia-focused efforts of the African Colonization Society. A contemporary claimed of Forten that "he sees in the great men of Hayti the deliverers and the avengers of his race."[19] This "deliverance" was also encouraged by the Haitian press: in an 1825 exchange with an anonymous white US Quaker, a Haitian editorialist (also anonymous) wrote in the Port-au-Prince-based newspaper *Le Télégraphe*:

> D'inexorables préjugés tourmentent, maîtrisent et aveuglent à un tel point les blancs de ces États, que ces fantômes ne leur laissent pas même la volonté de s'affranchir de leur joug. L'Américain, si orgeiuilleux de son indépendance, est même fier de cet esclavage! On plaindrait cette faiblesse si elle n'était pas cruelle...Notre Républiqué naissante, beaucoup moins populeuse, beaucoup moins riche que les États-Unis, a fait pour les malheureux hommes de couleur des États-Unis, ce que cette federation n'a jamais fait pour les émigrans blancs. (*Le Télégraphe* PAP 18 mars 1825)
>
> [Inexorable prejudices torment, enslave, and blind the whites of the States to such a point that these phantoms do not even permit them the desire to free themselves from their yoke. The American, so arrogant about his independence, is even proud of this slavery! One would pity this weakness if it weren't so cruel...Our nascent [*naissante*] Republic, much less populous and much less wealthy than the United States, has done more for those unhappy men of color of the United States, than this federation has ever done for its white emigrants.]

The author reverses the logics of white supremacy, revealing the "whites of the States" to be enslaved to their own prejudices, while the "nascent [*naissante*] republic" of Haiti offers an alternative pathway for people of African descent. Moreover, the author deploys language explicitly yoked to sexual reproduction by figuring the republic as the product of childbirth. While emigration to Haiti was ultimately unsuccessful for reasons beyond

[18] On Haitian emigration and African-American religious organizations, see Campbell, *Songs of Zion;* Fanning, *Caribbean Crossing;* Newman, *Freedom's Prophet*; and Power-Greene, *Against Wind and Tide.*

[19] Cited in Winch, *A Gentleman of Color,* 145.

the scope of this chapter, the idea of Haitian citizenship held a significant place in the imagination of African-Americans in the United States.[20] "Theresa" harnesses this imaginative power, converting the diplomatic public discourse of emigration into an intimate tale of love among women. It is no coincidence that Inginac concludes the tale by helping Theresa reunite with her family. Inginac was a vocal proponent of emigration, claiming that Haitians were "interested more than any other in the fate of the descendants of the Africans, whose blood runs in their veins... .the Haytiens form at this time a society whose end is to favour the emigration of our American brethren into the republic."[21] The author of "Theresa" thus suggests that Inginac, and by extension Boyer's policies of emigration, would reunite not just a fictional mother and her daughters but an entire diasporic family, fostering Black solidarity across national lines.

Yet, even as the tale embodies the diasporic ethos of *Freedom's Journal* and early Haitian state politics, it also departs from the publication's norms in striking ways. Although "Theresa" makes a few nods to female "virtue" (their male garb, for example, is designed to protect them from "shame"), the tale's women ultimately live on their own terms. Theresa foregoes the "fatherly protection" of Toussaint in favor of her mother's love; the women mourn messily and noisily, perhaps serving as an ironic rejoinder to Paul's injunction that "women are to keep silent in the churches" (1 Corinthians 14:34) or, for that matter, *Freedom's Journal*'s aphorism "Silence is the female ornament" (June 15, 1827). Most importantly, the author foregrounds Haitian heroism through spiritual encounters, including prophecy, possession, and fits of emotion, which are revealed to be not the foibles of female emotional excess but instead the very power that drives the family's political labor.

This stands as a remarkable departure from common sentimental and melodramatic tropes in *Freedom's Journal*, which frequently deployed women as props for masculine heroics, empty vessels, wilting girls, or mawkish mothers.[22] Constitutive of Black masculine identity, according to *Freedom's Journal*, was its duty to protect, manage, and contain expressions of women's sexuality. In a May 11, 1827 portrait of Toussaint, for example, the revolutionary hero is lauded for his investment in female

[20] Dixon, "Nineteenth Century African American Emigrationism"; Fanning, *Caribbean Crossing*, 109–11.

[21] Cited from Power-Greene, *Against Wind and Tide*, 28.

[22] On raced and gendered myths of sentiment and melodrama, see Williams, *Playing the Race Card*. See also Merrill, "May She Read Liberty in Your Eyes?"

"virtue": "He was particularly attentive to the means of reforming the loose and licentious manners of the females. . .His maxim was that women should always appear in public as if they were going to church" (May 11, 1827). As Daut has argued, such accounts served to "elide or circumscribe the experiences of women."[23] Indeed, Daut reminds us that the *Journal* only mentions a nonfictional Haitian woman once: Christophe's wife, Marie, who is described as "a good and virtuous wife, an affectionate mother" (May 11, 1827).[24] This effacement of Haitian women from Revolutionary iconography is consonant with *Freedom's Journal*'s performances of masculinity. As Bacon points out, "freedom was a central component of what it meant to be a man, and the struggle for liberty was often framed in terms of manhood."[25] In original articles and reprintings such as "A Self Made Man" (July 25, 1828), "Good Advice to Young Men" (January 9, 1829), and "I Wish I Was A Man" (June 1, 1827), masculine citizenry was figured as studious, temperate, vigorous, and, above all, protective of the "weaker sex." Meanwhile, editorialists lauded women for their "mildness, patience, benevolence, affection, and attachment" (April 11, 1828).

In particular, the journal celebrated Black mothers as bearers of race futurity. For example, a poem reprinted in *Freedom's Journal* on May 25, 1827 declares "See a fond mother, and her young ones round/Her soul soft-melting with maternal love/Some to her breast she clasps, and others prove/By kisses her affection." It is important to recognize the significance of the journal's valorization of Black kinship, which rebuked violent systems of reproductive Black labor, especially transracial surrogacy ("to her breast she clasps" her *own* "young ones"). Yet, this sentimentalization frequently circumscribed the agency of women and refused to understand motherhood as a politics in and of itself. Moreover, the sentimental troping of Black motherhood marginalized, and sometimes discursively punished, those women who chose not to become mothers. As a representative editorial put it:

> Women are not formed for great cares themselves, but to soften ours. Their tenderness is the proper reward for the dangers we undergo for their preservation. They are confined within the narrow limits of domestic assiduity and when they stray beyond them, they move out of their proper sphere and consequently without grace. (February 14, 1829)

[23] Daut, *Tropics of Haiti*, 313. [24] Ibid., 315. [25] Bacon, *Freedom's Journal*, 125.

These women "without grace" played an important role in the pages of *Freedom's Journal.* The newspaper frequently printed graphic scenes of violence against "fallen" Black girls, usually represented as housemaids or servants. While these victimized girls were sexually assaulted, whipped, and in one case blinded, the moral center of *Freedom's Journal*'s narratives of abjection was never the woman herself. Instead, the suffering of Black women became focalized through the feelings of Black men – often a brother or lover – who had failed to safeguard his female wards. As Nazera Sadiq Wright argues, "the abused and scarred bodies of Black girls [in *Freedom's Journal*] upheld the *potential* of Black men as protectors."[26] Unsurprisingly, Black women readers were not always happy with their portrayal in the pages of *Freedom's Journal.* In a letter to the editors, appearing in an issue from August 10, 1827, a woman who signed herself as "Matilda" wrote:

> Will you allow a female to offer a few remarks upon a subject that you must allow to be all-important. I don't know that in any of your papers you have said sufficient upon the education of females. I hope you are not to be classed with those, who think that our mathematical knowledge should be limited to "fathoming the dish-kettle," and that we have acquired enough of history, if we knew that our grandfathers lived and died.

Much like Matilda's challenge to *Freedom's Journal*'s norms, "Theresa" serves as a rejoinder to the newspaper's scenes of violent abuse and domestic sentimentality. The women of "Theresa" have no interest in "dish-kettles." In fact, not once in the narrative are they shown to be inside the household, instead preferring to travel through forests, sleep under the stars, and camp out at Toussaint's base. Moreover, these heroic women displace the very forms of historical patrilineage that Matilda deplores in her letter: "we have acquired enough of history, if we knew that our grandfathers lived and died." "Theresa" instead offers a lineage of Black diasporic mothers and grandmothers whose role in liberation struggles overshadows even the mythos of Toussaint Louverture. Through its critique of masculinist and often misogynistic politics, "Theresa" stands as a fictive response to Matilda's complaint.

Matilda's letter also reminds us of the wave of women's spiritual leadership that was soon to be inaugurated with what has been historicized

[26] Wright, *Black Girlhood in the Nineteenth Century*, 32.

as the Second Great Awakening.[27] While women provided a vital role in founding and governing the AME, organizing petitions, protesting discrimination, and uniting congregations, they were traditionally excluded from the episcopal hierarchy. It was not until 2000 that the Church began permitting female bishops and itinerant preachers like Jarena Lee were officially condemned by Church leadership.[28] Yet, women fostered leadership both within and outside of church structures. Preachers and prophets like Lee, Rebecca Cox Jackson, Maria Stewart, Zilpha Elaw, and Sojourner Truth found, in the Second Great Awakening, freedom to preach openly and publicly, in the words of Carla Peterson, "[merging]…religious ecstasy with the Godhead."[29] Indeed, Daut has identified Maria Stewart as a possible author of "Theresa," citing her investment in both Methodist justice and the Haitian Revolution.[30]

Born into a free family in Hartford, Connecticut, in 1803, Stewart was one of the first African-American women to make public antislavery speeches and the first American woman to deliver public speeches to interracial audiences. A friend to William Lloyd Garrison, Stewart harnessed both public speech and print media, arguing not only for Black civil rights but also for the inclusion of Black women within Church leadership. Stewart's early circle was, moreover, extremely invested in the first Black republic. Her intellectual milieu included David Walker, the activist and Boston agent of *Freedom's Journal*, who famously invoked Haiti as a cautionary tale of divine justice in his 1829 *Appeal to the Coloured Citizens of the World*, and Thomas Paul (great-grandfather of Pauline Hopkins), the AME preacher and missionary to Haiti. Stewart herself frequently upheld Haiti as an exemplar for the African-American community in her speeches and writing. In "An Address Delivered Before the Afric-American Female Intelligence Society of America," given in Boston in April 1832 and printed in *The Liberator* in the same month, Stewart

[27] See Andrews, *Sisters of the Spirit*; Humez, *Gifts of Power*; Moody, *Sentimental Confession*; Peterson, "*Doers of the* Word"; Pierce, *Hell without Fires*; West, *African Spirituality in Black Women's Fiction*; Washington, *Sojourner Truth's America*.

[28] Dodson, *Engendering Church*, especially 78–91.

[29] Peterson, "*Doers of the Word*", 18.

[30] Stewart, "An Address Delivered Before the African-American Female Intelligence Society of America," 67. For these reasons, Daut has suggested that Stewart may have authored the tale. (Daut also considers Sarah Louise Forten as a possible candidate.) Although she doesn't make a strong claim for authorship, only insisting: "I hope to continue to highlight the connection between gendered portrayals of the Haitian Revolution in the Atlantic world and the gendering of [(anonymous] revolutionary writing," her evidence is convincing. See Daut, *Tropics of Haiti*, 295.

describes a litany of downtrodden peoples, from the Greek War of Independence to the freedom struggle of American Indians. Included in this catalog is Haiti:

> Look at the French in the late rebellion; no traitors among them to expose their plans to the crowned heads of Europe. "Liberty or death" was their cry. And the Haytiens, though they have not been acknowledged yet as a nation, yet their firmness of character and independence of spirit have been greatly admired, and highly applauded.[31]

Drawing from what M. Shawn Copeland has termed a "theology of suffering," Stewart fashioned herself into a "humble instrument in the hands of God" whose prophetic vision reached toward the "not yet" of Haitian statehood: "though they have not been acknowledged yet as a nation."[32] As Joycelyn Moody has argued, Stewart "challenged the social and political hierarchies of her day by proclaiming God as determined to demolish those hierarchies and the immoral and profane institutions that devised and sustained them."[33] Stewart, like many other Black women, found in Methodism the freedom – indeed even the ecstasy – to transform her social roles into a divine instrument of justice.

3.2 Wearing Power: Transvestism and Revolutionary Iconography

"Theresa" expertly merges the growing religious power of Black women within and outside the AME with Haitian Revolutionary histories. While few among New York's free Black population experienced Haiti first-hand, many of *Freedom's Journal*'s readers may have been familiar with Haiti from print culture. This is particularly apparent in the tale's attention to cross-dressing, given the prevalence of the practice in the Haitian Revolutionary period. Although female identified figures, like Sanité Belair, Marie Jeanne Lamartinière, and the lwa Ezili, are well known in Haiti, the dominant global historiography of the Revolution traditionally emphasizes the role of men. Not only are women less likely to be recognized as heroes by predominantly non-Haitian audiences but also their forms of heroism are seldom commemorated in text and therefore do not easily circulate outside of Haiti. Instead, their stories persist through oral

31 Stewart, "An Address Delivered Before the African-American Female Intelligence Society of America."

32 Copeland, "'Wading Through Many Sorrows'"; Stewart, *Meditations*, 24. See also Copeland, *Enfleshing Freedom*; Peterson, "*Doers of the Word*," 57.

33 Moody, *Sentimental Confessions*, 26. I here take the formulation of the "not yet" from Coviello, *Tomorrow's Parties*.

history, songs, folklore, Vodou rites, and other embodied archival forms. The patriarchal logics of the archive not only obscure the importance of female and gender-variant revolutionaries in Haiti but also conscript purportedly cis-male heroes into a male/female binary sustained by European fictions of gender.

Yet, the construction of Haitian masculinity has always been proximate to, embedded within, or even amalgamated within performances of femininity which, although elided by predominantly textual European and Western celebrations of manhood, have persisted through embodied practices and collective memory throughout the diaspora. The role of women and gender-variant people in the revolutionary period effectively decenters global northern ideologies of gender and sexuality in Haitian Revolutionary histories. This pantheon includes Sanité Belair, a famed lieutenant in Toussaint Louverture's Army, who led Haitian troops into battle against the French, cross-dressed in male military uniform, and emerged as a political rival to Dessalines, leading ultimately to her execution.[34] Others include Marie Jeanne Lamartinière, who cross-dressed as a man and fought in the battle of Crête à Pierrot; Toya Montou, Dessalines's aunt, who commanded soldiers in battle; Marie-Claire Heureuse, the wife of Dessalines; Catherine Flon, who created the first Haitian flag; and perhaps even Romaine Rivière, also known as Romaine-la-Prophètesse, a free Black coffee farmer who claimed to be the godson of the Virgin Mary, dressed in women's clothing, and led key military campaigns in the revolution.[35]

As Charlotte Hammond has argued, "cross-dressing allows the Haitian, Martinican, or Guadeloupean subject to refract and redefine a colonial signifying system in their own terms and thus forms part of an ongoing process of decolonisation."[36] This sartorial redefinition of colonial systems has famously been explored in the following passage from Frantz Fanon's *Peau noire, masques blancs*:

[34] On the role of women in Haitian iconography, see Daut, *Tropics of Haiti*, especially 197–328; Dayan, *Haiti, History and the Gods*, especially 16–65; Gautier, *Les sœurs de solitude*; Narcisse, *Mémoire de Femmes*; Willson, "Catherine Flon, Material Testimony and Occluded Narratives of Female-Led Resistance in Haiti and the Haitian Dyaspora." See also Willson's collaborative research project entitled *Fanm Rebel*, sponsored by the Levehulme Truste and the Institute for Black Atlantic Research at the University of Central Lancashire (http://famnrebel.com).

[35] Although it would be anachronistic to apply a trans identity to Romaine, I follow Tinsley and Terry Rey in arguing that Romaine felt "female identifications" that were, in the words of Rey, "consistent with African notions of the penetration of feminized male human bodies by the spirits, raising the radical imagination of the prophetess being penetrated by his virgin godmother." Rey, *The Priest and the Prophetess*, 209; Tinsley, *Ezili's Mirrors*.

[36] Hammond, *Entangled Otherness*, 17.

> Recall, however, the existence of what are called there 'men dressed like ladies' or 'gossips' ['Ma Commère']. Most of the time, they wear shirts and skirts. But I am convinced they have normal sexual lives. They can take a punch like any other strapping man [note there is some ambiguity or even punning in this statement which has occasionally been translated as "they can swill punch"] and are not insensitive to the charms of market-women, selling fish or vegetables.[37]

Much has been written on Fanon's disavowal of gay Martinican identity, which paints an almost parodical portrait of Caribbean machismo to counter what he perceives as the Oedipal emasculation of colonized masculine identity. Yet, while these readings have focused largely on Fanon's relation to male sexuality, I want to turn my interest to those market women, pushed to the margins of *Peau noire*, the charming "femmes" who supposedly entice Fanon's *gaillard*. Although themselves not cross-dressing, these women – who control households and local economies, who slap, slice, and sell fish with other women – do not necessarily seem as if they would be interested in sampling Fanon's punch, so to speak. Market women, as Strongman and Tinsley argue, have historically forged homosocial and sometimes openly homosexual relationships.[38] As such, they articulate forms of same-sex bonding and queer desire outside the anxious parameters of Fanon's male-centric gaze. Fanon simultaneously highlights and marginalizes not only the experience of men who love men but also the possibility of same-sex-loving women. He also contributes to the overvisibility of male-to-female cross-dressing in the Caribbean, eliding historical forms of female-to-male cross-dressing that are deeply important to Haitian Revolutionary history.

Although many of Haiti's cross-dressing heroes likely had secular reasons to bend European cis-gender conventions, it is also important to recall the spiritual framework of Vodou, which problematizes the gender binary. As discussed in Chapter 1, Vodou permits a wide range of gender expression through possession, transcorporeality, and porous philosophies of personhood. Particularly relevant to "Theresa," and to histories of Caribbean cross-dressing more broadly, is the Vodou belief in the *marasa*

[37] "Rappelons toutefois l'existence de ce qu'on appelle là-bas 'des hommes habillés en dames' ou 'Ma Commère.' Ils ont la plupart du temps une veste et une jupe. Mais nous restons persuadé qu'il ont une vie sexuelle normale. Ils prennent le punch comme n'importe quel gaillard et ne sont pas insensibles aux charmes des femmes–marchandes de poissons, de legumes." Fanon, *Peau noire, masques blancs*, 146.

[38] See Manning, "Watching Dunham's Dances 1937–1945"; Strongman, *Queering Black Atlantic* Religions; Tinsley, *Ezili's Mirrors* and *Thiefing Sugar.*"

twa, or "twins of three." This practice, what Jana Evans Braziel calls an "interlocking corporeal mythos," celebrates twinning, generally represented as the pairing of a male and female, or *dosu* and *dosa*.[39] Yet, the formation of the pair ultimately subverts the binary logic it first appears to imply: the *marasa twa* only places two forms of gender identity into relation in order to engender a more perfect third (or *twa*) child. As Vèvè Clark has argued about the tradition:

> Marasa states the oppositions and invites participation in the formulation of another principle entirely... Marasa consciousness invites us to imagine beyond the binary. The ability to do so depends largely on our capacities to read the sign as a cyclical, spiral relationship. On the surface, marasa seems to be binary...the tension between oppositions leads to another norm of creativity – to interaction or deconstruction, as it were. In Vodoun, the philosophical and environmental contrasts embedded in the marasa sign and the belief system it represents are danced into another realm of discourse during Vodoun ceremonies.[40]

As a subversion of the heteropatriarchal colonial state, the tripartite nature of the *marasa twa* reflects the tripartite nature of Vodou personhood: gender identity is therefore open to multiple and fluid forms of performance, embodiment, worship, and erotics that exceed global northern understandings of personhood. The dichotomous relationships embodied in the *dosu/dosa* twinning produce a third space, beyond binaries of male/female. While critics and anthropologists have sometimes analogized the structure of the *marasa twa* relationship to that of the Hegelian dialectic, I would argue instead that, if we are to reach into global northern theory, we might look not to Hegel but instead to the "third space" of androgyny posited by Marjorie Garber.[41] Although operating under specific spiritual imperatives and sociohistorical conditions distinct from Garber's early modern European milieu, the ontological capaciousness of Vodou subverts the fiction of the self-identical individual in much the same way that Garber argues of the third space: "Three puts in question the idea of one: of identity, self-sufficiency, self-knowledge."[42] Without subsuming the *marasa twa* into Garber's history of androgyny – and indeed, I do not believe that androgyny is the correct word to describe the *marasa twa* tradition – the notion of the "third space" as a site that disrupts the self-

[39] Braziel, "Re-membering Défilée," 69. On the *marasa twa* tradition, see also Clarke, "Developing Diaspora Literacy and *Marasa* Consciousness"; Fleurant, *Dancing Spirits*, 26; Houlberg, "Ritual Cosmos of the Twins"; and Pressley-Sanon, "One Plus One Equals Three."

[40] Clark, "Developing Diaspora Literacy and *Marasa* Consciousness," 12.

[41] Garber, *Vested Interests*. [42] Ibid., 11.

same global northern subject allows us to productively think beyond binaries, forging new forms of relation that are imaginative, not empirical, spiraled, not straight.

Take, for example, the history of Dédée Bazile (also known as Défilée la Folle), the purportedly mad woman who was said to have collected the remains of Dessalines' body and carried them to his burial place. Her life was first narrated by early Haitian historians, Thomas Madiou and Alexis Beaubrun Ardouin, and her legacy was later solidified through oral testimonies recorded by Octave Petit and Jean Fouchard in the 1930s and 1950s, respectively.[43] More recently, Défilée has played a prominent role in Haitian diasporic literary narrative, notably Edwidge Danticat's *Krik? Krak!* and Myriam J. A. Chancy's *Spirit of Haiti*. In francophone Haitian historiography, Défilée is frequently portrayed as a Magdalene figure, a mourner at the brink of society whose role is merely to witness, lament, and weep for her lost savior. Yet, if we examine Défilée from the perspective of Vodou history, another image emerges: she not only sanctifies the legacy of Dessalines but, in doing so, queers the logics of revolutionary masculinity. As Braziel argues, Dessalines and Défilée form a binary pair, which produces a third space of Haitian independence in which an "embodied, fully immanent ritual – Défilée's gathering of Dessalines's remains – traverses and confounds boundaries dividing body and spirit, state and ritual, death and life, gesturing toward infinity."[44] I would add to Braziel's list of "confounded" boundaries, the category of gender. In this respect, Dessalines – powerful, heroic, masculine, and strong – is paired against Défilée – mad, weak, feminine, and elderly. Yet, rather than reify the gender binaries of this pairing, the tradition of *marasa twa* instead creates something new. Dessalines, as the only Haitian leader to be admitted to the Vodou pantheon, is not only sustained, mourned, and carried by a female figure but is also intertwined with the feminine in ways that disturb colonial classifications of gender.

While many nations can lay claim to cross-dressing women among their foundational myths, from Joan of Arc to Deborah Sampson to Catalina de Erauso, "Theresa" taps into both a secular and a spiritual tradition that queers the contours of revolutionary history. To give a concrete example, let us examine the portrait of the revolutionary cross-dressing soldier Sanité Belair on the Haitian ten-gourde bank note (see Figure 3.1). While nationalist myths across cultures frequently emphasize the maternal,

[43] On the legacies of Défilée, see Dayan, *Haiti, History and the Gods*, 39–47.

[44] Braziel, "Re-membering Défilée," 71.

Figure 3.1 "Sanité Belair" from 10 gourde banknote, Haiti, 2004

even fecund, potential of the nation, Sanité's portrait refuses cis-heteronormative signifiers of femininity. On the ten-gourde bank note, she does not present in a traditionally feminine visual language. Instead, she is decked in full military regalia, including a jaunty bicorne and heavy epaulets, her gaze raised and slightly wary as though looking beyond the consumer toward an approaching battle on the horizon. Circulating freely through the Haitian economy, the gourde neither obscures nor apologizes for Belair's cross-dressing but instead celebrates her in the same visual rhetoric used to depict figures like Toussaint Louverture and Jean-Jacques Dessalines. Even her one gold hoop earring refuses strictly feminine identifications: enslaved men and revolutionary fighters, including the General Georges Biassou, were regularly depicted wearing similar hoop earrings.

Sanité Belair's portrait extricates the female body from capitalist logics of monetary exchange value. The apposite question here is not what ten gourdes can buy you, or the conversion rate between gourdes and US dollars, but instead what it means to hold, carry, exchange, or earn the image of a person who so clearly troubles Western Enlightenment binaries of gender. And how does this disruption of cis-normative imagery resonate within global capitalist structures, which have historically depended *precisely* on the gendering and commodification of women's energy? Sanité is not the only woman to be featured on official icons of the Haitian state: Catherine Flon, who stitched the Haitian flag, appears on an earlier ten-gourde note; the image of Marie Jeanne Lamartinière was printed on both a 100-gourde coin and a 1954 stamp; and the initials of Henri-Christophe's Queen, Marie Louise, authorize an 1820 gourde coin.[45] While monetary representations of figures like Sanité, Catherine, or Marie Jeanne participate in the commodification of Black women – distilling their faces into liquid capital – these women also show powerful ways in which to elide those very capitalist logics, establishing a fugitive system of valuation, a system that allows women to reclaim their labor and redefine their worth outside global market structures. It is, in this respect, perhaps not coincidental that Theresa and her family circulate spiritual messages to each other on the bark of a "gourde" tree, a plant that gives its name to Haiti's currency, thus evoking at once the political, monetary, and ecological Haitian landscape.

3.3 "A Prophetic Vision of the Past": Embodying the Future

"Theresa" foregrounds Haitian spiritual structures within African-American print culture and in doing so produces a uniquely diasporic genealogy. This feminization and queering of Haitian history cannot be understood outside of the tale's spirituality. While Captain Inginac, President Boyer, John Russwurm, and Samuel Cornish pursued diasporic solidarity through public writing, governmental policy, and financial incentivization, the author of "Theresa" instead insists upon the private energies of spirituality. Cultural and spiritual practices such as cross-dressing and prophecy interrupt the forward thrust of masculinist print culture and instead archive a deeply rooted, transnational history of resistance. This worldview not only shapes Haitian Revolutionary historiography but disrupts the gender binary of global northern narratives.

"Theresa" theorizes religious experience, not as a retreat into the inner sanctum of the self, but instead as a practice that is intimately connected to political labor. This suturing of the spiritual and the political is concretized in her prophecies and visions, which structure the story's narrative arc. Indeed, although Theresa does very little by way of battle, diplomacy, or other institutional modes of resistance, she and her family undergo four distinct moments of spiritual prophecy, mysticism, and possession that

[45] Willson, *Fanm Rebel.*

help contribute to Haitian independence. In this concluding section, I would like to dwell on the specifics of Theresa's heightened vision, giving particular attention to the tale's unstable representation of temporality and its consequences for ideologies of reproduction. The queer and spiritual temporalities of "Theresa" ultimately subvert the linear determinism of heteronormative, profit-oriented genealogies of the global north. Thus, a close reading of "Theresa"'s spiritual framework not only sheds light on the rich theological syncretism of African-American religion but also has implications for non-normative constructions of desire, kinship, and Black futurity beyond the essentialist logics of heterosexual reproduction.

If the linear march of reproductive time is oriented toward the future, "Theresa" opens in a more temporally complex register. We know, due to the title, that Theresa's is a "Haytien tale;" however, the story begins with the line, "[d]uring the long and bloody contest in St. Domingo." In this respect, the author of the story turns to the colonial past or the "long and bloody contest" to propel the reader into a liberated future. Similarly, the author's terminology is temporally unstable: the warriors are sometimes called the "Islanders," recalling the Taíno civilization from which postrevolutionary Haiti (Ayiti) took its name. They are sometimes called the "sons of Africa," projecting the narrative into a precontact past. Finally, the author glimpses the future (or the present day for the readers of *Freedom's Journal*), naming the army "revolutionaries," "patriotic brethren," and "Haytiens."

These spatiotemporal slippages have concerned some critics. Daut, for example, argues that "it is painfully obvious that the writer of this brief tale had little or no first-hand knowledge or experience of either Haiti or Saint-Domingue."[46] Daut cites several historical anachronisms, such as the word "Hayti" in a pre-1804 context, as well as the fact that certain places in the tale, like Saint-Marie, are most likely fictional.[47] While acknowledging the problematic history of misrepresentations of colonial and postcolonial spaces, I worry that critics place too great a burden of verisimilitude upon writers of color. After all, no one faults Thomas Hardy for terming the southwest of England "Wessex" or Herman Melville for changing the date of the *Tyral* rebellion in his 1855 *Benito Cereno*. Some of the purported anachronisms of "Theresa" are indeed so dramatic that it seems clear that they serve a critical function. Take, for example, Theresa's supplication to God: "thou art alike the Father of the native of the burning desert, and of the more temperate, region" (January 25, 1828). Haiti has no desert, yet Theresa's topographical slippages invite a Biblical reading common in

[46] Daut, *Tropics of Haiti*, 309. [47] Ibid., 309–10.

African-American liberation traditions. Conflating Theresa's secular political demands with Mosaic emancipation, Theresa reminds God not only to protect Haiti but also to consistently apply Enlightenment imperatives of self-governance across revolutionary struggles.[48] Later in the tale, Theresa imagines "St. Domingo, once the granary of the West Indies." Haiti, of course, has a tropical climate and does not produce grain. Yet, many of *Freedom's Journal*'s readers, particularly northern free people of color, *did* live in grain-producing regions. Like the characters in "Theresa," these readers fought for self-determination, sovereignty, and civic personhood in the United States. The author thus embeds Haitian Revolutionary futurity within the reader's environment, deliberately altering the Haitian landscape in order to articulate trans-American linkages throughout a Black diasporic imaginary.

Other readers of the tale have been kinder to these anachronisms. Jean Lee Cole, for example, locates in the tale a strategy that would enable the reader to "imagine possibilities – what could happen? What might be possible?"[49] I would like to extend Cole's argument by suggesting that this vagueness not only creates the political conditions for revolutionary possibility but does so in a specifically spiritual register. Colonial history in "Theresa" is thus narrated through temporally complex, private, and queer spiritual modes, which include prophecy, possession, dream visions, mortification, and contemplation. The tale's anachronistic spatiotemporal emplotments create a private spiritual space similar to the *locus amoenus*, or "pleasant place" of the mystical dream vision: an enclosed "grove of peace" (January 5, 1828) from which the future can be glimpsed.

We might read, for example, one of Theresa's first prophecies:

> The vigour of her body was indeed much exhausted, but the emotions of her mind were more active than ever: she saw with the mind's eye the great services which might be rendered to her country; she brought to her imagination the once delightful fields of her native Hayti, now dy'd with the blood of her countrymen in their righteous struggle for liberty and for independence. Not less did she contemplate the once flourishing plantations ruined and St. Domingo once the granary of the West Indies, reduced to famine, now the island of misery, and the abode of wretchedness. (January 25, 1828)

The passage begins by juxtaposing corporeal mortification, or the "exhausted" body, against the activity of the mind. It is this corporeal

48 On the rhetorical significance of Egypt in *Freedom's Journal*, see Bacon, *Freedom's Journal*, 149–59. On the Exodus narrative in African-American culture, see also Glaude, *Exodus!*

49 Cole, "Theresa and Blake." See also Allewaert, *Tropologies*.

duality that creates the conditions for Theresa's mental state of "contemplation."[50] Through an explicitly spiritual practice, her "mind's eye" dilates to absorb an internal vista that simultaneously encompasses the past, the present, and the future. The first component of Theresa's vision collapses precontact, revolutionary, and postemancipation chronotopes within the formulation "delightful fields of her native Hayti." The notion of a "native Hayti" is both anachronistic (as Daut reminds us, Haiti did not exist as a political entity until 1804) and deeply historical: the word Ayiti comes from the Taíno word "land of high mountains" and Haitian revolutionaries frequently assumed affinities with the Taíno, perhaps most notably through the naming of Dessalines' *Armée indigène*. Moreover, this spatiotemporal confusion is overlaid with present-day violence: "now dy'd with the blood of her countrymen." In the second paragraph of her vision, Theresa continues to layer multiple temporal registers, replacing what were once the "delightful fields" with "plantations ruined." This is not, I believe, a lazy or ignorant slip but a thoughtful historical claim. Through her spiritual vision, "Theresa" shows the legacies of plantation violence against which ensues a "righteous struggle for liberty and independence." Theresa's pluralized temporal vision, although vast and nonlinear, possesses a rigorous logic: hand in hand with God, she writes a history of oppression in which the root causes of poverty, violence, and war are revealed to be the consequences of the colonial project. The historiographical "mind's eye" is explicitly named as a prophecy in the final vision of the tale. As Theresa searches for her mother and sister, she

> left the general's camp of hospitality, retracing her steps towards the grove of Pimento, where, at her departure, she left her dear mother and Amanda, enjoying calm repose; seated in a close carriage, her thoughts reverted to the deplorable state of her country; with a prophetic eye she saw the destruction of the French, and their final expulsion from her native island. She entreated the Creator, that he would bless the means, which through her agency, he had been pleased to put in the possession of her too long oppressed countrymen, and that all might be made useful to the cause of freedom (February 8, 1828).

The multiple temporalities of Theresa's prophetic vision culminate in a future that the 1828 reader of *Freedom's Journal* would have recognized as present-day Haiti. Moreover, the past Haitian "cause of freedom" would

[50] For a useful summary of Neoplatonic dualism, see Harrison, *Rethinking Augustine's Early Theology*, 85–7.

have resonated with a contemporary New York-based reader who had, just half a year prior, seen New York emancipation (which, as we will see in the following chapter, remained imperfect and incomplete). By physically retreating backward in time ("retracing her steps"), Theresa renders possible the conditions for forward-oriented prophecy, displacing herself within the narrative past in order to realize Haiti's future: "the destruction of the French, and their final expulsion from her native island." Furthermore, Theresa's role in this temporally complex vision is explicitly rendered active. Although she is a vessel of Haitian futurity in ways that recall philosophies of possession recounted in Chapter 1, she is not construed as passive. Instead, she is an active collaborator with her "Creator," whom she entreats "that he would bless the means, which through her agency, he had been pleased to put in the possession of her too long oppressed countrymen." This intimate negotiation between "her agency" and the Creator's "blessing," her "entreaty" and the Creator's "pleasure" creates the conditions for the "cause of freedom" in which the single woman's vehicular body is not a mere tool or pregnant vessel but instead an agentive and collaborative instrument of divine energy, operating across multiple spaces and points in time: from colonial Saint-Domingue to independent Haiti to the future and incomplete liberations of New York State emancipation, toward which the readers of *Freedom's Journal* labored.

This temporally plural mode of thinking rejects the logics of linear history and Enlightenment ideologies of the self-possessed person. As such, the story's religiosity not only elucidates the transnational contours of early African-American culture but also rethinks the ways in which futurity has historically been gendered and constrained to hetero- and cis-normative ideologies of reproduction. The author asks the audience to identify with Haiti's revolutionary past in order to better understand not just the present context of publication and circulation in Black New York but also the reader's future. This narrative strategy should be understood within the ongoing project of New York State emancipation, as well as the struggle of Haiti to be recognized as a sovereign nation. Indeed, although the author of "Theresa" respects the name Haitians chose for themselves (itself transtemporal, with attachments to a Taíno past), the United States would not recognize Haiti until 1862, and most white-authored discussions of the nation still referred to it as "San Domingo," "St. Domingue," or other versions of the colonial appellation.

This form of analeptic prolepsis, or a future narrated from within the confines of the past, recalls, in inverted form, Édouard Glissant's "prophetic vision of the past" (*une vision prophétique du passé*) in which the "relentless unveiling of the past, which has been distorted or obliterated by others, sometimes allows one to better handle [toucher] the present"("[l]'acharnement à dévoiler le passé, par d'autres dénaturé ou oblitéré, permet parfois de mieux toucher l'actuel" (8)).[51] Glissant's demand for a mode of historical consciousness bypasses the imperatives of linear, white supremacist, and ostensibly modern teleology; in doing so, he theorizes a temporal mode that resonates with the complex narrative structure of "Theresa." For Glissant, the past does not simply inhabit or shape the present. Instead, one must return to the past with future-oriented eyes in order to see beyond the epistemological limits of the colonized present and allow for new horizons of collective labor and human energy.

There is an explicitly spiritual and affective dimension to this future-oriented justice or what Theresa, in the tale, names prophecy. The prophetic mode, as Martin Munro reminds us, is an important concept within Haitian political and spiritual life:

> In Haiti. . .there are other conceptions of time and history at play, quite different to the linear model. Specifically, time is often judged to turn in circular or cyclical movements so that the idea of progressing through time in a linear fashion seems barely appropriate to an understanding of Haitian time and history.[52]

Munro turns to the intertwined phenomena of prophecy and apocalypse, giving particular attention to the 2010 earthquake that devastated Port-au-Prince. But "Theresa" points toward other futures that insist on apocalypse in its etymological sense: as an uncovering or revelation, a starting point for renarrating what Glissant would call the "distorted or obliterated" past and establishing a counterarchive to colonial forms of institutional memory.[53] Although Glissant would use the phrase "prophetic vision of the past" in other writings, notably *Introduction à une poétique du divers* (1996), it is important to recall that the term originated in the context of the play *Monsieur Toussaint* (1981), an embodied retelling of Haitian history. The explicitly corporeal elements of this prophetic vision are readily apparent in Glissant's diction: the word *l'archarnement* (unrelenting) derives from *chair* or flesh, while the insistence on understanding the present is conveyed through the verb *toucher*, to touch or realize. In this respect, the embodied prophecies of Glissant's *Toussaint* evoke the "sensory register" that Elizabeth Freeman has identified in studies of queer temporality, or the

[51] Glissant, "Avertissement" *Monsieur Toussaint* (version scénique), 9–10.
[52] Munro, *Tropical Apocalypse*, 26. [53] Glover, *Haiti Unbound.*

"sense-methods [that] rearrange the relations between past and present, linking contemporary bodies to those from other times in reformulations of ancestry and lineage."[54] Like Glissant, the author of "Theresa" insists on the sensory aspects of prophecy: the women of the tale repeatedly undergo overwhelmingly physical experiences, whether it be "calm sensation" at the touch of a cool breeze or the physical "shuddering" of grief, pouring from their eyes in "copious streams." This emphasis on the bodily aspects of possession and prophecy not only recall Christian theologies of bodily mortification but also tap into what Freeman would identify as a uniquely queer temporality of sense perception and futurity.

Yet, although the body is central to Theresa's prophecies, the author also refuses its instrumentalization, which would reduce the characters to sentimental mothers or virginal Marys. While the opening lines, for example, begin with explicitly reproductive language ("the white man, who flourished the child of sensuality"), the paragraph concludes with an image, not of fecund maternity, birthing futures, or gestating messiahs, but instead with a figure of solitary motherhood: "Madame Paulina was left a widow." As we recall from Chapter 1, Ezili Dantò, the lwa who launched the Haitian Revolution, is also a single mother and often figured as a lesbian. As the tale progresses, the women insist on protecting their strong familial ties and yet simultaneously subvert the biological essentialism of the family by refusing the logics of paternity and linear reproduction. Instead, they establish queer and racially ambiguous visual codes of dress (from cross-dressing to racial passing), which complicate the iconography of the colonial family and subvert the logics of colonial social structures.

In this respect, "Theresa" refuses the kind of reproductive futurity influentially theorized by Lee Edelman, in which the teleology of patrilineal succession – "the fantasy of reproduction as the seedbed of futurity" – forecloses the political potential of the present.[55] As many feminist and queer scholars of color have argued, Edelman's rejection of this reproductive "fantasy" retains the fantasy of a relatively privileged subject position (a middle-class, white man). In doing so, Edelman elides the experiences of those whose futures have historically been – and still are – denied by white ideologies. As Kara Keeling argues, "Calling for no future, it has been argued, might inform a (non)politics only for those for whom the future is given, even if undesirably so."[56] With its promises of future freedoms, its

[54] Freeman, *Time Binds*, 15. [55] Edelman, *No Future*, 132.

[56] Keeling, *Queer Times, Black Futures*, 89. On temporality and queerness, see Edelman, *No Future;* Freeman, *Time Binds*; Halberstam, *In a Queer Time and Place* 2005; and Muñoz, *Cruising Utopia.*

celebration of an all-female Black diasporic family, and its embrace of matrilineal (and possibly queer) kinship, I want to suggest that "Theresa" retains the "futurity" of Edelman's concept while rejecting ideologies of the "reproductive" in ways that recall José Muñoz's now canonical critique of Edelman. Muñoz argues that queerness structures a "mode of desiring that allows us to see and feel beyond the quagmire of the present."[57] Through collective love and labor, Muñoz imagines a horizon of the "not here yet" enabling pluralized temporal experiences without the linear chain of genealogical narratives:

> To see queerness as a horizon is to perceive it as a modality of ecstatic time in which the temporal stranglehold that I describe as straight time is interrupted or stepped out of. Ecstatic time is signaled at the moment one feels ecstasy, announced perhaps in a scream or grunt of pleasure, and more important during moments of contemplation when one looks back at a scene from one's past, present, or future.[58]

"Theresa," with its roots in both Christian and Afro-Caribbean forms of spiritual ecstasy, looks toward Muñoz's horizon, converting the exploitative energy extraction technologies of the plantation into forms of spiritual resistance among women who may or may not care to use their energy to reproduce. Embedded in multitemporal prophecy, communal possession, and love among women, the tale makes possible visions of Black futurity without reducing women to reproductive capital. Instead, "Theresa" rewrites the past, resounds in the present, and imagines a future for all: where Haiti can flourish as a sovereign state, where Black New Yorkers can realize the full rights and prerogatives of citizenship, and where motherhood is a choice and an acknowledged form of political labor (the tale certainly celebrates Paulina's love for her daughters) but not a social obligation or ontological state (Paulina's daughter, Theresa, is perfectly happy to fight in male garb, without giving any thought to romance, children, or men). Not unlike the many faces of the Ezili pantheon – from Ezili Freda to Ezili Dantò – both Paulina and Theresa represent equally valuable paths of spiritual and political action.

The unruly temporalities of Theresa's prophetic vision interrupt the kind of linear reproductive futurity that so often characterized women's lives in *Freedom's Journal*. If the future of the "race" was to be accorded to women, the author seems to suggest that the future is not embedded in a woman's ability to submit to a man's protection, bear children, or further

[57] Muñoz, *Cruising Utopia*, 1. [58] Ibid., 32.

the bloodline. Refusing to concede to typical scripts of Black womanhood, Theresa is emphatically *not* a victim of sexual assault, nor is she a passive girl to be rescued, nor is she a sentimental mother or reproductive vessel. Instead, the temporal structures of "Theresa" reject the logics of reproductive futurity and the exploitation of Black women's energy. Through these structures, "Theresa" defends Black kinship, Haitian sovereignty, and love among women, theorizing a philosophy of energy that imagines Black futures beyond the plantation, the household, or the hearth; beyond the colonial categories of gender and cis-heteronormative reproduction; and beyond the national categories that would circumscribe and isolate Haiti from the United States and, more broadly, the Americas.

CHAPTER 4

"A Wandering Maniac"
Sojourner Truth's Demonic Marronage

In Sojourner Truth's 1875 *Book of Life*, an unusual tribute to the activist appears: in a fragment recounting Truth's meeting with the minister George Truman, an anonymous New Jersey journalist claims that "Cosmopolitan in her nature, she calls the world her home."[1] Truth, who never left the United States, is an unlikely candidate for cosmopolitanism. As her chosen name would suggest, Truth *sojourned* extensively, living and lecturing throughout New England, the Midwest, New York, and Washington, DC, yet the most international Truth ever got was rather close to the Canadian border. However, the *Book of Life*, curated by the white reformer Frances Titus, suggests a broader global stage.[2] While Truth was often portrayed, particularly by white activists, as a homespun rustic, the anonymous journalist's interest in cosmopolitanism highlights, although unintentionally, a neglected aspect of her life and legacy. Born under the name Isabella Baumfree in Rifton, New York, Truth grew up in a cosmopolitan milieu inflected by Dutch, African, and Caribbean cultures; this milieu introduced her to hemispheric, creolized, and transculturated spiritual and folk traditions that exceeded the boundaries of the United States. Truth's first language was Dutch, her early spiritual beliefs were African, and her community was shaped through transnational channels of trade, labor, and revolution – particularly the Haitian Revolution. As such, Truth's early life

1 "George Truman and Sojourner Truth in Orange, New Jersey, 1874," cited in *The Narrative of Sojourner Truth.*

2 I do not take up the term "cosmopolitan" to intervene in traditional philosophical discourses of cosmopolitanism, with their interests in universal human rights and the cultivation of a global citizenry around shared obligations and responsibilities. Instead, my understanding of Truth's cosmopolitanism derives from eighteenth-century definitions of the term, what Diderot's and d'Alembert's *Encyclopédie* defines as a "man of no fixed abode, or a man who is nowhere a stranger." Less interested in rights-based discourses, world citizenship, or social contract theory, such approaches to cosmopolitanism focus instead on lives experienced in flux, both enmeshed in intimate locales and stretched over wider global circuits of contact and exchange.

puts pressure on the limitations of traditional Anglo-American nationalist narratives that have sought to define her. Moreover, Truth's "cosmopolitanism" – or rather her creolized background, a term I believe is more appropriate to describe her cultural contexts – highlights her lifelong mobility: a commitment to movement, wandering, and kinetic energy that has since been celebrated by later critics. This chapter aims not only to more fully adumbrate the Caribbean dimensions of Truth's early life in upstate New York but also to consider her within twentieth- and twenty-first-century theorizations of Black mobility. Ultimately, I argue, Truth's early milieu can be read within later intellectual genealogies of Black fugitivity, which propel her kinetic movement beyond the cliches of white reformist literature.[3]

As we saw with Marie Laveau in Chapter 2, Truth's life raises significant methodological and ethical challenges. A repository of facts and fiction, a collage of projections from white abolitionist culture, Truth represents, in Nell Irvin Painter's words, "the triumph of a symbol."[4] This symbol is sometimes composed of outright errors: For Frances Gage, Truth was a Southerner, speaking in the false thick dialect of the "Ain't I A Woman Speech"; for Harriet Beecher Stowe, she was born in Africa and already dead (Truth actually had another twenty years in her at the time of publication); and Olive Gilbert's *Narrative* wraps Truth in a sentimental bourgeois cloak of True Womanhood.[5] This tapestry of fiction and romance offers a valuable insight into the abuses of white women's abolitionist culture but often obscures Truth as a historical and agentive subject.[6] Later critics have read Truth beyond the parameters of white print culture, precisely by focusing on the "symbolic" dimensions of Painter's words. Perhaps most representative of such approaches, Donna Haraway interprets Truth as a trickster figure who "resist[s] representation, resist[s] literal figuration," a cipher whose meaning was perpetually in flight, or, in the words of Haraway, "the essential Truth would not settle down; that *was* her specificity."[7] Yet, this line of poststructuralist inquiry, as many Black feminist critics have argued, frequently gives way to

[3] Wynter, "Beyond Miranda's Meanings." See also McKittrick, *Demonic Grounds*.

[4] Painter, *Sojourner Truth*, 281.

[5] Stowe, "The Libyan Sibyl." On the inaccuracies of Gage, Gilbert, and Stowe, see Painter, *The Triumph of a Symbol*, especially 160–4. See also Adams, *Owning Up*.

[6] See Humez, "Reading the Narrative of Sojourner Truth as a Collaborative Text," 30; Mandziuk and Fitch, "The Rhetorical Construction of Sojourner Truth."

[7] Haraway, "Ecce Homo, Ain't (Ar'n't) I a Woman, and Inappropriate/d Others," 86, 102. See also Ernest, "The Floating Icon and the Fluid Text," 483.

abstractionist, ahistorical idioms of fluidity, flux, and rootless signifiers, which often reproduce the power structures they seek to erode.[8]

More successful have been attempts to situate Truth's mobility within epistemological and ontological models for Black women's spirituality and political labor. Patricia Hill Collins, for example, has emphasized Truth's "migratory status," unseating the assumption of "one center of power" within hierarchical relations constitutive of white supremacist societies.[9] For Daphne Brooks, Truth's mobility is better understood through the discourse of performativity. Building from Carla Peterson's notion of eccentricity as "freedom of movement stemming from lack of central control," Brooks emphasizes how Truth transformed her corporeality into a terrain that allowed her to "protect, empower, and *mobilize* herself at unlikely moments."[10] More recently, Sarah Jane Cervenak has understood Truth within a broader genealogy of Black wandering, arguing that Truth's itinerant paths led to a "philosophically performative spirit of ungovernability" that exceeds the immobilizing limitations of the rational, Enlightenment subject.[11] Whether figured as a cosmopolite, sojourner, migrant, eccentric, or wanderer, Truth's movements – in short, her kinetic energy – have motivated critical understandings of the activist, from our nameless journalist in 1875 to the present day.

This chapter contributes to the critical discourse on Truth's mobility by examining her peripatetic paths, not only as epistemological or ontological signifiers but as a set of energy practices rooted in historical networks representative of Truth's creolized milieu. Critics who have explored Truth's Afro-Dutch background tend to come from historical disciplinary backgrounds and therefore do not often engage in the philosophical implications of the activist's wandering. Similarly, more philosophically oriented critics often overlook – sometimes egregiously – the historical and social conditions that shaped Truth's worldview. This chapter brings these two approaches together, by arguing that Truth's spiritual kineticism must be understood within a broader hemispheric framework of self-emancipation and energy reclamation in the Americas. In particular, I analyze Truth within a genealogy of marronage, thus extending the spatial and temporal coordinates that have traditionally limited her to the Anglo-American nineteenth century. Instead, I argue that Truth should be read within

8 McDowell, "Recycling"; Smith, *Not Just Race, Not Just Gender*; Brooks, *Bodies in Dissent;* Homans, "'Women of Color' Writers and Feminist Theory."

9 Patricia Hill Collins, *Fighting Words,* 231.

10 Peterson, "Eccentric Bodies," xii; Brooks, *Bodies in Dissent,* 158.

11 Cervenak, *Wandering Philosophical Performances of Racial and Sexual Freedom,* 130.

kinetic freedom practices of Caribbean flight and in doing so stands as a precursor to twentieth-century celebrations of marronage in Négritude, Antillanité, and Créolité movements.

Yet, Truth also unsettles the masculinist assumptions of these later discourses. In transforming the profit-driven energetic demands of enslaved reproduction into emancipatory kineticism, Truth's marronage rewrites familiar twentieth-century Caribbean discourses of mobility and freedom. Truth thus not only highlights the role of women marrons/maroons but also exemplifies what Sylvia Wynter famously terms the "demonic grounds" of colonial geographies: a liberatory Black feminist cartography that operates as a counterdiscourse to white ideologies which have traditionally understood Black women as lacking, marginal, or oppositional to humanness. Suturing the demonic (an energy force that emerges from Wynter's study of nineteenth-century physics) with Caribbean practices of marronage (a kinetic practice of flight against the energy demands of chattel slavery), Truth, I argue, is not only a creolized subject but also can expand our understandings of twentieth- and twenty-first-century Caribbean philosophy and specifically Black women's energy in the Americas.

Born around 1797 in Rifton, New York, a town in the predominantly Dutch Ulster County, Truth grew up in a world shaped by Atlantic empires; steeped in African, Caribbean, Native American, Spanish, Dutch, and French histories; and shaking with the tremors of the Haitian Revolution. In considering Truth as a creolized figure, we displace the authority of white texts traditionally central to Truth's legacy. This chapter thus shifts from the white reformer's word to the global system, the fetishized individual body to networked collective bodies, from the *Narrative* to cultural, political, and historical apparatuses only briefly signaled by the discursive contexts of Truth's amanuenses. As with Marie Laveau, a woman whose histories have been overdetermined by white popular culture, I read Sojourner Truth's textual remains against their narrative grain and attempt to situate them in broader cultural frameworks (see Figure 4.1).

In this respect, I follow the methodological cues of several influential critics. Nell Irvin Painter's research on Truth was among the first to open up alternative spiritual paradigms, including witchcraft, for understanding African-American religious identity. As Painter argues, Truth's religious identity "was syncretic – which is the very essence of African-American culture – and also very much in flux."[12] Margaret Washington's magisterial *Sojourner Truth's America* builds from Painter's analysis of syncretism,

[12] Painter, "Sojourner Truth's Religion in Her Moment of Pentecostalism and Witchcraft," 147.

Figure 4.1 Grace Lynne Haynes, Sojourner Truth mural, Newark, New Jersey, 2020

foregrounding the importance of Afro-Dutch culture in Truth's "spiritual biography."[13] The first extended study of Truth's African and Dutch milieu, Washington's work developed critical avenues for further research into Truth's creolization, steering critical focus away from white Anglo-American biases. Drawing from a deep archive of Kongolese spiritual traditions, Washington has powerfully shown how Truth's spiritual beliefs and practices, including African song, dance, and a close relationship with the African *Nzambi*, developed within a contested cultural sphere overlooked by the hegemonic optics of white Anglo Protestantism later in Truth's life. For Washington, "African spirituality would later nudge [Truth] toward American spiritualism."[14] Yet, with the notable exception of Jeroen Dewulf, who has thoughtfully and thoroughly explored Truth's Dutch milieu, very few critics have since followed Painter's and Washington's groundbreaking injunctions to read Truth beyond US cultural frameworks.[15] This chapter aims to correct this critical lacuna by exploring not only Truth's syncretic cultural contexts but also, in particular, the Caribbean aspects of her early milieu.

In Ulster County, where Truth was born and raised, enslaved people comprised fourteen percent of the population, many of whom were from

[13] Washington, *Sojourner Truth's America,* 5. See also "'From Motives of Delicacy": Sexuality and Morality in the Narratives of Sojourner Truth and Harriet Jacobs," *The Journal of African American History* 92:1, 2007.

[14] Washington, *Truth's America*, 55.

[15] Dewulf, "The Many Languages of American Literature," 222. See also Dewulf, "A Strong Barbaric Accent," Dewulf, *The Pinkster King and the King of Kongo.*

or had traveled through the Caribbean.[16] Moreover, Truth was born in the middle of the Haitian Revolution and her personal road to freedom charted a parallel path to the first Black republic's liberation. As we saw in the previous chapter, the freedom time of New York State emancipation imaginatively coextended the temporalities of Haitian independence. Even in the heavily compromised texts of white print culture, there exist small hints of Truth's possible contact with Caribbean and African traditions throughout her life. Washington, for example, has called attention to Truth's skilled performance of Congo dances, many of which were practiced throughout the Caribbean and Latin America;[17] Truth's son Peter went to sea, sending her letters from the West Indies and perhaps news from Haiti;[18] even her garb of the Madras scarf described by Harriet Beecher Stowe in the 1864 "Libyan Sibyl" indicates possible West Indian sartorial strategies, albeit strategies misunderstood and romanticized by Stowe.[19]

Most strikingly, Truth's conversion narrative aligns with Pinkster, a Pentecostal holiday typically celebrated in Black Dutch communities in New York and New Jersey. Not only did the Pinkster of Truth's conversion in June 1828 take place a month before New York State emancipation (July 4, 1828), it also drew on the iconography and cultural memory of Black kingship in Haiti. Rather than reading Pinkster as oppositional to Truth's spirituality, as many commentators have done, I argue that the holiday allows us to interface the domestic pantomimes of enslaved festivities with the very real ascension of Black men to modern thrones in Haiti. In this respect, Truth's relation to Pinkster was both embedded in an Afro-diasporic past and attuned to a Haitian political future. That her own spiritual rebirth so closely coincides to a narrative of Black self-emancipation – in both upstate New York and Haiti – throws into relief Truth's Caribbean influences and draws together the palaces of Haitian kings and the farms of upstate New York.

Truth's "house of bondage" in Ulster County gives way to larger global networks structured by multilingual and overlapping scales of relation.[20]

16 Groth, *Slavery and Freedom in the Mid-Hudson Valley*; Davies, "New York's Black Line"; Armstead (ed.), *Mighty Change, Tall Within: Black Identity in the Hudson Valley* ; McManus, *A History of Negro Slavery in New York.*

17 Washington, *Truth's America*, 45.

18 Nantucket Historical Assocation, MS 15 box 8, folder 205.

19 On the Caribbean legacies of the Madras scarf, see Dillon, *New World Drama.* See also Buckridge, *African Lace-Bark in the Caribbean*; Riello and Parthasarathi (eds.), *The Spinning World*; Kobayashi, "Indian Cotton Textiles in the Eighteenth Century Atlantic Economy."

20 Like Margaret Washington, I will refer to Sojourner Truth as both Truth and Isabella in this chapter, generally using "Isabella" to refer to the period prior to her self-baptism in 1843.

Following the irregular domestic orbits of Truth's biography opens other nodes, which stretch and warp these familiar locales (New York, New England, Ohio, or Michigan) into vast transnational cartographies. Understanding Truth's Atlantic and hemispheric influences allows critics to glimpse the Netherlands, Curaçao, or Haiti embedded within the modest cultural circles of US national identity, and a radical revolutionary lurking beneath the benign guise of the sentimental portrait. Truth's creolized background and commitment to mobility not only expand critical understandings of African-American nineteenth-century culture but also redefine energy practices typically associated with Black women's enslavement. As such, Truth leads us to the unruly and fugitive paths of liberation, forging an alternative and energetic cartography beneath the Anglo-American sentiments of white abolitionist culture.

4.1 Creolizing Dutch New York

Truth's New York was built upon labor and knowledge stolen from enslaved people. When the Dutch invaded Manhattan Island in 1628, they imported African workers by way of the Caribbean, through the Dutch West India Company (WIC). According to Leslie Harris, enslaved people built roads, cleared land, burned limestone and oyster shells, cut timber and firewood, and – as the colony spread up the shores of island – cultivated the land on "bouwerys" or farms.[21] Because New Netherland attracted very few white indentured European workers, the colony was disproportionately dependent on enslaved labor. Yet, the African population was relatively small. Chattel slavery was not institutionalized, and Dutch settlers, rather than buying enslaved persons, often hired people of African descent directly from the WIC.[22] The seventeenth-century Dutch primarily directed their trade of enslaved Africans through the burgeoning plantation economies of the South Atlantic, especially Portuguese Brazil (over which it had assumed control in 1637). These territorial holdings left a strong Luso-African influence on Dutch culture in New Netherland. In fact, Isabella's name, as Washington has argued, almost certainly comes

[21] Harris, *In the Shadow of Slavery*, 13–14. See also Hodges, *Root and Branch*; Klooster, *The Dutch Moment*; Goodfried, "Burghers and Blacks; Heywood and Thornton, *Central Africans, Atlantic Creoles, and the Foundation of the Americas, 1585–1600;* Berlin, "From Creole to African; Rink," *Holland on the Hudson*.

[22] See Hodges, *Root and Branch*, 31. See also Jacobs, *The Colony of New Netherland*.

from a Luso-Congolese lineage of Isabellas, including the militant cross-dressing sister of the Kongo king Pedro IV.[23]

Although the comparison of slave systems offers specious moral comfort – as though any institution that systematically robs persons of their right to self-determination could be viewed as "better" than another – slavery in the early years of New Netherland offered a degree of legal flexibility to people of African descent. Early Dutch jurisprudence, in stark contrast to the model of civic death familiar to scholars of Anglo-American slavery, admitted, albeit reluctantly, Black legal personhood. New Netherland's Black population, whether enslaved or free, had the right to marry; own land, livestock, and other property; work for wages; testify in court; and bring lawsuits against white people.[24] This was a pragmatic rather than moral stance: Dutch officials hoped to secure African allies in their wars against Native Americans.[25] Moreover, many Africans were released from bondage only to find themselves in indentured servitude or poverty. Ill motivated as these concessions were, they had lasting consequences for Dutch Africans. A 1635 Dutch court witnessed what was perhaps one of the first successful equal pay lawsuits, when five Africans from New Amsterdam obtained a settlement from eight white guilders, guaranteeing the latter equal pay with white laborers.[26] Nearly a decade later, in 1644, a group of eleven Africans achieved the first known group manumission after petitioning Dutch officials for their freedom. They were eventually granted "half freedom" and were given land in what is now Greenwich Village.[27] Dutch jurisprudence even recognized the legal status of Black families, in 1644, allowing two men, Cleijn Antonio and Paulo d'Angola, to petition for freedom on the grounds that they needed to support their wives and children.[28] Truth perhaps inherited her own

[23] Washington. *Sojourner Truth's America,* 11; see also Dewulf, *The Pinkster King and the King of Kongo*, especially 95–104; Heywood and Thornton, "The Portuguese, Kongo and Ndongo and the Origins of Atlantic Creole Culture to 1607."

[24] Harris, *In the Shadow of Slavery*, 16. See also Jacobs, The Colony of *New Netherland*, 383–85; Romney, *New Netherland Connections*, 192–94; Moore, "A World of Possibilities, 47–49; Goodfried, "The Souls of New Amsterdam's African American Children," i.

[25] On black militias and manumission, see Dewulf, *The Pinkster King and the King of Kongo*, 135–49.

[26] Harris, *In the Shadow of Slavery*, 20.

[27] The notion of "half freedom" again emphasizes that Dutch manumission was far from true liberation but instead motivated by racist pragmatism. The men were required to pay for their freedom, entering into an indentured servitude in which they were obliged to pay the company "22½ bushels of maize, wheat, or corn, and one fat hog." Eight of the original eleven eventually achieved full freedom but, like many manumitted Africans, were likely forced to live in poverty. See Gomez, *Black Crescent,* 129.

[28] Van Zandt, *Brothers among Nations,* 143–4.

strategies of legal literacy from this Black Dutch juridical tradition: she sued for her own freedom from John Dumont in 1826; the following year, she successfully sued for her young son Peter's freedom. In 1835, she won a slander suit against a white couple, the Folgers, who had accused Truth of attempting to poison them during their involvement in the Matthias cult; later in her life, she won a lawsuit against a car conductor on charges of assault and battery.[29]

Yet, with the British conquest in 1664, slavery became recognized as a legal institution and even greater restrictions were imposed upon enslaved people. Under "Duke's Law" – named for the Duke of York, who incidentally had a controlling interest in the British Royal African Company – the religious instruction of enslaved Africans became illegal; fines were imposed for self-emancipated people as well as anyone who abetted them; and the colony (very ineffectually) attempted to limit celebrations, gatherings, and the consumption of alcohol among New York's Black population.[30] After the so-called "Slave Revolt" of 1712, which led to the execution of twenty-one enslaved people, the colony established a series of even more stringent laws, forbidding the congregation of groups of more than three African persons and imposing the death penalty on anyone of African descent who "wilfully" burned white dwellings.[31] This increased policing of Blackness was concomitant with England's rapid expansion of the New York slave trade. Due to the rapid industrialization of colonial Saint-Domingue, New York City saw a growth in trade, creating a need for manual labor that the comparatively meager white indentured population could not fulfill. Between 1737 and 1771, the Royal African Company imported 4394 enslaved people into New York, thirty percent of whom were from the Caribbean.[32] As Jill Lepore notes, a strong link was forged between this newly arrived Caribbean population and the specter of slave revolt (whether real or perceived): "Blacks who came to New York from the Caribbean brought with them tales of rebellion."[33] The New York Conspiracy of 1741 further yoked the perceived menace of revolution with Caribbean identity by

[29] For more detailed accounts of these trials, see Accomando, "Demanding a Voice among the Pettifoggers; see also Field, *The Struggle for Equal Adulthood*; Amuchie, "The Forgotten Victims"; DeLombard, *Slavery on Trial.*

[30] See Harris, *In the Shadow of Slavery,* 26–28; Hodges, *Root and Branch,* 10–12; Higginbotham, *In the Matter of Color*; Malone, *Between Freedom and Bondage*; Goodfriend, *Who Should Rule at Home?*

[31] Cited in Malone, *Between Freedom and Bondage,* 28; Hodges, *Root and Branch,* 98; Harris, *In the Shadow of Slavery,* 37–40; Foote, *Black and White Manhattan,* 133–38.

[32] Harris, *In the Shadow of Slavery,* 208.

[33] Lepore, *New York Burning,* 54.

muddling the specious threat of slave revolt with rumors of a "Popish" – and specifically Spanish Catholic – plot. Nearly 200 people were implicated in the conspiracy, leaving Spanish Caribbean peoples of African descent particularly vulnerable to the imbricating fears of Catholicism, Blackness, and the Caribbean. A violent witch hunt, fueled by rumor and racism, the New York Conspiracy nonetheless reveals the deepening alliances among New York's Black population across geographic and colonial lines. As Lepore notes, "Men born in New York, in the Caribbean, and in Africa – and perhaps especially . . . born in Africa and 'seasoned' in the Caribbean – forged bonds of fictive kinship."[34] These coalitions, built in the face of white supremacist violence, helped forge a creolized Black New York identity, one that brought together African, Caribbean, Dutch, English, and Native American practices, strategies, and belief systems.

Representative of this transnational coalition is the 1770 *Narrative of the Most Remarkable Particulars in the Life of James Albert Ukawsaw Gronniosaw, an African Prince*. Born in Borneo around 1710, Gronniosaw was kidnapped by a trader, shipped to Barbados, and eventually purchased by the Dutch Vanhorn family in New York City. In 1730, the Calvinist minister Theodorus Frelinghuysen purchased Gronniosaw and brought him to the predominantly Dutch community in Raritan Valley (New Jersey), where he lived for 18 years. Upon the death of Frelinghuysen's family, Gronniosaw departed for New York City, traveled the Caribbean, migrated to England and Amsterdam, and wrote his narrative through an amanuensis before his death in 1775. As Dewulf points out, Truth's and Gronniosaw's respective *Narratives* form distinct parallels, perhaps most convincingly in their mystical accounts of conversion. An 1810 edition of his life story was published in Catskill, not far from Truth's birthplace, and Dewulf speculates that Truth may have taken inspiration from Gronniosaw's *Narrative*.[35]

Although born nearly a century apart, the two figures shared common cultural ground. Gronniosaw's itinerant life – from his native Borneo to the Gold Coast, Barbados, New York, New Jersey, Saint-Domingue, Martinique, Havana, Amsterdam, London, and provincial England – prefigures Truth's similarly mobile cartographies. Upon the death of his enslavers, Gronniosaw, like many emancipated Black New Yorkers, was left impoverished. According to his *Narrative*, he accumulated three pounds of debt, which led to a term of bonded labor during which he served as cook on a British warship fighting in the Caribbean during the Seven Years War (1756–63). This re-enslavement with the formal name of

[34] Ibid., 47. [35] Dewulf, 'The Many Languages of American Literature," 230–4.

freedom sent Gronniosaw to the very heart of modern slavery – the coast of Saint-Domingue – where he reported fighting French merchant ships, as well as a fleet of thirty-six warships. One might imagine which other diasporic subjects Gronniosaw may have encountered and what alliances he may have formed with enslaved Africans of Saint-Domingue.

But creolized resistance did not only play out in the theater of war. As Joyce Goodfriend has argued, the intimate spaces of the household also became contested sites of Black autonomy, particularly for women. Goodfriend cites the case of Belinda, an enslaved female cook in New York, who in 1762 was sold for practicing what was likely an Afro-Caribbean religion.[36] As her enslaver John Watts wrote: "She is a simple creature and a very good cook . . . but her simplicity led her to triffle [sic] about charms which alarmed my female family too much to keep her."[37] Although Watts belittles Belinda's spiritual beliefs, his disproportionate reaction to her "triffles" reveals a deeper anxiety around Black religious autonomy. Not only did Watts arrange with a slavedealer to sell her in Virginia (a more violent place for enslaved people and, according to Craig Steven Wilder, an unusually severe punishment for a woman) but also her dismissal was grounded in the patriarchal logics of protecting Watts's "female family."[38] As Goodfriend has argued, Belinda's rejection of European Christianity "managed to disturb the fragile equilibrium between master and slaves."[39] I would add that Belinda also disturbs white masculine authority by introducing a private and specifically female form of spirituality into Watts's Dutch Protestant home. Evoking the Indian-Barbadian Tituba of the Salem witch trials, Belinda's racialized and gendered domestic influence troubled the white household with an emergent Black hemispheric identity. What kinds of contagion did Watts fear Belinda might spark among the white "females" under his roof? Her quiet spiritual rebellion prefigures the ways in Truth, a century later, would harness not only Protestantism but also the practices and rituals – dismissed as "trifles," "superstitions," and "charms" – of Afro-diasporic religions. Indeed, Painter, in her suggestive essay "Sojourner Truth's Religion in Her Moment," reads Truth's spirituality as a form of witchcraft, drawing from both African traditions and seventeenth-century New England. As she argues: "The coexistence of Pentecostalism and witchcraft in Isabella's

[36] Goodfriend, *Who Should Rule at Home?*, 172–3.

[37] John Watts to John Riddell, November 17, 1762, New York. *Letter Book of John Watts: Merchant and Coucillor of New York: January 1, 1762–December 22, 1765* (New York Historical Society 1928) 97.

[38] Wilder, *Ebony and Ivy*, 132.

[39] Goodfriend, *Who Should Rule at Home?*, 172.

[Truth's] life in 1828 demands a closer and more careful look at all the manifestations of what we call black religion."[40]

Both Belinda and Gronniosaw highlight the creolized identity of Dutch Africans. Like them, Truth would have been familiar with the stories, beliefs, and traditions of many imbricating cultures. In fact, her parents are representative of the kind of creole coalition described by Lepore and emblematized by Belinda and Gronniosaw. Although we do not know the date or specific place of birth for either James Baumfree or his wife Elizabeth, they were likely born in the western hemisphere or brought to it at a young age. Their dates of birth would have been decades after the New York Conspiracy (probably in the 1760s or 1770s), yet their upbringing reverberated with the accruing energies and anxieties of possible revolt. News of Tacky's War in Jamaica and the Abaco Revolt in the Bahamas would have reached the ears of New Yorkers, as would have news of Makandal's conspiracy in Saint-Domingue in the 1750s. Elizabeth – known as Betsy or "Mau-mau Bet" – was, according to Margaret Washington, likely of Kongolese descent. James's surname merged the Dutch word for tree ("bome" or "baum") with the English word "free," an etymology that, according to Washington, likely suggests a background in the inland Gold Coast, or present-day Ghana.[41] Truth's father may also have had ties to Native American cultures, as James was reportedly half "Mohawk Indian" (Kanien'kehá:ka). According to an 1880 letter from Eliza Seaman Leggett to Walt Whitman, Truth had reported that her "father's mother was a squaw."[42] Although we should be wary of too hastily accepting the myths imposed on Truth by white spectators, this kind of alliance was common for Dutch Africans in New York, who often worked as interpreters and traders, and married Native Americans.

Truth inherited from her parents Kongolese, Ghanean, possibly Kanien'kehá:ka and Caribbean cultural identities. But she had another parent as well: the Haitian Revolution. By 1797, the year of her birth, the Revolution had been making steady gains on the island for six years. That same year, Toussaint forced the Civil Commissioner and de facto ruler Léger Félicité Sonthonax to leave the island in a publicly humiliating expulsion. In the absence of Sonthonax, Toussaint consolidated his power. In the following year, the British withdrew from the war, and by 1801, Toussaint had abolished slavery in Saint-Domingue, declaring himself

40 Painter, *Spellbound,* 153–4. 41 Washington, *Sojourner Truth's America*, 9.

42 Ibid., 10. Eliza Seaman Leggett, letter to Walt Whitman, June 22, 1881, cited in Thomas C. Donaldson, *Walt Whitman: The Man* (New York: Frances P. Harper 1896) 244.

Governor General for Life (albeit still under the authority of Napoleon) of the entire island of Hispaniola. US newspapers were filled with the news of "this ill fated island," eagerly awaiting indications that trade could resume, offering support to white French émigrés, and (particularly in the Southern states) spreading ominous rumors of "French Negroes."[43]

While US tales of conspiracy were largely unfounded, Haiti's Revolution sparked other fights for freedom throughout the Caribbean. In 1795, the enslaved populations of both British Grenada and Dutch Curaçao attempted revolutions that took direct inspiration from Saint-Domingue. Truth's milieu in upstate New York would have been particularly sensitive to news from Curaçao. Ulster County was still predominantly Dutch, and many ancestors of the region's enslaved population – including, perhaps, Truth's parents – passed through the island on their way to New York. Established as a centralized depot for slave cargoes, Curaçao had been a major node in transatlantic commercial networks in the late seventeenth century. Between 1651 and 1700, Curaçao received over half of the 156,800 enslaved Africans the Dutch had kidnapped in Africa.[44] Although many enslaved people's experience on Curaçao were brief, they left stark and likely traumatic memories. As Michael Kammen explains, Curaçao served to "season" newly kidnapped Africans: "The brutal plantation experience there introduced them to European values[and] taught them what their white masters expected."[45] Although by the time of the Haitian Revolution, Curaçao was no longer the trade hub it had been in the seventeenth century, shipping records suggest sustained cultural contact between these two faded nodes in what was once a broader Dutch empire. Throughout the 1790s, North American ports maintained a brisk trade with Curaçao despite reports of slave rebellion, piracy, and French aggression. Indeed, nearly a quarter of ships entering and clearing Willemstad between 1796 and 1798 issued from the United States.[46]

Because Curaçao did not have a developed plantation economy, most of its African population were either transient laborers or sailors. This led to a highly mobile social structure that, according to Klooster and Oostindie,

[43] *The Farmer's Oracle*, August 22, 1797 (Troy, New York). See also Dun, *Dangerous Neighbors*; White, *Encountering Revolution*, 267; Hunt, *Haiti's Influence on Antebellum America*; On correctives to the narrative that Haiti suffered a "unilateral bad press," see Daut, "'Alpha and Omega' of Haitian Literature," 290.

[44] Rupert, *Creolization and Contraband*, 77. [45] Kammen, *Colonial New York*, 58.

[46] National Archief, West-Indisch Comité 1795–1800, Curaçao 141. Oostindie (Figures compiled by Pham Van Thuy) "Slave Resistance, Colour Lines, and the Impact of the French and Haitian Revolutions in Curaçao" in *Curaçao in the Age of Revolutions, 1795–1800*, eds. Wim Klooster, Gert Oostindie (Brill 2011) 1–22; see also Klooster, "Manumission in an Entrepôt."

"offered free and enslaved workers access to news and ideas from free and enslaved sailors direct contacts with numerous parts of the Caribbean and coastal North and South America."[47] The intra-Caribbean mobility of Curaçao's enslaved population permitted news of the Haitian Revolution to spread swiftly. In 1795, when the island erupted in revolt, Curaçao's revolutionary leaders looked to their Haitian neighbors for inspiration. For example, the revolution's leader Tula often went by the name of Rigaud after the renowned Haitian general.[48] The practice of choosing Haitian Revolutionary names seems a common practice among Curaçoan revolutionaries: Tula's right-hand man, Mercier, claimed the name Toussaint.[49] Both Tula and Mercier also invoked Haiti in speeches. Tula is reported to have declared, "We have been badly treated for too long, we do not want to do anybody harm, but we seek our freedom, the French blacks have been given their freedom ... hence we too must be free." Similarly, Mercier announced, in French, "Nous sommes ici pour vaincre ou mourir," consciously echoing the famous motto of the Haitian Revolution, *"Liberté ou la mort."*[50]

4.2 "Sing Carmanole and Libertie": Pinkster and the Revolutionary Atlantic

It was against this backdrop of hemispheric Black revolution that Isabella became Sojourner Truth. Her conversion is not only a central story in her myth-making, it also emphasizes her creolized milieu, excavating a revolutionary Caribbean from within the heart of upstate New York. According to the *Narrative*, Isabella's first direct encounter with God took place on June 4, 1827, exactly one month before New York State emancipation, during the Dutch holiday Pinkster, a Carnaval-like inversion of social roles celebrated during the Pentecostal period. Olive Gilbert frames Truth/Isabella's temptation as a return to Dumont, to enslavement, and to the merry-making festivities of what she calls "Pingster":

> She says she "looked back into Egypt" and everything looked "so pleasant there" as she saw retrospectively all her former companions enjoying their freedom for at least a little space, as well as their convivialities, and in her heart she longed to be with them. With this picture before her mind's eye,

[47] Klooster and Oostindie, *Curaçao*, vii.

[48] Rupert, *Creolization* and Contraband, 208; Oostindie, *Curaçao*, 10.

[49] Oostindie, *Curaçao*, 10.

[50] Geggus, "Slave Rebellion during the Age of Revolution," 33. See also Gaspar and Geggus (eds.), *A Turbulent Time.*

> she contrasted the quiet, peaceful life she was living with the excellent people of Wahkendall, and it seemed so dull and void of incident, that the very contrast served but to heighten her desire to return, that, at least she might enjoy with them, once more, the coming festivities. These feelings had occupied a secret corner of her breast for some time, when, one morning, she told Mrs. Van Wagener that her old master Dumont would come that day, and that she should go home with him on his return; They expressed some surprise and asked her where she obtained her information. She replied that no one had told her, but she felt that he would come.[51]

Filtered through Gilbert's cultural biases, Truth's/Isabella's backward glance "into Egypt" presents itself as a choice between enslavement and freedom, pagan pleasure and saintly salvation, Afro-Dutchness and white Protestantism. Yet, to dismiss Pinkster as a mere temptation is to overlook the complex cultural matrix in which the holiday developed, as well as the geopolitical stage against which it played. As Painter argues, "Pinkster in 1827 bore a bundle of meanings for Isabella: slavery and blackness, freedom and apprehension, hope and vice and pleasure, and commitment to a life of religious purity – the old world and the new order all at once."[52] These complicated but not necessarily paradoxical meanings have been obscured by Gilbert's anglocentric mistranslation of the holiday. As Dewulf notes, "[u]nfamiliar with both Dutch and African American traditions, Anglo-Americans perceived Pinkster either as an exotic tradition or a despicable custom. Due to a lack of familiarity, their accounts of Pinkster are fraught with cultural misunderstandings. . . . For Truth . . . Pinkster was part of normal life. For Gilbert, on the other hand, it was an exotic custom."[53] Careful exploration of Pinkster reveals not only Truth's/Isabella's creolized background but the geopolitical struggles – specifically, the Haitian Revolution – which unfolded during the earliest years of her life.

A syncretization of Dutch, African, and Caribbean religious practices, Pinkster was widely celebrated in Albany, the Hudson Valley, New York City, Long Island, and eastern New Jersey. Although the word derived from the Dutch name for Whitsuntide or Pentecost (*Pfingsten*), by the mid-eighteenth century, the celebration had become embedded in Black New York culture, where festivities were overseen by the Black pantomime "King Charley." The popularity of Pinkster became even more pronounced between the 1790s and the first decade of the nineteenth century – not coincidentally, the same period as the Haitian Revolution – at which point

[51] Gilbert, *Narrative*, 64–65. [52] Painter, *Spellbound*, 149.
[53] Dewulf, *The Pinkster King and the King of Kongo*, 38.

references to the holiday in contemporary literature sharply increased. The new and radical contours of Pinkster flourished until 1811, when the Albany City Council abolished the practice. Other cities soon followed suit, effectively containing the threat of Black autonomy within the burgeoning fantasy of an Anglo-Protestant white national identity. By the time Truth/Isabella confronted Pinkster, the holiday was already on the wane – although as we shall see, people of African descent at that point had other models for Black sovereignty.

Often mischaracterized as a "slave" celebration, Pinkster is perhaps more precisely understood as a creolized holiday whose participants cut across race, ethnicity, and class lines. With its emphasis on African traditions, including the use of Guinea drums, bangars, rattles, Luso-Kongolese monarchical iconography, and Dutch Protestantism, Pinkster festivities were, as Dewulf has argued, "neither Dutch nor something new but rather a North American variant of an Afro-Portugese, Atlantic Creole traditions."[54] This cultural heritage was reflected in the demographic makeup of Pinkster's practitioners. Brad Verter argues in his discussion of the holiday that Pinkster "fostered a democratic populism and spiritual exuberance that challenged the settled Power of the Federalist merchants who lorded over the local economy and state government."[55] Through dance, song, sport, and pantomime, Pinkster offered the illusion of Black self-determination even as it threatened its participants with horrifying discipline: it is not for nothing that Pinkster Hill, in Albany, was also the site of the city's gallows.[56] This disciplinary function becomes even more troubling in the context of sexual relations. The holiday's permissiveness around interracial relations certainly would have led to an increased opportunity for and visibility of sexual assault by white men. As Washington has argued, Pinkster permitted sexual "relations perilous to black women" (and surely Black men as well).[57] This explains, in part, the implication in Gilbert's *Narrative* that Isabella associated Pinkster with a "return" to her abusive relationship with Dumont. Pinkster could be both a site of radical revolution and utter abjection, of "freedom" and enslavement, of excess and its swift containment.

The character who best exemplified these paradoxes was Pinkster's pantomime leader King Charles or Charley, an "old Guinea Negro ...

[54] Dewulf, *Pinkster King and the King of Kongo*, 249; Hodges, *Root and Branch*, 88; Stuckey, *Going through the Storm*; Sweet, "The Hidden Histories of African Lisbon."
Verter, "Interracial Festivity and Power in Antebellum New York," 400.

[55] Ibid. [56] Dewulf, *Pinkster*, 59; White, *Somewhat More Independent*, 100.

[57] Washington, *Sojourner Truth's America*, 45.

whose authority is absolute and whose will is law during the Pinkster holidays."[58] The earliest references to the Pinkster King emerge in the early nineteenth century, specifically in two 1803 Albany publications, an anonymous letter published by "A.B" in the *Albany Centinel* and a pamphlet entitled the *Pinkster Ode*, dedicated to King Charles (or rather, Most Respectfully Dedicated to CAROLUS AFRICANUS, REX; Thus Rendered in English: King Charles) published under the name "Absalom Aimwell." The latter, a mock-heroic epic, vacillates between the high and the low, the classical and contemporary, the old world and the new. Indeed, the following passage from the *Ode* reveals the timely concerns bound within the holiday's revelry:

> On wing'd Pegasus, laureat Pye
> May raise king George above the sky;
> And Gallic poets strain their art,
> To swell the fame of Bonaparte;
> These bards of gas can never raise
> A song that's fit for Charley's praise.
> Tho' for a sceptre he was born,
> Tho' from his father's kingdom torn,
> And doom'd to be a slave; still he
> Retains his native majesty.[59]

The mock-heroic style of the *Ode* contains the revolutionary potential of Pinkster within the tight couplets of satire. Yet, the *Ode* also places the Pinkster King against a revolutionary geopolitical background that bristles with threats of, at once, French, Haitian, and US Revolutions. Moreover, the appellation of "Charley" references the Stuart Monarch executed in the English Civil War in 1649.[60] Within the *Ode,* a headless king and an abducted African, flanked by King George and Napoleon, thus register a series of conflicting tensions accruing around Blackness, a growing transatlantic wave of republicanism, and the US's own violent origins. A contemporary audience would have appreciated that both George and

[58] "A.B." June 13, 1803 Albany Centinel ; reprinted in New York's *Daily Advertiser*, June 29, 1803. Reproduced by Shane White, "Pinkster in Albany, 1803: A Contemporary Description," *New York History* 70 (1989): 191–9. Verter notes that the initials A.B may have been intended to invoke Aaron Burr, Verter, "Interracial Festivity and Power in Antebellum New York," 405–7.

[59] Aimwell, "Pinkster Ode for the Year 1803." Reprinted in Geraldine R. Pleat and Agnes N. Underwood, "Pinkster Ode, Albany, 1803," *New York Folklore Quarterly* 8 (1952), 31–45.

[60] Charles II, his son – who ascended to the throne upon the restoration of the monarchy – married the Portugese Catherine of Braganza. It is perhaps through this alliance of Portugese empire and British monarchy, that Pinkster – whose routes, prior to the Dutch, can be traced to Portugese settlements in the Congo – earned its Anglo-Saxon monarch.

Napoleon lost their empires to the Americas: in the case of the latter, through the US Revolutionary War, and in the case of the former, through the mutually entwined events of Haitian independence (1804) and the Louisiana Purchase (1803). But far from being a celebration of early US national identity, the specters of European leaders instead heighten a sense of malaise around revolutionary fervor, French republicanism, and Black liberation. If Charley comically surpasses the powers of European leaders, he also signals the void of political power left by King George and Napoleon in the Americas. This displacement is heightened by the concluding feminine rhyme of "he" with "majesty" – a sharp contrast with the steady, harsh beats of the stanza's previous masculine rhymes. This uncanny ending signals not only the failure of bardic glory that the poem laments but also an unsettling space in which the crown and its head do not line up. The topsy-turvy inversion of Pinkster seems to ask but refuses to answer the question: Whose head will roll? Will it be high or low, royalist or republican, tossed in a basket, displayed on a pike, or shorn with a guillotine?

Later in the *Ode,* the connection among the rise of Charley and the consolidation of US identity becomes even more explicit:

> There you'll see brave mountaineers–
> The independent Vermonteers.
> You'll hear them ask for warlike news,
> Of Bonaparte and Jarsey blues.
> Then point out all the ways and means,
> To drive the French from New-Orleans;
> Where jealous Spain, our trade to stop,
> Has damm'd the Mississippi up.

The *Ode*'s invocation of New Orleans is remarkably topical: the Louisiana Purchase Treaty was signed on April 30, exactly a month before the celebration of Pinkster on May 30, 1803. In this respect, the *Ode* constitutes a kind of lyric journalism, far more invested in current affairs than in Dutch colonial nostalgia. The largest acquisition of territory in US history, the Louisiana Purchase, expanded United States sovereignty across the Mississippi River, nearly doubling the country's size. The US gained 827,000 square miles of land, the equivalent of fifteen current US states and two Canadian provinces.[61] The transfer of such a vast territory was far from simple. Although France had possessed the Louisiana territory since

[61] Bush, *The Louisiana Purchase*; Dubois, "The Haitian Revolution and the Sale of Louisiana"; Kastor, *The Nation's Crucible*; Rothman, *Slave Country*.

1699, it had ceded control to Spain in 1762 as part of the Treaty of Fontainebleau, concluding the French and Indian War.[62] Napoleon, who had nominally regained possession of Louisiana in 1800, initially planned to expand the French colonial project in the Western hemisphere. Yet, the territory remained under de facto Spanish control and the legality of France's claims to Louisiana territory were fiercely disputed by both the Spanish and US Federalists. Spain was a tenuous ally of the United States and had – as the *Ode* references – blockaded the Mississippi for nearly twenty-five years in order to halt US expansion.

This complex struggle of Old and New World powers was adumbrated by the ascension of Haitian independence. The Haitian Revolution had been a significant factor in Napoleon's decision to abandon his colonial empire in the Western hemisphere. The failure of the Leclerc expedition to reseize control in Saint-Domingue, compounded by growing international support for the abolition of the slave trade, led Napoleon to conclude in 1802: "I already consider the colony [the Louisiana Territory] as entirely lost."[63] As Laurent Dubois has noted, "what is often remembered as a remarkably 'peaceful' transfer of land was in fact predicated on events of enormous violence that took place in the Caribbean."[64] Hence perhaps the surprisingly bellicose language of the *Ode*, in which imaginary troops of "Vermonteers" and "Jarsey blues" march into New Orleans. If the Louisiana Purchase has been historicized as a diplomatic rather than a militaristic feat, the *Ode's* rhetorical emphasis on warfare – "driving out" the French – disguises and displaces other wars throughout the Americas. King Charley – and with him Toussaint Louverture, Jean-Jacques Dessalines, and other leaders of Haitian independence – fall out of the *Ode*, with Black liberation struggles overshadowed by a fiction of a cohesive US military identity.

But no sooner is the Haitian Revolution "silenced" from the history of the Louisiana Purchase than it resurfaces again.[65] Following the invocation of New Orleans, the author composes a catalog of national, regional, and ethnic identities: "All the world in miniature." We are introduced to the "honest German," the Dutch "Burgomaster," "Papists, Turks, and

[62] McMichael, *Atlantic Loyalties*; Weber, *The Spanish Frontier in North America.*

[63] Bonaparte to Ledere, July 1, 1802, in Paul Roussier ed. 1937. *Lettres du Général Ledere, commandant en chef de l'armée de Saint-Domingue en 1802.* (Paris: Société de l'histoire des colonies françaises et E. Leroux 1937) 305–6. Cited in and translated by Dubois, "The Haitian Revolution and the Sale of Louisiana," 32.

[64] Dubois, "The Haitian Revolution and the Sale of Louisiana," 18–19.

[65] Trouillot, *Silencing the Past.*

stubborn Jews," beef-eating gentlemen from "Albion's isle," and several other national and ethnic caricatures. Amid this pageant appears a new, unnamed, but highly legible power:

> Brisk French Monsieurs, who come from far,
> Talk all at once, we, we, be gar;
> Sing Carmanole and libertie,
> With footre jang and sac cra je.

Haiti is not explicitly referenced but the specter of Black republicanism is clearly, if mockingly, rendered. The anglicization of French (roughly translated as "yes, yes, by Jove/Sing Carmagnole and liberté/With lay-abouts and sacré Dieu.")[66] crudely creolizes French republicanism through its invocation of the revolutionary song *la Carmagnole*.[67] The Carmagnole, a sarcastic revolutionary song and dance, is often compared unfavorably to the more stately *Marseillaise* – as Victor Hugo claimed, "With just the 'Carmagnole' to sing [a Parisian] will only overthrow Louis XVI; but give him the 'Marseillaise' and he will redeem the world."[68] This condescending comparison is, moreover, racialized: although originally a metropolitan revolutionary song, the Carmagnole was often used to invoke the Haitian Revolution, reproducing the racist logics that considers the French Revolution as the dignified model (the Marseillaise) for its rough-hewn Haitian "copy." In the United States, for example, the Carmagnole was often performed in minstrelsy antecedents, such as Sambo performances.

While white commentators have yoked the perceived crudity of the Carmagnole to mockeries of Black liberation, diasporic traditions have embraced its revolutionary potential. In the Haitian city of Gonaïves, streets were named for the Carmagnole; in Louisiana, free people of color reportedly sang the Carmagnole while "awaiting the order from Saint-Domingue" in the 1790s; and Haitian armies were said to perform the song from the Revolution well into the nineteenth century.[69] Kate Hodgson, for example, has located a reference to the Carmagnole in an

[66] There is some ambiguity around "be gar". It may be an anglicization of *prends gard* or "beware." It also may be a transposition of the English phrase "be gar" "be gar" or "by God" as popularized in the works of Walter Scott and Shakespeare. I have chosen *bigre* or "by Jove"' as it seems a likely phonetic strategy within the *Ode*'s use of *franglais*. As for *jean-foutre*, I have selected a mild translation of quite a vulgar word. I am thankful to Grégory Pierrot, James Wood, and Emma and Izumi Bérat for some help deciphering this passage.

[67] For a more detailed reading of the Carmagnole, see Brécy, ""La Chanson Révolutionnaire de 1789 à 1799." McClellan, "Counterrevolution in Concert"; Nora and Kritzman (eds.), *Realms of Memory*.

[68] "Tant qu'il n'a pour refrain que la *Carmagnole*, il ne renverse que Louis XVI; faites-lui chanter la *Marseillaise*, il délivrera le monde." Hugo, *Les Misérables*.

[69] Livre, *En Haïti*, 319; Faber, *Building the Land of Dreams*, 36; Hodgson, "*Pays-la chaviré*."

1840s Kreyòl political song used during the attempted Haitian invasion into what is now the Dominican Republic:

> Rivier té parti pour réduir pagnol;
> Yo fai li dansé la carimagnol:
> Pagnol ba li canon; (Ter)
> Li touné derrier, li mandé padon.
>
> Rivière [a Haitian General] went to put down the Spanish;
> They made him dance the carmagnole
> The Spanish fired their cannons at him; (x3)
> He ran away, asking for forgiveness.[70]

Hodgson's "archaeological" approach to Haitian folk music reveals that the Carmagnole, despite being mocked by white audiences, harnessed considerable political, popular, and military power in Haiti. Therefore, while the Pinkster *Ode* satirizes Black sovereignty, parodies Haitian revolutionaries, and displaces the Haitian role in the Louisiana Purchase, it also reveals the powerful ways in which the Haitian Revolution influenced global Black freedom struggles, spanning from the Dutch empire to small towns in upstate New York. A consideration of the *Ode* reveals Pinkster to be, far from a quaint Dutch Pentecostal tradition, a creolized and extremely modern political engagement with the revolutionary Atlantic. When we consider Truth's conversion, it is thus important to situate her within this global political context. Pinkster was not, as per Gilbert, a symbol of the heathenish provincialism of Afro-Dutchness, but instead powerfully linked with global Black emancipation, radiating from New York State abolition to the ascendancy of Haiti.

In the thirty years between the rise of Pinkster and its fall – which incidentally coincide with Isabella's birth and conversion – the world would have been well acquainted with a Black king, one whose power extended beyond the ephemeral crown of Charley. Between 1810 and 1820, Haiti was divided into two states, one a republic governed by Alexandre Pétion in the South and the other a monarchy governed by the Roi Henry Christophe in the North. The latter carefully crafted his image abroad not just as a sovereign leader but as the head of a British-style constitutional monarchy after the manner of George III.[71] Henry Christophe consolidated the North's authority through specifically monarchical institutions, including court accoutrements, the establishment of a nobility, and perhaps most famously the construction of the palace Sans

[70] Cited in Hodgson, "Pays-la chaviré," 28.
[71] Racine, "Britannia's Bold Brother."

Souci. In doing so, he became the first truly modern Black king: not the "noble savage" popularized by figures such as Aphra Behn's Oroonoko, nor the caricature of Black authority celebrated at Pinkster, but rather a leader who claimed the same geopolitical stage, spoke the same imperial language, and traded in the same visual symbols as the great European powers.

In 1827, the reign of Pinkster in New York was already in its twilight. Yet, to argue that Truth's/Isabella's, and by extension, the African-American community's, rejection of Pinkster constituted a rejection of diasporic kinship is misleading and fails to understand Pinkster's complex cultural network. On the contrary, by 1827, Truth and others need not have worshipped a pantomime king. If they wanted a model of Black sovereignty, they had a very real example: a kingship in Haiti, one that made Black rights a far more tangible political project than anything people of African descent could attain in the United States. While Gilbert's account frames Pinkster as oppositional to Truth's religiosity, we can instead think of the holiday within Atlantic cultural histories, revolutionary modernity, and Haitian political sovereignty. Viewed from within the prison-house of Gilbert's narrative, Truth's/Isabella's "rejection" of Pinkster resembles a rejection of African culture, a conversion from the diabolical paganism of Isabella to the holy script of Truth. Yet, a careful consideration of Pinkster yields other perspectives: Pinkster was not only a complex, creolized holiday. Its fantasies and theatrics played out against the political reality of Haitian sovereignty, with the Pinkster King gradually eclipsed by a series of true crowns, thrones, and Black heads of state.

4.3 Kinetic Power

Understanding the creolized and specifically Haitian context of Truth's conversion narrative demands that we take her itinerancy seriously. This itinerancy is not only a metaphor for spiritual freedom but also serves as a model for alternative forms of Black energy, which intertwine with diasporic philosophical movements across cartographies of freedom and enslavement. While critics such as Haraway have celebrated Truth's mobility in abstractionist terms often consistent with postmodern thought, I would like, in this concluding section, to offer a set of concrete and historical contexts of Atlantic flight – specifically the phenomenon of marronage – that channeled Truth's wandering energy and itinerant spiritual paths into political projects of Black freedom. Consider, for example, the following passage in Gilbert's *Narrative*, from a section titled "Some of Her Views and Reasonings":

> When it became known to her children, that Sojourner had left New York, they were filled with wonder and alarm. Where could she have gone, and why had she left? were questions no one could answer satisfactorily. Now, their imaginations painted her as a wandering maniac – and again they feared she had been left to commit suicide; and many were the tears they shed at the loss of her.[72]

While Gilbert elsewhere in the *Narrative* celebrates Truth as a figure of personal freedom, religious ecstasy, or spiritual abandon, she here frames Truth's liberation as a problem of abandonment. Gilbert not only positions Truth's itinerancy as antithetical to motherhood, pathologizing her pursuit of freedom within familiar white reformist narratives of the fallen Black woman.[73] She also locates and implicitly condemns a specific practice central to Truth's spiritual emancipation: her physical mobility, her itinerancy, and her self-baptismal namesake *Sojourner*.

Gilbert's genteel condemnation of this "wandering mania" forms a counterpoise to one of the most iconic images of Truth: her celebrated "Walk to Freedom" away from the Dumont farm in October, 1826, carrying her three-month-old daughter Sophia in her arms.[74] Yet, while that sentimental tableau allows maternity to soften the transgressive potential of Black woman's autonomy, Gilbert's condemnation of Truth's later "wandering" speaks to the limits imposed on Black flight by white reformers. As Jean Humez has argued, "there was a vast difference in perspective between Gilbert and Truth on the meaning of motherhood," a difference that subtends the *Narrative* as the two women negotiate gendered and racialized expectations of love, care, and kinship.[75] In this concluding section, I will focalize this negotiation around not only representations of Black maternity but also how Truth's maternity intersects with her mobility. Her celebrated wandering, I argue, not only reveals a rift between Truth's and Gilbert's understandings of motherhood but also highlights tensions between Truth's creolized background and Gilbert's Anglo-American whiteness. Truth's mobility, I argue, should be read within an archive of hemispheric marronage – a practice that allowed

[72] Gilbert, *Narrative*, 109. [73] Roberts, *Killing the Black Body*; Foreman, *Activist Sentiment*.

[74] This image of fugitive maternity anticipates, and perhaps even influenced, Harriet Beecher Stowe's portrait of Eliza crossing the ice two years later in *Uncle Tom's Cabin*. Like Gilbert, Stowe would also insist on Truth's maternity in her 1863 *Atlantic* profile of Truth, concluding with a comparison of Truth to a Libyan "mother of myriads." See Stowe, "The Libyan Sibyl," 481.

[75] Humez, "Reading the Narrative of Sojourner Truth as a Collaborative Text," 42.

Black women to reclaim their bodies from plantation economies and convert their reproductive energy into political and spiritual projects of freedom. In doing so, Truth's "mania" for wandering rewrites the scripts of Black motherhood, refusing white reformist narratives of propriety. Instead, Truth's itinerancy allows for other ways of reading Black women's cartographies of freedom throughout the western hemisphere.

While Gilbert semantically attempts to redomesticate Truth through her narrative, Truth's wandering subverts the white sentimental policing of Black conduct by operating within and expanding broader Caribbean philosophical traditions of marronage. In twentieth- and twenty-first-century postcolonial discourses, we see many variations on Truth's mobile poetics: figures like the errant, the castaway, the fugitive, the exile, the migrant, and the marron/maroon populate and unsettle Caribbean networks of belonging. While I am reluctant to subsume Truth's performances of mobility into a modern critical paradigm, I suggest that we might extend critical timelines of Caribbean philosophy to include Truth, whose nomadic identity shares as much philosophical ground with these later figures as it did with the Protestant and millenarian theologies of US revivalism and certainly more than it did with Gilbert's sentimental paradigms of maternity.

What would it mean to think of Truth's sojourning within a broader history of Atlantic fugitivity? And how might this sojourning disrupt traditionally masculinist accounts of fugitivity? Her mobility, in this respect, can be read within a longer history of marronage, or the process by which enslaved Africans in the Americas escaped slavery and cultivated projects of freedom outside plantation systems. Most scholars locate the term's etymology in the Spanish *cimarrón,* denoting domestic cattle that had escaped into the wild. Yet, its meaning in diasporic memory has expanded to index centuries of enslaved resistance, survival, and cartographies of both individual and collective freedom.[76] More than a mere physical escape from slavery, marronage, in the words of Neil Roberts, "cultivat[es] freedom on their own terms within a demarcated social space that allows for the enactment of subversive speech acts, gestures, and social practices antithetical to the ideals of [enslavers]."[77] These subversive acts

[76] The literature on maroon communities is vast. For a brief overview of maroon life in the Americas, see Price, *The Guiana Maroons*; Price (ed.), *Maroon Societies*; Fouchard, *Les marrons de la liberté*; Hall, *Africans in Colonial Louisiana*; Schwartz, *Slaves, Peasants, and Rebels*; Landers, *Black Society in Spanish Florida*; Geggus, *Haitian Revolutionary Studies;* Thompson, *Flight to Freedom*; Diouf, *Slavery's Exiles*; Gonzalez, *Maroon Nation*; Hahn, *The Political Worlds of Slavery and Freedom.*

[77] Roberts, *Freedom as Marronage*, 5.

were articulated on scales large and small. In what historians have identified as "grand" marronage, self-emancipated Africans established permanent and self-sustaining free communities, some of which endured for centuries. In contrast, "petit" marronage consisted of individuals temporarily leaving the plantation, a more intimate act of resistance consistent with Isabella's early departures and returns to the Dumont household.[78] The kinetic power of marronage – as much a verb as a noun, as Aimé Césaire reminds us – transforms traditional epistemologies of freedom from a static category to a mobile, energetic, and lived concept.[79]

Truth's peripatetic paths intersect with these hemispheric histories. As mythologized in the *Narrative*, she did not "escape" or "flee" her enslaver Dumont. Instead, she merely walked off: "'No, I did not run away; I walked away by day-light.'"[80] The distinction Truth draws between running and walking is significant and is one she returns to at multiple points in the *Narrative*. If to run away implies pursuit, panic, and subterfuge, it also invites the contraction of the act "to run away" into the noun "runaway." In doing so, it reifies the freedom projects Truth sought to build both outside Dumont's farm and throughout her errant career. In contrast, walking emphasizes not only the dignity but also the *kineticism* of the walker. Truth walked toward freedom, slowly, but constantly, ambulating in open defiance of her enslaver. In doing so, she laid claim to the kinetic energy of the sojourner, imbuing her rebirth and self-baptismal name with the movement of a verb – to sojourn, wander, or *marroner*, thus insisting on Black life as mobile, active, and generative beyond the energy demands of enslaved labor.

While studies of marronage tend to focus on Caribbean and Latin American societies or, in the case of the United States, on the Gulf region or "Dismal Swamp" marshlands of Virginia and North Carolina, practices of self-emancipation also shaped Black culture in Sojourner Truth's New

[78] This distinction is not always neat, nor does it encompass the many freedom practices that enslaved people engaged in throughout the Americas. For example, market marronage, or the engagement of enslaved people within internal market systems, especially in Jamaica, is neither precisely petit or grand marronage and yet in the words of Shauna J. Sweeney, it "constitute[d] an infrastructure of freedom within slavery" "Market Marronage," 221. See also Mintz and Hall, "The Origins of the Jamaican Internal Marketing System"; Brown-Glaude, *Higglers in Kingston: Women's Informal Work in Jamaica*; and Tinsley *Thiefing Sugar*, especially 73–7.

[79] First published *Présence africaine* in 1955 under the title "Réponse à Depestre poète haïtien (éléments d'un art poétique)," the poem is better known as "Le verbe marronner" *La poésie*, eds. Daniel Maximin and Gilbert Carpentier (Paris: Seuil 2006) 481–3.

[80] Gilbert, *Narrative*, 43.

York.[81] Although enslaved people have always sought freedom, reports of self-emancipation sharply increased, beginning in 1799 with New York's gradual emancipation law.[82] Enslaved people had little reason to trust that their enslavers would follow state law: it was common practice for enslavers to recoup their anticipated financial losses by reporting their workforce as fugitive slaves (permissible under the Fugitive Slave Act of 1793) and selling them in the South.[83] Indeed, this is precisely what happened to Isabella's five-year-old son Peter, whom Dumont illegally sold to a plantation in Alabama immediately prior to general New York State emancipation. As a pre-emptive measure against these further incursions on their freedom, record numbers of enslaved Africans in New York emancipated themselves throughout the early nineteenth century.

Not only did New York State emancipation laws encourage extralegal self-emancipation but the Haitian Revolution – and with it, nascent myths of institutional, or what Roberts might call sociogenic, marronage – likely played a role in New York's rise in fugitive slaves.[84] According to Shane White, the majority of self-emancipated Africans in the New York region had been born in the West Indies and were most likely the former property of Saint-Dominguan émigrés who had fled to New York in the 1790s.[85] Upon arrival, these would-be revolutionaries carried the large-scale revolt in Haiti into their intimate lives, fleeing their enslavers in droves and perhaps transmitting stories of what would soon become the first Black republic. In short, they brought marronage – both petit and grand – from the sugar plantations of Saint-Domingue to the farms, shops, and taverns of New York. For example, in 1796, an eleven-year-old "French mulatto" named Catherine was reported by the New York newspaper *Argus* to have run away; she had justified her independence to curious inquirers by claiming that her "master had gone away to Santo Domingo."[86] Moreover, as we saw in Chapter 3, Haiti's free soil policies, established in 1805, effectively created a space of asylum to all Black people who

[81] See Sayers, *A Desolate Place for a Defiant People*; Nevius, *City of Refuge* ; Maris-Wolf, "Hidden in Plain Sight"; Delle, *The Limits of Tyranny*; Lockley, *Maroon Communities*.

[82] Harris, *In the Shadow of Slavery*, 72.

[83] U.S. Constitution, article IV, section 2, clause 3.

[84] Roberts distinguishes between "sovereign" and "sociogenic" marronage, the latter of which entails "macropolitical flight whereby agents flee slavery through non-fleeting acts of naming . . . liberation. It is a non-sovereign state of being whose conception of freedom is shaped by . . . the experiences of masses." For Roberts, sociogenic marronage includes institutional and symbolic political action, such as the adoption of the name Haiti or the redefinition of blackness as a political category in the nascent republic's constitution. Roberts, *Freedom as Marronage*, 116–17.

[85] White, *Somewhat More Independent*, 91.

[86] Cited in White, *Somewhat More Independent*, 122.

escaped from slavery, thus institutionalizing the fugitive promise of individual marronage within official structures of Haitian statehood.[87]

Truth's movements not only extend the timeline and geographic remit of northern Black freedom. Her act of "walking away" from Dumont, child in her arms, also demands a reckoning with the gendered imperatives of traditional historiographical and epistemological understandings of Black flight. If we are to take seriously Kamau Brathwaite's claim that Haiti is "the greatest and most successful Maroon polity of them all," I would like to look away from individual male figures of marronage typically celebrated by folk traditions. (See, for example, the legacy of Makandal.)[88] Instead, we can trace the success of marronage across a wider network of revolutionary actors: in the nameless people of Haiti's maroon colonies, in eleven-year-old girls in New York City, and in Isabella's sojourn toward freedom throughout the northern United States. To consider marronage as a Black feminist cartographic practice goes against the grain of twentieth-century intellectual genealogies of marronage. These genealogies have typically relied on the masculinist heroic narratives of Négritude, Antillanité, and Créolité, for which, as Édouard Glissant claims, the maroon was "the only true popular heros of the Antilles" ("le seul vrai heros populaires des Antilles").[89] This emphasis on individual masculine strength has elided not only the collective labor of maroon colonies but also the central role of women to the Haitian Revolution. As Lorna Moore has argued, the maroon celebrated by Négritude "appears in mythified form as an agonistic, supermale hero, more virile than the dominant Other."[90] In his poem "Le verbe marroner," for example, Césaire celebrates Dessalines and the "demented chant of Boukman" ("chant dement de Boukman"), but makes no mention of Marie-Jeanne Lamartinière, Sanité Bélair, Ezili Dantò, Cécile Fatiman, or many of the other women who participated in the Haitian Revolution.[91] Indeed, when women maroons emerge in Négritude, they often take the form of the romanticized erotic figure seen in Césaire's 1946 *Autre saison*, throughout

[87] On the historiographical debate around marronage and its role in the Haitian Revolution, see Debien, "Marronage in the French Caribbean"; Debien *Les esclaves aux Antilles français aux 17e et 18e siecles*; Geggus, *Haitian Revolutionary Studies;* Fick, *The Making of Haiti;* Blackburn, *The Overthrow of Colonial Slavery.*

[88] Brathwaite, *Roots*, 231.

[89] Glissant, *Le discours antillais,* 104. On the genealogy of the maroon in twentieth-century Caribbean thought, see also Bernabé, Chamoiseau, and Confiant, *Éloge de la Créolité*; Césaire, *Cahier d'un retour au pays natal* and "Les chiens se taisaient"; Glissant, *La case du commandeur* and *Le quatrième siècle.*

[90] Milne, "Sex, Gender and the Right to Write," 60.

[91] Césaire, "Le verbe marronner."

which the figure of the "femme marron" (the "maroon wife" or "maroon woman") repeats as a kind of refrain: "Où allez-vous ma femme marron ma restituée ma cimarronne?" (Where are you going my maroon wife my restored one my cimarronne?").[92] While the men of "Le verbe marroner" drink, fight, and escape in traditionally virile images of rebellion, the "femme marron" is an object to be longed for, pursued, and possessed. The very act of placing the possessive pronoun "ma" before the "femme marron" circumscribes the emancipatory potential of the female maroon, her fugitivity semantically repropertied and reproduced in the language of cis-masculine sexual desire.

This poetic aggrandisement of masculinity is equally true of traditional historiographical approaches to marronage, which have typically elided women from celebratory histories of flight. Female maroons appear, if they are discussed at all in the historical literature, as indexes of cis-sexist assumptions unsubstantiated by the archival record. Historians have traditionally justified what they consider a lack of women from histories of marronage, through clichés such as inherent biological weakness, the supposed burden of pregnancy and motherhood, and alleged female loyalty to white enslavers.[93] Equally troubling is the historiographical tendency to claim that female maroons did not self-emancipate willingly but were instead abducted by enslaved men.[94] Yet, this assumption merely reproduces racist colonialist constructions of Black masculine hypersexuality and female passivity, a fetishization of Black sexuality far more aligned with the governor of Jamaica's 1739 complaint that "in all [the maroons'] plunderings, they are [more] industrious in procuring Negro women, girls, and female children" than to critical understandings of Black women's agency.[95] What could only appear to an enslaver as abduction was to many "Negro women, girls, and female children" an act of self-emancipation that rejected colonial scripts of female passivity and sexual vulnerability. Historians would thus do well to interrogate the ideological assumptions behind language of sexual "plundering" within the unevenly represented archive of colonial history.[96]

92 Césaire, "Autre saison," 117.

93 Schwartz, "The Mocambo," 218–19. See also Debien, "Marronage in the French Caribbean," 140; Lokken, "A Maroon Moment," 52. For counter-narratives to this argument, see Gautier, *Les soeurs de solitude*, 31–7.

94 Beckles, 'Freeing Slavery,"210.

95 Cited in Kopytoff, "The Early Political Development of Jamaican Maroon Societies," 301.

96 Wim Hoogbergen makes a similar point in "Maronnage and Slave Rebellion in Surinam," 175.

While few self-emancipated enslaved people left first-hand accounts of marronage, it is unlikely that they would have described their experiences through the same language as their enslavers. Moreover, the historiographical amplification of "abduction" detracts from the very real political and symbolic power women exerted in maroon communities. Despite their relatively small numbers, maroon settlements throughout the Americas were frequently named for women, including Magdalena, María Angola, and María Embuyla in Colombia; Guarda Mujeres in Cuba; Molly's Town, Diana's Town, and – perhaps most famously – Nanny Town in Jamaica.[97] Nanny in particular proves an exception to the masculinist narratives that have dominated twentieth-century understandings of marronage. Perhaps the most famous figure associated with the Windward Maroon community, Grand Nanny or Queen Mother Granny, has been celebrated as a guerrilla warrior, Obeah woman, and freedom fighter who led maroon troops against the British from 1728 to 1734.[98] Although neglected by the (largely male and francophone) movements that have over-represented marronage in the twentieth century, Jamaica's Grand Nanny is nevertheless honored and celebrated in statues, reggae songs, and public holidays, and her image is emblazoned on the Jamaican $500 bill (known informally as a "Nanny").[99]

Despite this symbolic power, it is likely that women were in the minority of many maroon communities. Arlette Gautier, Gabriel Debien, Jean Fouchard, and David Geggus have all estimated the percentage of fugitive women in Saint-Dominguan marron societies at around 12 to 20 percent.[100] Yet, given the general gender imbalance of Saint-Dominguan society, a paucity of women in these settlements was to be expected. A 1775 census reports that enslaved women in Saint-Domingue composed 44 percent of the enslaved population, and the numbers of newly arrived African women were even lower, with 179 men for every 100

[97] Thompson "Gender and Marronage in the Caribbean," 263.

[98] Gottlieb, *The Mother of Us All.* For an exploration of Nanny's afterlives, see also Brown, *The Repeating Body.*

[99] As a recent example of the significance of Grand Nanny in popular culture, the Granny Nanny Cultural Group in Moore Town, Jamaica recorded an album of songs and oral histories entitled *Granny Nanny Come Oh: Jamaican Maroon Kromanti and Kumina Music and Other Oral Traditions* (Harcourt Fuller, executive producer, 2016; 2 Compact Discs, 156 min). See also the film *Queen Nanny: Legendary Maroon Chieftainess*, director Roy T. Anderson (2015); and Renée Cox's photographic series *Queen Nanny of the Maroons* (2004–5).

[100] Cited in Daniels, *Recovering the Fugitive History of Marronage*, 133. Gautier, "Les esclaves femmes aux Antilles françaises"; Debien, "Marrons autour du Cap," 794; Debien and Fouchard, "Aspects de l'esclavage aux Antilles françaises," 55; Geggus, "On the Eve of the Haitian Revolution," 117.

women, or roughly 35 percent of the population.[101] Given that maroons tended to be newly arrived African laborers, the demographic composition of maroon settlements is likely more reflective of the gender disparity in Saint-Domingue's general population than it is an indictment of women's predisposition (or lack thereof) to seek freedom. Moreover, some of Saint-Domingue's most famous maroon communities boasted remarkably high numbers of women. In the celebrated Bahoruco settlement on the current Haitian-Dominican border, for example, women played a vital role in community life. In 1785, there was a ratio of 75 males to 58 females, or 44 percent of the population – that is to say, in precise proportion to the general ratio of enslaved men to enslaved women determined ten years earlier on the island.[102]

Historians who have highlighted the significance of female maroons tend to cite the self-sustaining nature of long-standing communities of grand marronage. Gautier, for example, claims that eighty percent of the 133 inhabitants of the Bahoruco settlement had been born there by the 1780s, and Alvin O. Thompson reiterates Moreau de Saint Méry's claim that many had never lived anywhere but the forests in which they had been born.[103] This certainly indicates that a substantial number of what historians call "women" – more specifically, the exceedingly narrow category of people with certain reproductive organs, who were of reproductive age and ability – contributed to maroon societies. But this methodology has striking, even absurd, faults. First, it leaves itself vulnerable to the "abduction" narratives favored by many historians as elucidated above. Second, conflating sexual reproductive capacity with gender elides the experiences of many people who did not adhere to the gender binary, who could not bear children, or who chose not to bear children. Finally, the self-sustaining reproductive narrative also restricts Black freedom by channeling an individual's energy from one form of heteropatriarchal reproduction to another. But the most famous female maroons, such as Grand Nanny, are not known to be mothers. And Truth did not birth a single child once she freed herself from bondage; instead, Truth and Grand Nanny found

[101] No general census for Saint-Domingue exists after the U.S. Revolutionary War and it is thus difficult to estimate the extent to which Bahuroco's demographics were representative of the general population. However, the 1780s saw a marked increased in imported African labor – which skewed heavily male – likely impacting the overall gender ratio in Saint-Domingue. See Doyle, *Old Regime France,* 135; see also King, *Blue Coat or Powdered Wig,* 79.

[102] Thompson, "Gender and Marronage in the Caribbean," 267.

[103] Gautier, *Les soeurs de solitude,* 231; Moreau de Saint-Méry, "The Border Maroons of Saint Domingue," 140. Cited from Thompson "Gender and Marronage in the Caribbean," 265.

themselves freed from maternity once they began to wander. Defining the nomenclature of "grandmother" as a political rather than biological category, they tended to their biological *as well as* spiritual children, be they worshippers or revolutionaries. Much as we saw in Chapter 3's discussion of "Theresa," marronage allowed for multiple forms of care – for some, through birthing and parenting, but for many others through rejecting maternity altogether, or redefining maternity along spiritual and political coordinates.

In her study of Black mobility, Sarah Jane Cervenak explores wandering as a Black feminist corrective to hegemonic geographic logics, arguing "the philosophically generative act of phantasmatic travel engendered by the unpredictability of spirit and desire questions racialist logics that presume that bodies of color can only be moved by an outside force and not from within."[104] Although Cervenak does not discuss marronage, her emphasis on Truth's "phantasmatic travel" shares both historical and conceptual groundwork with these fugitive histories of flight and freedom.[105] While Truth's white ameneunses attempted to move her body through sentimental nineteenth-century narratives of True Womanhood, and more recent critics of marronage assume that Black women could only be moved to freedom by the projects, desires, and expectations of Black men (the amount of passive voice in the scholarship on female maroons is astonishing), I insist that we read Truth's "wandering mania" in the active voice, as a form of kinetic energy that channeled Black women's power away from the reproductive structures of enslavement, the prison-house of white reformist sentimentality, and instead toward practices of freedom.

To think of Truth's movement in the active voice is to reject the logics of her white amanuenses and instead conceptualize the energetic – or perhaps what Sylvia Wynter would call the "demonic" – geography of fugitive terrain beyond the totalizing exploitation of enslavers and white reformists alike.[106] Wynter's conceptualization of the demonic offers an alternative geography outside of the territorialization of Enlightenment projects, instead establishing a new model of the human, or what Katherine McKittrick identifies as "the grounds from which we can imagine the world and more workable human geographies."[107] Wynter's interrogation of "Western Man" develops, in part, from a particular

[104] Cervenak, *Wandering: Philosophical Performances of Racial and Sexual Freedom*, 13.
[105] Ibid., 130.
[106] Wynter, "Beyond Miranda's Meanings." See also McKittrick, *Demonic Grounds*.
[107] McKittrick, *Demonic Grounds*, xxv; Wynter, "Beyond Miranda's Meanings," 364.

understanding of the demonic, which emerges from physics and computer science. As Wynter argues, the demonic is a concept

> posited by physicists who seek to conceive of a vantage point outside the space-time orientation of the humuncular observer . . . . The possibility of such a vantage point, we argue, towards which the diacritical term "womanist" (i.e. these readings as both gender, and not-gender readings, as both Caribbean/Black nationalist and not-Caribbean/Black nationalist, Marxian and not-Marxian readings) point can only be projected from a "demonic model" generated, parallely to the vantage point/demonic model with which the laity intelligentsia of Western Europe effected the first rupture of humans with their/our supernaturally guaranteed narrative schemas of origin.[108]

In her critique of global northern discourses of the human, Wynter reaches to, as Sarah Haley has argued, theories of nineteenth-century French mathematician Pierre Simon Laplace.[109] Laplace famously theorized that, under the logics of universal Newtownian laws, an intelligent being (a "demon") might achieve epistemic omniscience. For Laplace, the demon was

> An intelligence knowing all the forces acting in nature at a given instant, as well as the momentary positions of all things in the universe, would be able to comprehend in one single formula the motions of the largest bodies as well as the lightest atoms in the world, provided that its intellect were sufficiently powerful to subject all data to analysis; to it nothing would be uncertain, the future as well as the past would be present to its eyes.[110]

Situated at the crossroads between Enlightenment determinism and the burgeoning fields of probability theory and statistics, Laplace's demon could predict events, anticipating the carceral calculations that would come to systematically police Black life. In traditional energy histories, Laplace's demonic is, far from the liberatory grounds of McKittrick and Wynter, instead a panoptic mechanism of containment and deterministic foresight central to nineteenth-century fields of criminology, reform, and social work premised on the (perceived) predictability of an individual's actions based on the (perceived) behavior of the statistical aggregate.

Wynter elsewhere critiques the Newtonian homogeneity that would "exult" in the belief that "all parts of the universe were made of the same forces, of the same matter [and] one could now be able to extrapolate from the bodies nearest to us . . . what the bodies furthest from us had

108 Wynter "Beyond Miranda's Meanings," 364.

109 Haley, *No Mercy Here*, 229–30.

110 Laplace, *Essai philosophique sur les probabilités*.

necessarily to be."[111] Yet, she also reimagines these experiments as not the pseudo-universalism of "Man as Rational Self" but instead, in the words of McKittrick, a "process that is hinged on uncertainty and nonlinearity."[112] Wynter's redefinition of deterministic nineteenth-century energy production effectively upends the spatial and temporal coordinates through which women of African descent were denied kinship, space, and humanity. In this way, she anticipates Chanda Prescod-Weinstein's recent call to denaturalize and historicize the racist conditions of labor that produce the perceived universality of modern quantum mechanics: "[I]t may be that what we think we know is incomplete and will not be complete until we are able to think beyond how white men are trained to think in a Western educational setting."[113] In pushing beyond these limits, Wynter and Prescod-Weinstein (albeit through very different discursive frameworks) both plot new spaces outside racist territoriality, allowing Black thinkers to move beyond the exclusionary maps of global northern conceptions of the universal human.

Truth's demonic marronage thus disrupts not only the laws of antebellum America and reformist decorum but even the laws of thermodynamics. As Zakiyyah Iman Jackson has argued, Wynter's demonic "bring[s] about another mode of science altogether" by creating an unimaginable respatialization of Black womanhood.[114] Not unlike Trouillot's famous formulation of the Haitian Revolution as "unthinkable," these unimaginable, demonic geographies operate outside of Enlightenment epistemologies, or as McKittrick claims, "[i]f identity and place are mutually constructed, the uninhabitable spatializes a human Other category of the unimaginable/native/black."[115] Truth's marronage produces new and kinetic cartographies, converting the fuel of enslaved labor into the demonic energy of freedom. In doing so, she rejects the determinism of traditional energy structures, be they reproductive, capitalist, or thermodynamic.

If critics are to take Truth's creolized mobility seriously, they must then think of her not only as a progenitor of the US Civil Rights movement but also of modern conceptions of diasporic Black feminist identity, Caribbean understandings of marronage, and even recent theorizations of Black science, energy, and thermodynamics. Moving through the demonic circuits of history, Truth was an errant subject, unbound to fictions of nation, even as she was shaped by the intimate locales of her domestic

[111] Wynter, "Unsettling the Coloniality of Being/Power/Truth/Freedom", 281.
[112] McKittrick, *Demonic Grounds*, xxiv. [113] Prescod-Weinstein, *The Disordered Cosmos*, 26.
[114] Jackson, "Theorizing in a Void," 620. [115] McKittrick, *Demonic Grounds*, 130.

sphere, generating new epistemological and ontological models for people of African descent. Through her peripatetic paths, Truth traced Afro-diasporic histories of marronage, flight, and self-emancipation. Dwelling within the circuits of migrations, both forced and voluntary, her freedom projects simultaneously embed themselves within specific sites of domestic regionalism and radiate beyond US borders. Truth's wandering exceeds the parameters of white Anglo-American print culture, instead performing an elastic, ungovernable, and erratic set of circuits which warp and wend from Haiti to Curaçao to upstate New York. These circuits not only help us understand Black feminist mobility but also help us redefine traditional accounts of energy, labor, and modernity. If traditional understandings of enslaved labor are generally limited to capitalist ideologies of profit, consumption, exploitation, and reproductive injustice, Truth shows us other relationships people of African descent cultivated with energy. Her celebrated wandering reveals itself to be, far from a "mania," instead a philosophy and practice of kineticism, a way of reclaiming her energy and redirecting her power toward projects of liberation.

CHAPTER 5

Mesmeric Revolution

Hopkins's Matrilineal Haiti

Throughout this book, we have seen people of African descent channel the energy of plants, divine possession, prophetic futurity, and kinetic flight into strategies of resistance against the biocapitalist imperatives of energy production. Although each of these people expressed their energy in historically and culturally distinct times and places, they share a project of what we might consider an alternative practice of energy unbound to capitalist ideologies of supply, demand, extraction, and consumption. A careful consideration of these subjects replaces familiar narratives of human and nonhuman exploitation, anthropogenic crisis, and what would eventually become late capitalist globalization with another history of energy, one which is both deeply local and widely diasporic. This history of energy destabilizes the category of the human which has traditionally structured Enlightenment and post-Enlightenment projects of modernity; instead, the practices described in this project unsuture the human from binaristic structures of domination and submission, supply and demand, accessibility and extraction, which have come to inform contemporary understandings of modernity. To generate energy is not necessarily to be modern, or perhaps it is to be modern in ways that conventional histories of capitalist and anthropogenic exploitation cannot encompass. Instead, a new politics of energy emerges from these lives, a politics which adumbrates the complex relationships between human, nonhuman, and spiritual forces.

In this final chapter, we will consider Pauline Hopkins's novel *Of One Blood* (serialized in *The Colored American* 1902–3) as an early articulation of these new energy politics. Through its engagement with Black women's energy practices, Hopkins's novel not only foregrounds Haiti within domestic US histories, it also forges an alternative to global northern capitalist understandings of modernity. As one of the first African-American novels to feature both African characters and take place in

Africa, *Of One Blood* has been celebrated as one of the earliest fictional representations of Black internationalism. Yet, while critics have traditionally focused on Egypt or Ethiopia in relation to Hopkins's diasporic commitments, fewer have considered the novel within the context of Afro-Caribbean political and spiritual histories. I argue that the energy practices of the novel's women – specifically mesmerism, but also rootwork, possession, prophecy, and legacies of marronage – point the reader not only to Africa but also toward Haiti.[1] This chapter extends the coordinates of Hopkins's global commitments, charting an alternative geography beneath the Africa-oriented *Of One Blood* in which Haiti emerges at key moments of resistance. Moreover, Hopkins explicitly genders these moments of resistance as feminine. Focusing on the matrilineage of the characters Hannah, Mira, and Dianthe, I argue that women in the novel carry specifically Haitian valences: from colonial Saint-Dominguan mesmerism to the poison of Makandal, to the legacy of marronage. This muted Caribbean geography recenters women at the heart of the narrative, deepens Hopkins's anti-imperialist politics, imagines Black history beyond national lines, and subverts the energy politics of plantation genealogies.

5.1 Shadows of Toussaint

Because readers, even those familiar with *Of One Blood*, may have forgotten these women, I will offer a brief plot summary. When Reuel Briggs quits Boston for Africa, he leaves behind the sickly, beautiful Dianthe Lusk, who exerts a powerful mesmeric pull on men but is also, herself, mesmerized and controlled by Reuel, his colleague Livingston, and the medical community. Although Hopkins romanticizes Reuel's "courtship" of Dianthe, the coercive nature of his pursuit and Dianthe's fatigued acquiescence ("with the sigh of a tired child") make questionable the degree to which she consents.[2] Reuel's colleague Aubrey Livingston takes advantage of his friend's absence by coercing Dianthe into a sexual relationship, suggesting that Reuel has abandoned Dianthe because he knows of her mixed-raced heritage: Aubrey alone – or so he claims – can offer her protection. Aubrey then manages to convince both Dianthe and

[1] On Hopkins and internationalism, see O'Brien, "Blacks in all Quarters of the Globe"; Aljoe, "Aria for Ethiopia"; Peterson, "Unsettled Frontiers"; Goyal, *Romance, Diaspora, and Black Atlantic Literature.*

[2] Hopkins, *Of One Blood*, 492.

Reuel that the other is dead. The plot twists and turns, with spying servants, drowned fiancées, and leopard attacks rounding out the melodrama. In the final pages of the novel, the old medicine woman Aunt Hannah emerges from a hut at the edge of society. She reveals to Dianthe that Reuel is alive, before disclosing the darker origins of this romantic triangle: Hannah is Dianthe's grandmother and the mother of Mira, a mysterious woman who has appeared in the narrative as a flashback, a ghost, and a prophetic spirit. Mira is the product of Hannah's assault by Livingston Sr. and the only child of ten whom Hannah was allowed to raise. Mira was herself assaulted by Livingston's son and bore three children: Dianthe, Reuel, and Aubrey Livingston. Dianthe and Reuel were raised outside the Livingston family, but Hannah swapped the dying "legitimate" child of Livingston with the mixed-race child of Livingston and Mira. Horrified by these revelations, Dianthe attempts to poison Livingston; however, he suspects Dianthe's motivations and forces her to drink the poison instead. With Hannah at her side, Dianthe dies. Reuel returns from the mythical land of Telassar in time to bid farewell to Dianthe. After Dianthe dies, Reuel (who has, by this time, found a new bride) then returns to rule Telassar.

Although Haiti is never explicitly mentioned, this plot summary makes clear that energy practices we have come to see as Haitian, or more broadly, Afro-Caribbean, shape the lives of the novel's women: Dianthe is both controlled by disciplinary technologies of magnetic energy and is herself a mesmeric practitioner, ensnaring those around her with a possessing and possessed frequency of vibration; Mira, the novel's ghost, prophesies emancipatory futures from beyond the grave; and Hannah, the old medicine woman and grandmother of the novel, manipulates roots and plants from the margins of society, echoing histories of female marronage, midwifery, and rootwork. The novel's interest in the first Black republic also resonates with Hopkins's anti-imperialist commitments. Hopkins wrote extensively on Haiti in the *Colored American* and solicited essays on the nation as the editor of the short-lived *New Era* (1916).[3] She had a

[3] A prospectus for the *New Era* advertises an article called "Hayti – Political and historical," which promises the following: "Mr. E.H. Leonard, a native of Hayti having served in the army in that country ... will do research work for our magazine. Mr. Leonard is an able scholar in several languages, including French, German, and Italian and will give us many interesting happenings, both political and historical." Although I have been unable to locate the original article, other content in the journal critiques imperial projects in Liberia, Puerto Rico, the British West Indies, and the Congo, as well as racism within U.S. borders. (Unlike in the *CAM*, Hopkins has the editorial freedom to report on lynching in the March 1916 issue; the journal also condemns D.W. Griffith's 1915 *The Birth of a Nation*.)

personal interest in the island as well; her great uncle Thomas Paul served as a missionary to Haiti in the 1820s, taking advantage of President Jean-Pierre Boyer's immigration policies, which courted US free people of color.[4] Most scholarly interest in Hopkins's connection to Haiti has, however, focused on her Toussaint profile in the series "Famous Men of the Negro Race," which appeared in November 1900 in the *Colored American.* In this profile, Hopkins inaugurates her series on shores beyond the United States, beginning her anthology of Black heroism not in New York, Philadelphia, or Washington but rather in Haiti, under the aegis of Toussaint Louverture.[5] In doing so, Hopkins implicitly redefines the *Colored American* as the Black Americas, locating the origins of the "Negro race" at the roots of the tree of liberty: that is to say, the Haitian Revolution. But Hopkins figures Haiti neither as a cradle of civilization nor as nurturing womb, nor benevolent father of a diasporic family. Instead, Toussaint appears as a specter or, as Hopkins terms him, "Napoleon's black shadow."[6] That Hopkins privileges the trope of the shadow should not surprise; her corpus bristles with counterfactuals, alternative genealogies, unquiet ghosts, and fantastic timelines. But given the Afrocentric bent of her fiction, one might wonder why Hopkins, in this crucial first installment, turned neither to Africa nor to a mythical past, but instead to a republic borne of the violent tremors of modernity or, in Hopkins's words, "a stepping stone from the old world to the new."[7]

The answer might be found in situating Hopkins's profile of Toussaint within her journalism more broadly. While early US and European representations of Toussaint merely sought to deploy his figure as evidence of Black humanity – and as a result often neutered his political radicalism – Hopkins, throughout her journalistic career, frames him as the figurehead for divine-sanctioned resistance to imperialism, exemplifying what Colleen O'Brien has termed an "insurgent cosmopolitanism."[8] Early in her Toussaint essay, Hopkins writes: "In the history of this island – the sole possession of the Negro race in America – we find what we seek: the point of interest for all Negroes, whether Frenchmen, Spaniards, Americans, or Africans – the point of interest for all students of the black race. The voice

[4] Brown, *Pauline Elizabeth Hopkins*, 10–12.

[5] *Famous Men* is a twelve-part installment that, which includes profiles of Frederick Douglass and William Wells Brown, among others. The series appeared in the *Colored American* from November 1900 (beginning with Toussaint) to October 1901 (ending with a far less laudatory profile of Booker T. Washington).

[6] Hopkins, "Toussaint Louverture," 9. [7] Ibid.

[8] O'Brien, "'Blacks in all Quarters of the Globe,'" 249.

of history is the voice of God."[9] This investment in providential justice knitting together an oppressed global south is equally apparent in her anticolonial writings elsewhere, especially her series *The Dark Races of the Twentieth Century*, published in the *Voice of the Negro* (February–July 1905), which despite its sometimes troubling pseudoscientific typologies, explicitly condemns Western "imperialist fever" concluding with the powerful assertion: "Men . . . will teach the Anglo-Saxon that 'all men were created equal' and that '*all men*' are not *white* men."[10] Read within this context, Hopkins's Toussaint stands not as benign martyr or the "miserable Chieftain" of Wordsworth's sonnet, but rather as a flashpoint for global resistance to imperialism.

In the decades leading up to the US Occupation, Hopkins was carefully attuned to the nation's fragile sovereignty. In an essay criticizing William Pickens's speech "Misrule in Haiti," Hopkins, writing under the pseudonym J. Shirley Shadrac, announces: "I rolled up my sleeves and went in for a good chance to make a philanthropical and magnificent plea for the non-interference of the outside world in Haytien affairs."[11] And she concludes her defense of Haitian self-determination with lines directly lifted from her portrait of Toussaint: "Let us have no fears for the future of Hayti, or for that of our entire race. We feel with the late Frederick Douglass that, as the north star is eternal in the heavens, so will Hayti remain forever in the firmament of nations."[12] Similarly, in an essay on Douglass, the second installment of her *Famous Men*, series, Hopkins commends the "veritable and historic sage" for his defense of Haiti during the US attempted occupation of the Môle St. Nicolas: "The government has not yet acquired the Môle St. Nicolas from Hayti, and it is doubtful if it ever does" she exults.[13]

An examination of Hopkins's journalism reveals that Haiti may very well be the "black shadow" of the novel's fictional uncolonized kingdom Telassar, which – like so much of the Caribbean – is threatened by the imperialist "advance of mighty nations."[14] *Of One Blood*'s carefully chosen names and symbols not only bear specifically Haitian connotations but, following P. Gabrielle Foreman's concept of "simultextuality," I believe it likely that many of these connotations would have been legible to a contemporary readership.[15] In a novel where names undertake most of the work of character exposition – the evil "Doctor Livingston," for

[9] Hopkins, "Toussaint Louverture," 10. [10] Ibid.
[11] "William Pickens, Yale University," *CAM* (July 1903), 520. [12] Ibid., 529.
[13] Hopkins, "Frederick Douglass,"131. [14] Hopkins, *Of One Blood*, 621.
[15] Foreman, *Activist Sentiments*.

example, essentially does what it says on the tin – such choices should not be overlooked. Dianthe Lusk shares a name with the first wife of John Brown, whose raid on Harper's Ferry took the Haitian Revolution as its source of inspiration. Moreover, Dianthe – the seemingly passive, mesmerized subject – also goes under the name Felice, the name of a woman reputed to have been turned into a *zombi* in Port-au-Prince (most famously, Zora Neale Hurston would later write of Felice in *Tell My Horse* (1938), but the *zombi*'s mythology had long circulated in the nineteenth-century press).[16] Early in the novel, Reuel obtains his tickets to the Fisk Jubilee Concert (and thus encounters Dianthe) through a servant named Redpath: the biographer of both Brown and Toussaint, whose writings did much to concretize the connection between Harper's Ferry and the Haitian Revolution in the public imagination; Redpath was also the Haitian government's official "Official General Agent of Emigration to Hayti for the United States and Canada."[17] (Hopkins's early theatrical work with the Hyers sisters, which was sponsored by the Redpath Agency, may have brought her into contact with Redpath or at least his estate).[18] Even the lily marks that appear on the skin of the royal family evoke and reappropriate the fleur-de-lys brandings that, under the French Code Noir, were inflicted as punishment on enslaved people.[19]

But Haiti's influence goes beyond names and symbols: we can also excavate Haitian histories of energy from the novel's three most prominent women. Hopkins portrays a lineage of three revolutionary women, all of whom evoke Haitian energy practices which resist the biocapitalist demands of white ideologies. In what follows, I would like to ask: Why is this muted Afro-Caribbean insurrection threaded through the matrilineal line? Given Hopkins's proclaimed interest in Toussaint, wouldn't we expect a noble masculine character such as Reuel to father Black futurity?

16 See Hurston, *Tell My Horse.*

17 On the triangulation of Brown, Redpath, and Toussaint, see Clavin, *Toussaint Louverture and the American Civil War: The Promise and Peril of a Second Haitian Revolution.*

18 See Patterson, "Remaking the Minstrel." See also Southern (ed.), *Nineteenth-Century American Musical Theater.*

19 Article XVI of the 1685 Code Noir states: "Défendons pareillement aux esclaves appartenant à différents maîtres de s'attrouper le jour ou la nuit sous prétexte de noces ou autrement, soit chez l'un de leurs maîtres ou ailleurs, et encore moins dans les grands chemins ou lieux écartés, à peine de punition corporelle qui ne pourra être moindre que du fouet et de la fleur de lys" ("In the same way we forbid slaves belonging to different masters to gather in the day or night whether claiming for wedding or otherwise, whether on their master's property or elsewhere, and still less in the main roads or faraway places, on pain of corporal punishment, which will not be less than the whip and the fleur de lys." *Le Code Noir ou Recueil des reglements rendus jusqu'à present* (Paris: Prault, 1767) [1980 reprd. by the Societé, d'Histoire de la Guadeloupe]. Trans. John Garrigus.

To make sense of the novel's matrilineage and particularly their Caribbean influences, we might turn to Hopkins's profile series "Famous Women of the Negro Race," which followed "Famous Men" in eleven installments between November 1901 and October 1902. In this series, Hopkins makes the unusual decision to frame a Black woman – Sojourner Truth – as an inheritor of Toussaint Louverture's legacy, comparing "the depths from which men such as ... Toussaint Louverture ... [has] sprung" to the "mules, horses, sheep, and old wagons!" of Sojourner Truth's upstate New York farm. Moreover, while Truth appears as a female version of Toussaint and an implicit bearer of hemispheric Black emancipation, Hopkins concludes the "Famous Men" series with less optimism. The last profile in the men's series, an ambivalent portrait of Booker T. Washington, culminates with the invocation of a man antithetical to Black liberation: Napoleon Bonaparte. The final lines of Hopkins's "Famous Men" do not predict uplift, emancipation, or revolution but instead ominously foretell that "Dr. Washington's motives will be open to as many constructions and discussions as those of Napoleon today." While Truth is a homespun hero, evoking Toussaint Louverture and the enslaved masses who liberated Haiti, "Famous Men" ends with the man who ordered Toussaint's capture and reinstated slavery throughout the French Caribbean. This is not to say that Hopkins necessarily follows a strict gender binary in which Haiti would be the female subaltern warrior to Booker T. Washington's implied chauvinistic imperialism; however, it does suggest an interest in understanding the Haitian Revolution beyond the romantic masculinist narratives that dominated US print culture.

Not only does Hopkins nuance our understandings of gender and revolution through her unlikely comparison of Sojourner Truth to Toussaint. She also, in "Famous Women," questions the heroic logics of individual action. Unlike "Famous Men," Hopkins's series of women focuses on collective, rather than individual, female heroism. Only Sojourner Truth and Harriet Tubman are given full profiles: the other nine installments of the series instead shift from individual lives to what Ira Dworkin calls "collective biograph[ies]" including "Phenomenal Vocalists," "Literary Workers," "Educators," and "Artists."[20] Not unlike *Of One Blood*, where the communal labor of Hannah, Mira, and Dianthe is seemingly overshadowed by the heroics of Reuel's quest for self realization, "Famous Women" at first glance appears to subordinate female collectivism to masculine individual heroics. And yet, "Famous Women"

[20] Dworkin, *Daughter of the Revolution: Major Nonfiction Works*, 111.

points us to other ways of conceiving political labor, which extend beyond the "colossal schemes" of the "Famous Men" series.[21] Shifting from the individual to the collective, the heroic to the communal, "Famous Women" achieves a global scope as Hopkins details the modest, quotidian, and sometimes nameless efforts of Black women's political and social organization across the diaspora. Concluding the series in the installment "Higher Education of Colored Women," Hopkins writes:

> And the world has need for all the higher work of which women is capable. In cities, villages, prisons, workhouses, in art galleries, and in letters, in all branches of industry, the world is the debtor of the woman of any race who can do it better.
>
> We who are near to the heart of the Negro – we know that a wonderful transformation is going on within the secret forces of his being. We do not fear the future, but we look forward with confidence to the time when Phoenix-like, he shall arise from the ashes of his past and become the wonder of ages yet unborn. The current of human progress is slow, sometimes apparently backward, but never permanently checked.[22]

Here, the "higher work" of nameless women across the globe creates an activist network which sutures the modest labor of Black women educators, singers, nurses, and club members with a nearly eschatological vision of human rebirth. Crucially, however, this rebirth is not linear: "Famous Women" concludes with a vision of futurity that resists the deterministic paths of genealogical time. Instead, the "slow, sometimes apparently backward" path of human progress speaks to both a faith in Black futurity and a way of conceiving of futurity beyond linear genealogies. Her final invocation of the Phoenix's burning energy creates a cyclical and unruly temporal horizon, in which the past repeats and compounds through women's labor.

Of One Blood's gendered energy practices and Caribbean influences similarly alter heteronormative narratives of Black reproduction. In one respect, the matrilineage of Hannah, Mira, and Dianthe – each sexually assaulted and torn from their children and mothers – is symptomatic of the kind of racial-sexual violence that structured and fueled chattel slavery throughout the Americas. And yet, Hopkins also shows us how to think of Black motherhood as independent of these violent political, biological, and economic regimes of reproduction and the exploitation of Black women's

[21] Hopkins, "Booker T. Washington," *Daughter of the Revolution: Major Nonfiction Works*, 110.

[22] Hopkins, "Higher Education of Colored Women," *Daughter of the Revolution: Major Nonfiction Works*, 198.

energy. Instead, she subverts her narrative of sexual abjection and natal alienation through Caribbean, and specifically Haitian, energy practices. As we will see, the novel's investment in these alternative energy practices allows for an unfolding of time, in which mothers, grandmothers, and daughters collapse into a nonlinear genealogy of haunted but powerful forms of care. Haiti's past warps reproductive channels, thwarts the forward thrust of propagation, and sends the reader backward to a revolutionary past, and forwards to a startlingly empty utopian future. In the following pages, I will ask: What histories emerge when we look beyond Toussaint? What happens when Boston meets the Caribbean, the Caribbean meets Africa, and the haunted circuits of history meet the linear paths of genealogy?

5.2 "Vital Energy": Mesmerism in the Caribbean

Although scholarship on the novel is dominated by its representations of mesmerism, very few critical approaches to *Of One Blood* have historicized mesmerism's transatlantic and hemispheric roots, instead situating the practice in domestic histories of spiritualism, reform, and the New Psychology movement of the late nineteenth century.[23] But mesmerism's path to Hopkins's Boston was a complex and deeply transnational one. The practice was developed by the Vienna-born physician Franz Anton Mesmer, who, upon his arrival in Paris in 1778, began peddling a vulgarization of electric experiments made popular by scientists like John Hunter, Joseph Priestley, Benjamin Franklin, and Luigi Galvani. Like these electricians, Mesmer subscribed to the Newtonian theory which held that an invisible and ethereal substance permeated all matter. For Newton, this substance was "a certain most subtle spirit which pervades and lies hid in all gross bodies" and which would explain all the universe's attractions and repulsions.[24] Yet, unlike conventional scientists of the time, Mesmer claimed that he could channel this invisible substance without the aid of electricity. Instead, he positioned his own body as a conduit of what he called "vital energy," highlighting the tactile and affective dimensions of

[23] A sampling of this very large body of work includes Gillman, "Pauline Hopkins and the Occult"; Schrager, "Pauline Hopkins and William James"; Lam, "Uncanny Compulsions"; Unlike the majority of critics, who tend to read the novel's supernatural dimensions from an Anglo-European perspective, Otten, ("Pauline Hopkins and the Hidden Self of Race,") examines the role of "hoodoo" in the novel. However, he does not consider the transnational dimensions of African-American spiritual practices.

[24] Newton, *Scholium Generale*, 93.

Enlightenment science in order to manipulate the universal fluid that had been popularized by electrical experiments earlier in the century.[25]

Mesmer's embodied spectacle became wildly fashionable in Paris's elite circles: wealthy patients congregated in the city's salons where, surrounded by perfumes and the music of Mesmer's mystical glass harmonica, they would encircle *baquets*, or tubs, which had been filled with what Mesmer claimed was magnetized water. Drawing inspiration from the experiments of the Leyden jar, Mesmer invited his audience to hold hands in a human chain and grasp hold of an iron rod which he placed within the baquet, and which purportedly transmitted energy from the water to the crowd. But while the Leyden jar's effectiveness was in its transmission of an electric shock, Mesmer himself embodied the energetic "charge" that linked his patients: once his audience had clasped their hands around the tub, Mesmer would theatrically enter the room, touching each patient, frequently holding eye contact, and leading patients into what he called a state of *crise* (a crisis, trance, attack, or seizure). These *crises* purportedly unblocked the stagnant flow of human energy, re-energized his patients' circulation, and cured complaints including blindness, fever, gout, nervousness, and labor pains.[26]

For Mesmer, "all bodies . . . were like the magnet, capable of communicating [the] magnetic principle" which "penetrated everything."[27] Yet, this notion of all-encompassing penetration led to deep seated anxieties within the medical establishment. Shortly after Mesmer's arrival in Paris, Louis XIV appointed five members of the Academy of the Sciences, chaired by Benjamin Franklin, to investigate Mesmer's experiments.[28] The Commission unequivocally debunked Mesmer's methods, attributing the reactions of his patients to the "mechanical imagination" of his patients:

> [T]hey concluded unanimously, on the question of the existence & utility of Magnetism, that nothing proves the existence of animal magnetic fluid; that this nonexistent fluid is by consequence without any utility; that the

[25] Indeed, much metropolitan anxiety around Mesmer's practice stemmed from its frankly erotic emphasis on touch. One witness, for example, noted that Mesmer's hand "is applied to the diaphragm area and sometimes lower over the ovaries. So touch is applied to many areas at once and in the vicinity of some of the most sensitive parts of the body." *Royal Commission Secret Report.* Quoted in Crabtree, *From Mesmer to Freud*, 93.

[26] Benz, *The Theology of Electricity*; Darnton, *Mesmerism and the End of the Enlightenment in France*; Ogden, *Credulity*.

[27] Mesmer, *Mémoire sur la découverte du magnétisme animal*, 36. See also Ogden, *Credulity*.

[28] Lopez, "Franklin and Mesmer."

> violent effects observed in public treatments can be credited to the touch, to the imagination, the actuation, & to this mechanical imitation that impels us, despite ourselves, to repeat what strikes our senses.[29]

Despite its official censure in hexagonal France, mesmerism found a home in the colonies. In the same year that the Franklin Commission officially condemned mesmerism in Paris, a former student of Mesmer's, the Comte de Chastenet Antoine-Hyacinth de Puységur, arrived in Cap François, Saint-Domingue. He soon established magnetic treatments throughout the colony: unlike in hexagonal France, where mesmerism was largely an elite practice, it crossed social and racial boundaries in the colonial sphere. Although denounced by the elite scientific *Cercle*, who took their cues from the Franklin Commission, mesmerism remained popular with the fashionable *grand blancs* of the island; it was also deployed in poorhouses, such as the Maison de Providence des Hommes in Cap François, and eventually spread to the plantation system. It was particularly embraced by Saint-Dominguan enslavers, physicians, and merchants, who manipulated the trend into a disciplinary technology. It became common practice to channel Mesmer's "energetic fluid" through African bodies in order to appreciate the value of enslaved people (through either (allegedly) healing their ailments or (allegedly) training them to work more efficiently).[30]

As the next decades would prove, however, these disciplinary medical strategies failed to produce the docile laborer desired by colonial practitioners: by 1786, mesmerism had spread from enslavers to the enslaved community, where the practice's emphasis on emancipatory possession, enchanted refuge, and temporary removal from bondage, syncretized with Vodou practices.[31] The May 16 1786 minutes of the *Conseil Supérieur du Cap* reported two incidents of enslaved gatherings in which mesmerism was practiced: according to these reports, the affinities between mesmerism and the "mad fantaticism" of Vodou practitioners – referred to as a "class

[29] The original reads "ils ont conclu d'une voix unanime, sur la question de l'existence & de l'utilité du Magnétisme, que rien ne prouve l'existence du fluide magnétique animal; que ce fluide sans existence est par consequent sans utilité; que les violens effets que l'on observe au traitement public, appartiennent a l'attouchement, à l'imagination mise en action, & à cette imitation machinale qui nous porte malgré nous à repeter ce qui frappe nos sens." *Rapport des Commissaires chargés par le Roi de l'Examen du magnétisme animal*, 62.

[30] McLellan, *Colonialism and Science*, 178.

[31] See Fick, *The Making of Haiti*; Murphy, "Magic and Mesmerism in Saint-Domingue" and "The Occult Atlantic"; Weaver, *Medical Revolutionaries.*

of Macandals" – were cited as justification for outlawing the practice of magnetism for people of African descent.[32] As Karol Ann Weaver writes, "White residents saw mesmerist activity as the dangerous breakdown of hierarchy, the deterioration of social position, and the destruction of Saint-Domingue's slave society. The enslaved supporters of magnetism saw it differently; for them mesmerism offered freedom."[33]This offer of freedom was not impeded by colonial interdictions. In the year following the 1786 ban on African-led mesmerism, two enslaved men named Jérome Poteau and Télémaque began organizing mass rallies of enslaved people in several Marmalade plantations: these rallies purportedly included the distribution of iron rods, the utterance of incantations, and calls for liberty which not only syncretized Vodou with mesmeric practices but also foreshadowed the uprising of Bwa Kayiman. By the end of the decade, Moreau de Saint-Méry (conflating what he termed "Vaudoux" with mesmerism) boldly claimed that all mesmerists "preached rebellion."[34] And by 1824, Mesmer himself reportedly claimed that "the new republic [of Haiti] owed its independence to [him]."[35]

This syncretic form of Vodou and mesmerism came to the United States via multiple pathways. Around the Gulf basin, it emerged in creolized "voodoo" practices, perhaps most famously exemplified in the royal personality of Marie Laveau, who was said to control the New Orleans police force through hypnosis. However, if one follows the routes of white bodies, the revolutionary pulse of mesmerism decelerates: Emily Ogden, for example, traces the practice through the Guadeloupean sugar planter Charles Poyen, who introduced mesmerism to New England mill towns in the 1830s, where it was used as a disciplinary technique on (mostly female) factory laborers.[36] Whether punitive or revolutionary, mesmerism and its Caribbean origins were assimilated into the white and nebulous contours of spiritualism by the 1850s – not incidentally, the same decade in which New Orleans authorities began to crack down on "voodoo" rituals and African-American congregations.[37] The radical

[32] Cited in Weaver, *Medical Revolutionaries*, 104. [33] Ibid., 10.

[34] Moreau de Saint-Méry, *Description topographique, physique, civile, politique et historique de la partie française de l'isle Saint-Domingue*, 1:275.

[35] Cited from Ellenberger, *The Discovery of the Unconscious*, 73.

[36] Ogden, *Credulity*. Perhaps because Ogden frames her work as an intervention in narratives of emancipatory enchantment, she does not discuss Haiti in this cultural history.

[37] Fandrich, "Defiant African Sisterhoods"; see also Castronovo, "The antislavery unconscious: Mesmerism, vodun, and 'equality.'"

freedom of Saint-Domingue was thus quietly absorbed into the genteel violence of Anglo-American bourgeois culture.

Hopkins understood, however, that the domestic respectability of mystical congregation so popular in the later half of the nineteenth century did not just displace revolution: it also displaced other forms of "congress" between bodies, many of which were violent and nonconsensual. What brings *Of One Blood*'s women together are not just their supernatural abilities but acts of racial-sexual violence that enable Hopkins's royal genealogy. At the end of the novel, the grandmother and medicine woman Hannah reveals that Livingston's grandfather assaulted her ("As soon as I was growed up, my mistress changed in her treatment of me, for she soon knowed my relations with mass"[38]) and, moreover, Livingston's father assaulted her daughter (and Dianthe's mother) Mira ("she made de house too hot to hol' Mira"[39]). Dianthe's seemingly passive suffering at the hands of her brothers Reuel and Livingston is thus revealed to be, far from a melodramatic flourish, simply a common consequence of plantation violence. Moreover, Hopkins portrays the emancipated Dianthe, rather than legally enslaved Mira and Hannah, as the most abject of the triad, assaulted and coerced by not one but two men. The violence of slavery, Hopkins suggests, does not end with 1865: rather, historical trauma accumulates, repeats, and compounds in the vehicular body of the formally free woman.

Most scholarship on Dianthe focuses on her status as a mesmerized subject, often situating her within the discursive limits of US and European spiritualism and psychoanalysis. Yet, to limit our reading of Dianthe to the works of William James, Freud, or Lacan overlooks Hopkins's diasporic and hemispheric influences.[40] This overemphasis on global northern epistemologies fails to consider the radical potential of Black spiritual practices, an elision all the more marked given the well-established critical lineage celebrating the emancipatory uses of (white) women's spiritualism.[41] But Ann Braude's "radical spirits" very seldom stir criticism of Dianthe: Jennie Kassanoff, for example, diagnoses the character as a "passive object of exchange"; Claudia Tate argues that Dianthe's lack of agency leads to a negation of "the efficacy of social protest . . . as a remedy for racial injustice"; JoAnn Pavletich considers the novel's purportedly regressive gender politics alongside Hopkins's frustration with the

38 Hopkins, *Of One Blood*, 605. 39 Ibid.

40 See Bergman, "The Motherless Child in Pauline Hopkins's *Of One Blood*"; Horvitz, "Hysteria and Trauma in Pauline Hopkins's *Of One Blood*"; Luciano, "Passing Shadows; Schrager, "Pauline Hopkins and William James"; Tate, *Psychoanalysis and Black Novels.*

41 This lineage is most closely identified with Braude, *Radical Spirits.*

tragic mulatta cliché; and Jolie A. Sheffer reads Dianthe's trance state as "an illustration of the forced abjection of black women under American racism and slavery."[42] Perhaps the strongest counterpoint to these interpretations is Daphne Brooks's reading of the novel, which situates Dianthe within the history of the Fisk Jubilee Singers and Hopkins's own stage career, thus making a convincing case for Dianthe's "resistant alterity."[43] For Brooks, Dianthe musical talents "open up transgeographical frontiers and negotiate chronotopical fields to reconnect her character with an individual past as a solo choirist and a collective history of black subjugation and spiritual survival embedded in the lyrics of the spirituals."[44] Although Brooks is concerned with Dianthe as diva, we can expand these deft traversals of geographies and chronotopes beyond strategies of song, focusing on how Dianthe's "collective history" encompasses Haitian histories of electricity, magnetism, and revolutionary energy.

Specifically, Dianthe's mesmeric practices tap into a dual history of Saint Dominguan magnetism as both a disciplinary and emancipatory practice. When Dianthe first appears, her solo of "Go Down Moses" "dazes," "thrills," and renders "spellbound" the weeping and enchanted audience; she is said to have "enthralled [the] senses by her wonderful singing";[45] and Reuel himself is particularly moved – quite literally "carried out of himself" – by the magnetic power of Dianthe's voice. Indeed, her commanding performance seems to echo the enchantingly dangerous power of Mesmer's practice, as described by the Franklin Commission as:

> All subjugate themselves to the magnetizer. They may seem satisfied to be in an apparent state of drowsiness, but his voice or a look or a sign from him will drawn them out. One cannot help but note . . . a great power than moves the patients and masters them. The result is that the magnetizer seems to be their absolute ruler.[46]

Dianthe subjugates – or in a more genteel register "charms" – everyone with whom she comes into contact: not only Reuel, who insists on a "mysterious mesmeric affinity existing between them,"[47] but also Aubrey

[42] Kassanoff, "Fate Has Linked Us Together," 176; Tate, *Domestic Allegories of Political Desire*, 7. Pavletich, "Pauline Hopkins and the Death of the Tragic Mulatta"; Sheffer, *The Romance of Race*, 39.

[43] Brooks, *Bodies in Dissent*, 292. Brooks also argues for a more expansive definition of nineteenth-century spiritualism, calling attention (via Joseph Roach) to the Native American and African-American Ghost Dance of 1880s Louisiana (323).

[44] Ibid., 319. [45] Hopkins, *Of One Blood*, 475.

[46] *Rapport des commissaires chargés par le roi de l'examen du magnétisme animal*, quoted in Crabtree, 25.

[47] Hopkins, *Of One Blood*, 466.

Livingston, who falls into a "trance of delight" in her presence,[48] and his sister Molly, who "surrendered unconditionally . . . drawn by an irresistible bond" to Dianthe.

But Dianthe is also a victim of mesmerism's forceful pull. Both Reuel and Aubrey Livingston justify their invasive sexual advances through metaphors of magnetism, reproducing the tired trope of cis-male desire as a violent but ineluctable natural force elicited by his "magnetic" attraction to the female body. Even more explicitly, however, Dianthe is literally mesmerized and remesmerized: first by an unknown sorcerer, who pulls her into a deathlike trance, and second, by the Boston medical community. As Reuel claims, "This woman has long and persistently been subjected to mesmeric influences, and the nervous shock induced by the excitement of the accident has thrown her into a cataleptic state."[49] Through a countercurrent of mesmerism, Reuel claims to save her, combining the "magnetic" pull of his invasive sexual desire with the sterilized magnetism of his medical practice. According to Reuel:

> The secret of life lies in what we call volatile magnetism–it exists in the free atmosphere. . . . This subtile magnetic agent is constantly drawn into the body through the lungs, absorbed, and held in bounds until chemical combination has occurred through the medium of mineral agents always present in normal animal tissue. When respiration ceases this magnetism cannot be drawn into the lungs. It must be artificially supplied. This, gentleman, is my discovery. I supply this magnetism.[50]

While Dianthe's magnetic power is articulated through the language of mysticism, charm, and witchcraft, Reuel resituates magnetism within the pseudoscientific discourses of white colonial containment and discipline which were historically weaponized against Black bodies. But even this medicalization of magnetic energy harnesses Haitian influences. Reuel proposes a remedy astonishingly similar to those recommended for recovery from zombification: salt. The specificity of this cure ("This salt is saturated with oleo resin and then exposed for several hours in an atmosphere of free ammonia. The product becomes a powder, and that brings the seeming dead to life"[51]) evokes the Haitian belief that the *zombi* can break her master's spell when she ingests salt. For example, Haitian diplomat Hannibal Price's 1900 treatise *De la réhabilitation de la race noire par la République d'Haïti* discusses the folkloric history of a man named Bigarette, "a zombie who had eaten salt which he had saved from his

[48] Ibid., 475. [49] Ibid., 463. [50] Ibid., 468. [51] Ibid., 469.

mapou [a tree associated with Vodou, and which historically provided refuge for self-emancipated slaves]."[52] Reuel and Dianthe's magnetic connection taps deep into a Caribbean history of mutually entwined currents of subjugation and emancipation, syncretizing the Haitian zombi with the New England medicinal community.

Dianthe is not the only mesmerized woman of the novel. Her mother, Mira, is also presented as a clinical and ostensibly passive object for white observation. In a flashback recounted by Livingston Jr., we learn that Mira was frequently mesmerized by her enslavers. Livingston Jr. describes how his father, the senior Dr. Livingston, cajoled Mira into "perform[ing] tricks of mind-reading for the amusement of visitors," forcibly throwing her "into a trance-state."[53] First presented in the narrative without a name or history, Mira is initially framed as an object, quite literally a curio: "Nothing could be more curious than to see her and hear her"[54] recalls Livingston Jr. Yet, through the "peculiar metamorphosis"[55] of the elder Livingston's mesmerism, a prophet emerges. When asked what the future holds for the party's guests, Mira responds:

> You will not like it captain; but if I must, I must. All the women will be widows and the men shall sleep in early graves. They come from the north, from the east, from the west, they sweep to the gulf through a trail of blood. Your houses shall burn, your fields be laid waste, and a down-trodden race shall rule in your land. For you, captain, a prison cell and pauper's grave.[56]

Even confined within the straits of possession – a thraldom underscored by the submissively tautological preface "if I must, I must" – Mira voices what are perhaps the most radical lines of the novel. Mira's prophecy does not simply augur the Civil War: it rewrites postbellum history as a utopic revolution, one in which "a down-trodden race" is not only liberated but "shall rule in your land." Mira's visions, in tragic contrast to Hopkins's postbellum reality, establish a true revolution: a radical returning to a triumphant Reconstruction past and emancipated visionary future. It is fitting, then, that the broken bonds of kinship symptomatic of plantation economies (and so key to the narrative of the novel) are redirected toward white enslavers. Mira begins her prophecy with the declaration that "all the women will be widows," effectively destroying the white familial structure which upheld racist systems of oppression and obscured the reality of racial-sexual violence – indeed, although Livingston claims that Mira was

[52] The original reads "un zombi qui avait mangé du sel qui s'était sauvé de son *mapou*." Price, *De la réhabilitation de la race noire par la République d'Haïti*, 454.

[53] Hopkins, *Of One Blood*, 486. [54] Ibid., 487. [55] Ibid., 486. [56] Ibid., 487.

dismissed because of her audacious prophecy, Hannah later reveals that Mira was expulsed for having roused the jealousy of Mrs. Livingston.

Although aspects of both Mira and Dianthe reference the musical, mystical, and passive character of Mirah in *Daniel Deronda*, Hopkins rewrites Eliot's Jewish diasporic romance along powerfully female lines. Far from a mere instrument in the male protagonist's quest of self-discovery, Hopkins's Mira is a prophet, a sorceress, and a bearer of hexes, curses, visions, and blistering glimpses of future justice. Not only does Mira envisage the upheaval of revolutionary justice from within the confines of misogynistic and racist violence, she also explicitly echoes two prophets central to Hopkins's creative projects: John Brown and Toussaint Louverture. Livingston, although presumably not yet in the military, is twice addressed with Brown's title of militia "captain." Similarly, the "prison cell" and "pauper's grave" evoke the romanticized final days of Louverture and Brown in Fort-de-Joux and Charles Town, respectively. In both her fiction and biographical essays, Hopkins identified the two leaders as prophets, tapping into Christian eschatology, classical histories of the "black Spartacus" and Haitian Vodou practices. Like the John Brown of Hopkins's 1902 *Winona*, heroically described as a "prophet of old," Mira embodies a historical tradition of visionary calls for justice.[57] One need only change the gender pronouns of *Winona*'s description of Brown to recognize Mira in her antebellum parlor: "[L]ightning flashed from *her* mild eyes and sword-thrusts fell from *her* tongue."[58] If Mira's prophecy ("if I must, I must") takes the form of tautology, a neutering of meaning, it also reveals how to work outside of tautological confines. The past does not stupidly repeat the violence so prevalent in *Of One Blood*. Instead, as we shall see, Mira's prophecy contributes to a circum-Caribbean network of radical cosmologies and resistant energy flows.

5.3 Hannah's Roots

If Mira rebels against the straits of white supremacist mesmerism through a prophetic trance-state reminiscent of Theresa's prophecies in Chapter 3, Dianthe similarly subverts the racist and misogynistic medical disciplining of mesmerism through Caribbean energy practices. Turning away from the vital flows of mesmerism and prophecy, I will conclude this chapter with a

[57] It is not for nothing that the John Brown of *Winona* utters the line: "He hath made of one blood all the nations of the earth." See Hopkins, *Winona*, 374.

[58] Hopkins, *Winona*, 379.

consideration of Dianthe's most striking act of resistance: her attempt to poison Livingston. Dianthe's and her grandmother Hannah's manipulation of plants, I argue, harnesses a hemispheric history of botanical energy, rootwork, and poison. Removing her magnetic fluid or "vital energy" from the medical experiments and sexual violations of Reuel and Livingston, Dianthe instead offers an alternative paradigm of energy, one cultivated not in the laboratory, the plantation, or the factory, but instead hidden in the outskirts of the Black woman's garden.

Dianthe's quiet rebellion against Livingston places her within a long lineage of female poisoners; it is not for nothing that, shortly before the attempted murder, Dianthe references her classical education in Rome.[59] Yet, the kitchen looked different in the Americas. Poison was a widespread strategy of resistance and tool of protection, especially for enslaved women, who often worked as household cooks or nurses.[60] These women made use of their tools at hand – liberty tenderly cultivated in the garden and cupboard – not only to debilitate or kill their masters but also, as we saw in Chapter 2, to control their own reproductive systems, further straining the already tenuous legal boundaries between what were considered personal and property crimes. The constricted domestic spaces of the poisoner's kitchen, however, give way to a wider transnational network: not only was poison gendered as feminine but it also carried, as Diana Paton has argued, specifically French Caribbean valences.[61] Returning to Hopkins's Toussaint article, it is therefore significant that she emphasizes, along with his martial and political talents, his healing skills: "He knew something of herbs too."[62]

At the heart of this lineage is the legacy of Makandal, the first known enslaved person in Saint-Domingue to organize a mass-scale resistance against the plantation system.[63] Working within the cosmologies of Vodou, Islam, and Christianity, Makandal was a master pharmacist, prophet, and *houngan*, compounding complex poisons and fetishes, which he then distributed to slaves with the instruction that they were to serve them to their enslavers. Eventually caught by colonial authorities, he was burned at the stake but not without a struggle: according to eyewitnesses,

[59] Hopkins, *Of One Blood*, 608.

[60] See Crosby, *The Poisonous Muse*; Genovese, *Within the Plantation Household*; Wright, *Ar'n't I a Woman?*

[61] See Paton, "Witchcraft, Poison, Law, and Atlantic Slavery." [62] Hopkins, "Toussaint," 15–18.

[63] On the legacy of Makandal, see Dubois, *Avengers of the New World*, especially 50–9; Fick, *The Making of Haiti*, 62–70; Geggus, "Marronage, Vodou, and the Slave Revolt of 1791," in *Haitian Revolutionary* Weaver, *Medical Revolutionaries*, especially 93–7. Ramsey, *The Spirits and the Law*, 33–5; Mintz and Trouillot, "The Social History of Haitian Vodou," 123–47.

he escaped his binds before being retied and burned again. Folk tales, Vodou songs, and oral histories insist, however, that he was not killed: some claim that he turned into a fly, others to smoke.[64] Makandal's rebellion nurtured long afterlives among both Europeans, who evoked Makandal as proof of African iniquity, and Black diasporic traditions which wrote his purported shape-shifting abilities into a poetics of fugitivity. Dianthe's attempted murder of Livingston traces the contours of this fugitivity, revealing the ways in which people of both the US and the Caribbean made use of the non-human world for emancipatory ends.

When Dianthe first encounters her grandmother or "Aunt" Hannah, the old woman is murmuring a "funeral chant commonly sung by the Negroes over the dead"[65] and tending to a "stimulating"[66] brew. "The most noted 'voodoo' doctor or witch in the country"[67] Hannah has reason to mourn: witness to assaults passed down from generation to generation, she is issued by the narrative to not only resolve the tale but also see Dianthe from the world of the living into the world of the dead. To use the language of Haitian Vodou, she serves as a kind of *Kalfu*, or spiritual crossroads.[68] But Hannah is not merely the administrator of the "healing antidote of narrative" as Kassanoff has argued.[69] For every soothed brow, for every backstory restored, Hannah also administers a promise of revenge. When Dianthe reveals Livingston's abuse, Hannah has a ready rejoinder: "Yer granny knows de whole circumstance. I seed it all las' night in my dreams. Vengeance is mine; I will repay."[70] Like so many tropes of and about Haiti, Hannah is figured as a debtor, prophet, and, in the style of Jean-Jacques Dessalines, an "avenger of the Americas." Indeed, in the brief and obscure meeting which presumably condemns Livingston to death, Hannah joins Ai, Abdadis, and Reuel at the enchanted tribunal, a surprisingly folkish, female presence among the stately men of Telassar. Take a moment to appreciate this: at the height of Jim Crow, Hopkins allows a Black woman to issue a death sentence against her granddaughter's rapist and, by extension, the chain of sexual predators who assaulted her granddaughter, her daughter, and herself. Furthermore, the law is not only on her side; she *is* the law. Seen in this light, we might read Hannah as, not merely antidote, but rather as remedy, poison, and scapegoat – the mad witch at the margins of the plantation, the vengeful shadow of the Haitian

[64] For an example of one such song, see Laurent and Josué, "Le vodou, miroir de l'histoire." Cited in "Afro-Atlantic Music as Archive," paper for *Africa N'Ko: La bibliothèque coloniale en débat.*

[65] Hopkins, *Of One Blood*, 604. [66] Ibid., 603. [67] Ibid., 603.

[68] On the significance of crossroads in Haitian Vodou, see Rigaud, *Secrets of Vodou.*

[69] Kassanoff, "Fate," 176. [70] Hopkins, *Of One Blood*, 613.

Revolution, and the restorative hand of justice that quietly redresses the intergenerational trauma of racial-sexual suffering.

Through this modest figure of cosmic justice, the past erupts from the narrative like an originary wound: at once a reliquary old woman of the plantation and a distant shadow of an "African princess,"[71] Hannah punctuates the postemancipation present with vast, incommensurate, and overlapping temporal scales. Yet, even as Hannah harnesses the past, both near and distant, she also guides the reader forward. Vengeance – as the Haitian Revolution reminds us – looks simultaneously backward and forward, through its potential to redress historical injustice. Hannah is as much of the past as she is of the future, both an early victim of antebellum violence and a cosmic springboard into a pan-African utopian future. Indeed, she is the only African-American character (besides Reuel) in the novel to gain entrance to Telassar: "Briggs returned to the Hidden City with his faithful subjects, and old Aunt Hannah."[72] Moreover, Hannah returns to Telassar not *qua* grandmother nor even "faithful subject" – in fact, it is unclear whether Reuel realizes his relation to Hannah is one of blood, rather than "of one blood" – but instead as emissary of an as yet unacknowledged state of subterranean female sovereignty.

What would it mean to think of Hannah as diplomat, princess, or judge, rather than Hannah as grandmother? Although the narrative invests in fictions of maternity, it also subverts the logics of descent. Structurally, the narrative exposition of the Dianthe–Mira–Hannah family unravels the matrilineal line. Hopkins not only pushes the narrative backward in time (the originary matriarch does not make an appearance until the final pages of the novel) but also refuses the kind of linear chronology which governed the reproductive energy logics of slave holding economies. Instead, ghosts, visions, and specters rustle through the pages of the novel, punctuating the imperialist drive of Reuel's African mission with the persistent tug of slavery's past. The traumatic reverberations of racial-sexual violence unfix linear genealogical structures, even as they offer alternative modes of kinship within the temporally unbound triad of female figures. Mira is a future-oriented prophet, as well as a ghost heavy with the past. Hannah collapses the linear familial structure altogether, both revealing the origins of the novel's incest plot and moving beyond, into the future fields of Telassar. It is not for nothing that Dianthe addresses Hannah as "Aunt," "Mother," and "Granny" at various points in the final scenes. Not unlike the "locus of confounded identities" that Hortense Spillers catalogs in the

[71] Ibid., 603. [72] Ibid., 621.

opening of her pivotal essay "Mama's Baby, Papa's Maybe," she inhabits all these roles, and perhaps more, for Hannah embodies a form of kinship that cannot be contained within a fixed temporal frame. Yet, this act of unmothering creates new possibilities of relation. Hannah and Dianthe share the most – perhaps the only – intimate relationship in the novel, however their affective bonds, I would argue, run deeper than sentimental tropes of family reunion with their facile promises of bourgeois restoration.

Instead, these scenes of care between women reappropriate the painful movements of magnetism, converting violatory possession at the hands of white enslavers into a realm of collective healing. Hannah first appears as a mesmeric force. When she invites her lost granddaughter to rest in her home, Dianthe "obeyed without a murmur; in truth, she seemed again to have lost her own will in another's.[73] In effect, Hannah mesmerizes Dianthe with narrative. Listening to her grandmother's disclosure of the novel's incestuous backstory, Dianthe is "like a stone woman"[74] and suffers "some hideous trance."[75] But unlike the invasive force we see in Reuel or Livingston, Hannah suffers with her granddaughter. She "moans and rocks and weeps"[76] as though in "physical pain."[77] This shared pain is predicated on violence, but the novel reminds us that other forms of relation exist. As we saw in Chapter 1, Vodou "possessions" are not experienced as proprietary invasions of individual bodies but instead generate what Colin Dayan has called a "collective physical remembrance" that commemorates sexual violence, or, as Dayan euphemistically puts it, what was "most often experienced by women under another name, something called 'love."[78] Standing upon this memory of false and violent "love," the two women are not old grandmother and young granddaughter, wise woman and naïve child, but instead two survivors meeting on the same ground. This meeting upends conventional hierarchies and linear models of descent, eroding the borders of personal identity. The youthful Dianthe is said to grow as old as a grandmother: "bending a little, as though very weak, and leaning heavily upon her old grandmother's arm . . . [h]er face was lined and old with suffering."[79] And it is only after this "possession" that Dianthe, perhaps under the influence of Hannah's supernatural justice, is compelled to poison Livingston. Even the forms of their resistance are similar: Dianthe silently exchanges one glass of water for another, not unlike the way Hannah slipped one baby into the place of another.

[73] Ibid., 603. [74] Ibid., 606. [75] Ibid., 607. [76] Ibid., 606. [77] Ibid., 604.
[78] Dayan, *Haiti, History, and the Gods*, 56. [79] Hopkins, *Of One Blood*, 607.

I would therefore suggest that the women of the novel defy the ideologies of True Womanhood so often attributed to Hopkins.[80] Rather than enshrine the mother under the auspices of bourgeois respectability, Hopkins instead imagines a world with different forms of mothering.[81] In doing so, Hopkins respects the long birth pangs of history, or Hartman's "belly of the world," while also imagining alternative forms of kinship that operate outside the speculative value of reproducible racial capital.[82] It is not for nothing, I believe, that in the last scene between Hannah and Dianthe, the former is not a grandmother but instead "Old Aunt Hannah" and the latter is not a granddaughter but "the dying girl."[83] Unbound from the language of linear descent, Hopkins instead gestures to a way of loving that registers, without hierarchizing, both past and future and that fosters alternative forms of kinship, relation, and care.

Underneath racist misogynistic narratives of the transfixed, prone, and mesmerized female subject flows not only a current of insurrection but also a radical rejection of reproductive logics and the politics of energy which underwrote them. The time-traveling, continent-hopping "old Aunt Hannah" may, in this respect, be seen as a fugitive interlocutor, although not quite an answer, to Hartman's question: "Where does the impossible domestic fit into the general strike? What is the text of her insurgency and the genre of her refusal? What visions of the future world encourage her to run or propel her flight?"[84] We do not see Hannah's life in Telassar, and I am not sure we can assign her a "text" or "genre," but we do see this recalcitrant "impossible domestic" flourish outside the logics of traditional lines of kinship, energy politics, and beyond the imperial geographies of the United States. Both formed by and untethered from violent plantation structures premised on property relations, extraction, profit, and energy consumption, Hannah and her fugitive family instead create alternative forms of energy that unsettle national, temporal, and genealogical lines.

80 Ammons, *Conflicting Stories*; Carby, *Reconstructing Womanhood*; Tate, *Domestic Allegories of Political Desire.*

81 Sharpe, *Wake,* 32.

82 Hartman, "The Belly of the World," 170.

83 Hopkins, *Of One Blood*, 616.

84 Hartman, "The Belly of the World," 171.

Coda
Effluent Futures

In N. K. Jemisin's science fiction short story "The Effluent Engine" (2011), Jessaline, a Haitian spy and "natural" daughter of Toussaint Louverture, arrives in New Orleans in the early years of Haitian independence. Her world is both like and unlike our own: in the tale, Haitians have learned to convert gases from sugarcane distilleries into fuel for airships. Turning "our torment to our advantage," as Jessaline puts it, Haiti effectively bombed French ships to win the Revolution; became the world's leading manufacturer of dirigibles; and secured diplomatic standing in the United States, even constructing an embassy in New Orleans.[1] And yet, despite Haiti's steampunkesque political and technological power, there is much in "The Effluent Engine" that recalls a less optimistic history. The French are still "hell-bent upon re-enslaving" the nascent republic; although the United States begrudgingly recognizes Haiti, it remains "the stuff of American nightmare"; and Jessaline confronts white supremacist terrorism and the threat of racial-sexual violence in the US South, where she fights the Order of the White Camellia.

Jessaline's mission in New Orleans is to make contact with a wealthy engineer, a Louisiana-born *homme de couleur* whose experiments may help Haitians refine an extraction process that would convert rum effluent into methane. Yet, the engineer proves to be useless: the true brains behind the operation is his sister, the untrained but brilliant scientist Eugenie Rillieux, who promptly agrees to design the technology that would allow for this extraction process and thus "help a nation of free folk *stay* free."[2] Eugenie's interest in Haitian sovereignty is compounded by an overwhelming (and enthusiastically reciprocated) attraction she feels for Jessaline. With frankly sensual language of flushed cheeks, licking lips, and "sweetest, wildest" kisses, Jemisin allows for an unabashedly queer narrative *eros*, which places Black women's desire at the center of Haitian sovereignty and Atlantic

[1] Jemisin, "The Effluent Engine" in *How Long 'til Black Future Month*, 92. [2] Ibid.

modernity.[3] The tale ends with the two women escaping to Port-au-Prince where Eugenie vows, between passionate embraces with Jessaline, to rebuild her methane extractor, protect Haiti's independence, and marry her lover.

"The Effluent Engine" powerfully inverts – or, to use a more appropriately energetic vocabulary, *converts* – a host of negative stereotypes surrounding Haiti. Far from an island mired in disaster, Haiti instead stands as a beacon of hope to African-Americans, who cluster around the Haitian embassy in New Orleans, "gazing enviously"[4]; the two female protagonists seek refuge in Haiti, thus inverting contemporary clichés of impoverished victims and asylum seekers; parodying the typical seduction narrative of heterosexual spy novels, Jemisin presents Jessaline's and Eugenie's desire as not a conquest but a negotiation between two equally powerful parties; and rather than reproducing traditional patriarchal structures of state power, Jessaline makes clear that women in Haiti "run factories and farms," are "highly placed in government," and ascend to positions of spiritual power ("the houngans are mostly women now")[5].

Published two years after the earthquake that devastated Port-au-Prince and six years after Hurricane Katrina, Jemisin's tale of love between women and shared political power between Haiti and New Orleans stands in stark contrast to the after-tremors of disaster capitalism and neoliberal managerial strategies of containment masquerading as "relief." In this respect, Jemisin's tale echoes Deborah Jenson's injunction to refuse the metonymic association of Haiti with disaster. This association, in Jenson's words, "unintentionally closes the loop with that earlier tradition regarding the advent of a black state as disaster, and replaces a whole national tradition with a kind of apocalyptic signifier, as if nothing were there but what might replace it . . . Haiti, dear Haiti, no matter how tested and remapped by disaster, is not, in itself, disaster."[6] Instead, Jemisin renarrates a history of energy that operates outside of global northern markets and neocolonial intervention. "The Effluent Engine" is a tale of the Haitian Revolution, but it is also a tale of energy injustice throughout Haitian and Louisiana history: it reverberates along nodes that evoke at once the systematic deforestation of Hispaniola; the Clinton-era energy embargo of Haiti; the outdated and irresilient power grid in Louisiana; the boom and bust cycle of jatropha; and it anticipates the Petrocaribe crisis; the gas shortage experienced in Louisiana following Hurricane Ida; and many other contemporary forms of energy injustice. And yet, Jemisin refuses to reproduce the dehumanizing tropes of alterity that rhetorically repudiate

[3] ibid, 109. [4] ibid, 100. [5] ibid, 95. [6] Jenson, "The Writing of Disaster in Haiti," 111.

Black sovereignty. Her counterhistory instead asks how this deep timeline of energy exploitation might be reconfigured and renarrated from the standpoint of a temporally complex cartography of political sovereignty, queer desire, and modern alliances between US and Caribbean people of African descent.

I turn to Jemisin's tale in these final pages to emphasize the role fiction might play in establishing this alternative cartography of modernity. While some of the stories recounted in this study are clearly fictional (for example, *Of One Blood* or "Theresa"), others are told from deeply compromised archival forms. However, counterhistories, such as Jemisin's "Effluent Engine," collapse the distinction between the archive and the fictive. As such, they offer a methodology for not only rethinking the past but also interrogating, in the words of Ann Laura Stoler, "the conditions of possibility that shaped what could be written . . . what stories [could and] could not be told, and what [could and] could not be said."[7] We might even think of the history of Haiti itself as a counterhistory, articulated, by Michel Rolph Trouillot, in the language of fantastical or speculative fiction as "unimaginable" and "unthinkable"; what Glissant might call an "imposed nonhistory"; or what Hartman has described as "an asterisk in the grand narrative of history."[8] A history of alternative energy practices is not easily discerned within conventional methods of historiographical narration because it refuses the very logics that would make energy legible to a global northern audience. Hemispheric counterhistory – speculative, fleeting, and gesturing toward other futures – reconfigures the past as a dynamic force that continues to shape political and social struggles. As Brian Connolly and Marisa Fuentes have argued, "we might begin to see here that the production and constitution of 'a really livable world' emerges out of the archives of domination and their incomplete trajectories."[9] These incomplete trajectories are not only a lamentable gap but also a starting point for a more equitable way of inhabiting the world.

The brilliance of Jemisin's tale is that although certain plot points are obviously fabulated, many of these energy "conversions" are grounded in fact. As this book has shown, Black people throughout the Americas asserted spiritual and political power, albeit often extrainstitutionally; Haiti inspired freedom practices in people of African descent across the diaspora; and women and gender-variant people forged connections that

7 Stoler, "Colonial Archives and the Arts of Governance," 91.
8 Glissant, *Discours Antillais*; Hartman, "Venus"; and Trouillot; *Silencing*.
9 Connolly and Fuentes, "Introduction," 114.

subverted traditional heteropatriarchal structures of power. While traditional narratives of capitalist modernity focus on processes of extraction, commodification, and the subjugation of Black bodies, Jemisin's story redefines modernity outside the scope of global northern markets, capital accrual, and white supremacist violence. Instead, it assembles an archive of Black modernity that reclaims energy for practices founded in principles of mutual care and support rather than the extractive logics of capitalist consumption and expenditure.

In this respect, Jemisin's counterhistory – and I hope this project as well – contributes to reassessments of modernity in a Black Atlantic, hemispheric, and trans-American framework. Since Paul Gilroy's groundbreaking *Black Atlantic*, the paradigm of modernity has been central to narratives of Black life and culture in the Americas. Contesting the parochialism ascribed to national identities, Gilroy instead argues for an Atlantic subjectivity within a "webbed network" of interactions "between the local and the global" that constituted what we now signify as the modern, or, in Gilroy's words, "the concentrated intensity of the slave experience is something that marked out Blacks as the first truly modern people."[10] While the Black Atlantic paradigm has generated lively debate in the past three decades, it has laid the groundwork for reappraisals of modernity, disputing assumptions that would distinguish between the margin and the center, the colonial periphery and the European metropole, and the modern and the subaltern.[11] Gilroy's work has particularly influenced Caribbeanist scholars who have extended the Black Atlantic into reappraisals of the Haitian Revolution, reading the independence of the first Black republic as a uniquely modern event that shaped and

[10] Gilroy, *The Black Atlantic* 221.

[11] Since the publication of *The Black Atlantic*, critics have put pressure on Gilroy's privileging of the U.S. expanding the black Atlantic consciousness to a wider range of diasporic experiences. This expansion includes influential paradigms such as the Black Pacific (Shilliam, *The Black Pacific;* Taketani, *The Black Pacific Narrative;* and Weaver, *The Red Atlantic)* as well as attention to linguistic difference within the diaspora (Edwards, *The Practice of Diaspora)*. Other critics have questioned Gilroy's dismissal of the nation-state more generally, drawing criticism toward theories of "hybridity" in postcolonial studies (Giles' *Transatlantic Insurrections;* Puri, *The Caribbean Postcolonial*). Still others have insisted on the importance of the global structures of finance capital, which complicate Gilroy's abstractionist paradigm (Lazarus, "Nationalism and Cultural Practice in the Postcolonial World"; and Rothberg, "Small Acts, Global Acts"). Critics have also argued for a more capacious understanding of gender and sexuality in the Black Atlantic paradigm (Pinto, *Difficult Diasporas;* Schindler, "Home, or the Limits of the Black Atlantic"; and Tinsley, "Black Atlantic, Queer Atlantic"). For a pithy summary of some of these critiques, I turn to Hortense Spillers: "Actually what I think about the Black Atlantic is that it really is a very close funky little room with all the men in it and they're all speaking English" ("Whatcha Gonna Do?" 305).

unsettled the dominant paradigm of Enlightenment thought. Certain scholars, such as Susan Buck-Morss and Nick Nesbitt, have emphasized the mutual constitution of Haiti and European Enlightenment traditions, for example, in the theorization of the Hegelian dialectic or Spinozan conception of universal emancipation.[12] Other scholars, such as Marlene Daut, have convincingly argued for the inclusion of Haitian thinkers, such as the Baron de Vastey, within the Enlightenment canon, constituting what Daut has called "Black Atlantic humanism."[13] Others, including David Scott, have put pressure on the exclusionary function of the human in ideologies of modernity, and with it assumptions about teleological progress and linear self-determination. As Scott argues, in his reading of C.L.R. James's *Black Jacobins*: "[t]he lives of the African slaves. . .had been irrevocably transformed in a modern direction by the relations of power of New World plantation slavery. The choice, insofar as there was a choice, it was not between modernity and something else, but within modernity."[14] What Scott influentially calls a "conscription" into modernity reveals the ways in which Haitian revolutionaries, and more broadly Black freedom fighters in the Atlantic world, were both constituted by and transformed within dehumanizing systems of power relations often aligned with the modern. Or, as Sybille Fisher argues, "Would it not be surprising if the distinctively modern form of oppression and exploitation that developed in the Caribbean left no traces in people's everyday lives, their idea of liberation, and their practices of resistance?"[15]

This book has attempted to contributes to this lineage of political thought, dislodging the jurisdiction of the modern from white European intellectual history. Yet, unlike these important studies, *Energies of Resistance* has departed from institutional histories, which would locate the modern in the state, traditional philosophy, or as a precursor to late capitalist exploitation. Instead, I have foregrounded energy practices – rootwork, prophecy, midwifery, possession, or appeals to God - typically dismissed as pastoral, premodern, domestic, queer, or feminine. Bringing Black Atlantic critiques of modernity into the burgeoning discourse of the energy humanities, this project aims to destabilize assumptions about developmental progress, supply, demand, and consumption now considered constitutive of the supposedly "modern" anthropocene. I thus look

[12] Buck-Morss, *Hegel, Haiti and Universal History*; Nesbitt, *Universal Emancipation*. See also Dubois, *Avengers of the New World;* Garraway, *Tree of Liberty*; Jean-Marie, "Kant and Trouillot on the Unthinkability of the Haitian Revolution; and Popkin, *You Are All Free*.

[13] Daut, *Baron de Vastey and the Origins of Black Atlantic.*

[14] Scott, *Conscripts of Modernity,* 164.

[15] Fisher, *Modernity Disavowed,* 12.

beyond the electric grid, the extraction of fossil fuels, or the exploitation of Black people's bodies and instead toward the rustling gods and spirits, the caring medicine women and priestesses, the burgeoning plants and poisons, the future-oriented prophets, and – in the case of Jemisin – the spies, scientists, and lovers – who redirected their power away from the violent demands of white supremacist, capitalist ideologies.

In doing so, I hope to dislodge the recalcitrance of these ideologies, rescripting the seemingly constrained and gendered local on a global scale. In emphasizing Black women's political and spiritual labor, we can adumbrate an alternative epistemology of energy: one not premised on violent extraction but on collective action, communal ties, and political and spiritual labor. People of African descent found ways to resist the synecdochal violence that broke them into bellies, wombs, and the detritus of reproductive capital. These acts of resistance were carried out on scales large and small: from the constrained corners of the garden plot to the expansive circuits of global migration. Cultivating poison and medicine, reclaiming their bodily economies through rootwork, midwifery, and appeals to God, channeling the divine through acts of possession and prophecy, the subjects of this book made claims to self-sovereignty, redefined kinship, and protected their bodies from the violence of white ideologies through alternative forms of energy. When we unsuture the concept of energy from narratives of capital accrual, global expansion, and commercial consumption, new stories become legible, stories that center Black women at the heart of a pulsating, revolutionary world.

Bibliography

Accomando, Christina, "Demanding a Voice among the Pettifoggers: Sojourner Truth as Legal Actor," *MELUS* 28:1 (2003), 61–86.

Adams, Katherine, *Owning Up: Privacy, Property, and Belonging in U.S. Women's Life Writing, 1840–1890* (New York: Oxford University Press, 2009).

Adebimpe, Victor R., "American Blacks and Psychiatry," *Transcultural Psychiatric Research Review* 21:2 (1984), 83–111.

Africanus, *Freedom's Journal*, October 12, 1827.

Aimwell, Absalom, "'*Pinkster Ode* for the Year *1803:* Most Respectfully Dedicated to Carolus Africanus, Rex,' in Geraldine R. Pleat and Agnes N. Underwood, *Pinkster Ode*, Albany. *1803*," *New York Folklore Quarterly* 8 (1952), 31–45.

Albanese, Mary Grace, "Caribbean Visions: Revolutionary Mysticism in 'Theresa, A Haytien Tale'," *ESQ* 62:4 (2016), 569–609.

Aljoe, Nicole N., "Aria for Ethiopia: The Operatic Aesthetic of Pauline Hopkins's *Of One Blood*," *African American Review* 45:3 (Fall 2012), 277–90.

Alexander, M. Jacqui, *Pedagogies of Crossing: Meditations on Feminism, Sexual Politics, Memory, and the Sacred* (Durham: Duke University Press, 2005).

Allain, J. M., "Infanticide as Slave Resistance: Evidence from Barbados, Jamaica, and Saint-Domingue," *Inquiries Journal/Student Pulse* 6:4 (2014).

Allende, Isabel, *El Zorro: Comienza la leyenda* (Barcelona: Plaza & Janés, 2005).

Allewaert, Monique, "The Geopolitics and Tropologies of the American Turn," in Hester Blum (ed.), *Turns of Event: Nineteenth-Century American Literary Studies in Motion* (Philadelphia: University of Pennsylvania Press, 2016), 111–126.

Ammons, Elizabeth, *Conflicting Stories: American Women Writers at the Turn into the Twentieth Century* (New York: Oxford University Press, 1992).

Amuchie, Nnennaya, "'The Forgotten Victims': How Racialized Gender Stereotypes Lead to Police Violence against Black Women and Girls: Incorporating an Analysis of Police Violence into Feminist Jurisprudence and Community Activism," *Seattle Journal for Social Justice* 14:3 (2016), 617–668.

Andrews, William L. (ed.), *Sisters of the Spirit: Three Black Women's Autobiographies of the Nineteenth Century* (Bloomington: Indiana University Press, 1986).

Armstead, Myra B. Young (ed.), *Mighty Change, Tall Within: Black Identity in the Hudson Valley* (Albany: State University of New York Press, 2003).

Aslakson, Kenneth R., *Making Race in the Courtroom: The Legal Construction of Three Races in Early New Orleans* (New York: New York University Press, 2014).

"The 'Quadroon-Plaçage' Myth of Antebellum New Orleans: Anglo-American (Mis)interpretations of a French-Caribbean Phenomenon," *Journal of Social History* 45:3 (Spring 2012), 709–34.

Aubert, Guillaume, "'To Establish One Law and Definite Rules': Race, Religions and the Transatlantic Origins of the Louisiana Code Noir," in Cécile Vidal (ed.), *Louisiana: Crossroads of the Atlantic World* (Philadelphia: University of Pennsylvania Press, 2014), 21–43.

Bacon, Jacqueline, *Freedom's Journal: The First African American Newspaper* (Lanham, MD: Lexington Books, 2007).

Baer, Hans A., "Prophets and Advisors in Black Spiritual Churches: Therapy, Palliative, or Opiate?" *Culture, Medicine and Psychiatry* 5:1 (1981), 145–70.

Bailey, Eric J., "Hypertension: An Analysis of Detroit African American Health Care Treatment Patterns," *Human Organization* 50:3 (1991), 287–96.

Bailey, Moya, *Misogynoir Transformed: Black Women's Digital Resistance* (New York: New York University Press, 2020).

Bannister, C., "Meddlesome Midwifery," *Boston Medical and Surgical Journal* (1849), 339–40.

Bao, Junzhe, Li, Xudong, and Yu, Chuanhua, "The Construction and Validation of the Heat Vulnerability Index: A Review," *International Journal of Environmental Research and Public Health* 12:7 (2015), 7220–34.

Barnett, Ross, and Worden, Daniel (eds.), *Oil Culture* (Minneapolis: University of Minnesota Press, 2014).

Baucom, Ian, *Specters of the Atlantic: Finance Capital, Slavery, and the Philosophy of History* (Durham, NC: Duke University Press, 2005).

Bauer, Raymond A., and Bauer, Alice H., "Day to Day Resistance to Slavery," in Paul Finkelman (ed.), *Rebellions, Resistance, and Runaways within the Slave South* (New York and London: Garland Publishing, 1989), 388–419.

Beauvoir, Max, "Herbs and Energy: The Holistic Medical System of the Haitian People," in Patrick Bellegarde-Smith and Claudine Michel (eds.), *Haitian Vodou: Spirit, Myth, and Reality* (Bloomington: Indiana University Press, 2006), 112–33.

Beckett, Greg, *There Is No More Haiti: Between Life and Death in Port-au-Prince* (Berkeley: University of California Press, 2019).

Beckles, Hilary, "Freeing Slavery: Gender Paradigms in the Social History of Caribbean Slavery," in Brian L. Moore, B. W. Higman, Carl Campbell, and Patrick Bryan (eds.), *Slavery, Freedom and Gender: The Dynamics of Caribbean Society* (Kingston: University of the West Indies Press, 2003), 197–231.

Bellegarde, Dantes, *Histoire du peuple haitien (1492–1952)* (Port-au-Prince: Librairie Larose, 1951).

Bellegarde-Smith, Patrick, and Michel, Claudine, "Danbala/Ayida as Cosmic Prism: The Lwa as Trope for Understanding Metaphysics in Haitian Vodou and Beyond," *Journal of Africana Religions* 1:4 (2013), 458–9.

Benz, Ernst, *The Theology of Electricity: On the Encounter and Explanation of Theology and Science in the 17th and 18th Centuries* (Eugene, OR: Wipf and Stock, 1989).

Bergman, Jill, "The Motherless Child in Pauline Hopkins's *Of One Blood*," *Legacy* 2:2 (2008), 286–98.

Berlin, Ira, and Morgan, Philip D. (eds.), *The Slaves' Economy: Independent Production by Slaves in the Americas* (London: Frank Cass, 1991).

Berman, Carolyn, *Creole Crossings: Domestic Reform and the Reform of Colonial Slavery* (Ithaca, NY: Cornell University Press, 2005), 144–69.

Bernier, Celeste-Marie, *Characters of Blood: Black Heroism in the Transatlantic Imagination* (Charlottesville: University of Virginia Press, 2012).

Berry, Daina Ramey, and Harris, Leslie Maria (eds.), *Sexuality and Slavery: Reclaiming Intimate Histories in the Americas* (Athens: University of Georgia Press, 2018).

Blackburn, Robin, *The Overthrow of Colonial Slavery 1776–1848* (New York and London: Verso, 2011).

Boisvert, Jayne, "Colonial Hell and Female Slave Resistance in Saint-Domingue," *Journal of Haitian Studies* 7:1 (Spring 2001), 61–76.

Boyce Davies, Carole, "Sisters Outside: Tracing the Caribbean/Black Radical Intellectual Tradition," *Small Axe* 13:1 (2009), 217–29.

Boyer, Dominic, *Energopolitics: Wind and Power in the Anthropocene* (Durham, NC: Duke University Press, 2019).

Boyer, Dominic, and Szeman, Imre (eds.), *Energy Humanities: An Anthology* (Baltimore: Johns Hopkins University Press, 2017).

Boyer, Jean-Pierre, "'Perfectly Proper and Conciliating': Jean-Pierre Boyer, Freemasonry, and the Revolutionary Atlantic in Eastern Connecticut, 1800–1801," *Atlantic Studies* 16:3 (2019), 364–85.

Braude, Ann, *Radical Spirits: Spiritualism and Women's Rights in Nineteenth-Century America* (Bloomington: Indiana University Press, 1989).

Braziel, Jana Evans, "*Atis Rezistans* (Resistance Artists): Vodou Street Sculpture at the Grand Rue, Port-au-Prince," *Callaloo* 39:2 (2016), 419–37.

"Re-membering Défilé: Dédée Bazile as Revolutionary *Lieu de Mémoire*," *Small Axe* 9:2 (2005), 57–85.

Brécy, Robert, "La chanson révolutionnaire de 1789 à 1799," *Annales historiques de la Révolution française* No. 244 (1981), 279–303.

Brickell, D. Warren, "Introductory Lecture Delivered by D. Warren Brickell M.D.," November 3, 1857" (New Orleans: Bulletin Office, 1857).

"Two Cases of Vesico Vaginal Fistula Cured," *New Orleans Medical News and Hospital Gazette* 5 (November 1858), 577–585.

Brickhouse, Anna, *Transamerican Literary Relations and the Nineteenth-Century Public Sphere* (New York: Cambridge University Press, 2004).
Brodie, Janet Farrell, *Contraception and Abortion in Nineteenth-Century America* (Ithaca: Cornell University Press, 1994).
Brooks, Daphne, *Bodies in Dissent: Spectacular Performances of Race and Freedom, 1850–1910* (Durham, NC: Duke University Press, 2006).
Bodies in Dissent: Spectacular Performances of Race and Freedom, 1850–1910 (Princeton: Princeton University Press, 2007).
Brooks, David, "The Underlying Tragedy," *New York Times*, January 15, 2010.
Brown, Kimberly Juanita, *The Repeating Body: Slavery's Visual Resonance in the Contemporary* (Durham, NC: Duke University Press, 2015).
Brown, Lois, *Pauline Elizabeth Hopkins: Black Daughter of the Revolution* (Chapel Hill: University of North Carolina Press, 2012).
Brown-Glaude, Winnifred R., *Higglers in Kingston: Women's Informal Work in Jamaica* (Nashville: Vanderbilt University Press, 2011).
Buck-Morss, Susan, *Hegel, Haiti and Universal History* (Pittsburgh: University of Pittsburgh Press, 2012).
Buckridge, Steven, *African Lace-Bark in the Caribbean: The Construction of Race, Class, and Gender* (London: Bloomsbury Publishing, 2016).
Bush, Robert D., *The Louisiana Purchase: A Global Context* (New York: Routledge, 2013).
Bush-Slimani, Barbara, "Hard Labour: Women, Childbirth and Resistance in British Caribbean Slave Societies," *History Workshop Journal* 36:1 (1993), 83–99.
Byrd, Brandon. *The Black Republic: African Americans and the Fate of Haiti* (Philadelphia: University of Pennsylvania Press, 2019).
Cable, George Washington, "Creole Slave Songs," *The Century Magazine* 13:6 (April 1886).
The Grandissimes: A Story of Creole Life (New York: Charles Scribner's Sons, 1887).
Camp, Stephanie M. H., *Closer to Freedom: Enslaved Women and Everyday Resistance in the Plantation South* (Chapel Hill: University of North Carolina Press, 2004).
Campbell, James T., *Songs of Zion: The African Methodist Episcopal Church in the United States and South Africa* (Oxford: Oxford University Press, 1995).
Carby, Hazel, *Reconstructing Womanhood: The Emergence of the Afro-American Woman Novelist* (Oxford: Oxford University Press, 1989).
Castronovo, Russ, "The Antislavery Unconscious: Mesmerism, Vodun, and 'Equality'," *The Mississippi Quarterly* 53:1 (Winter 1999/2000), 41–56.
Cervenak, Sarah Jane, *Wandering Philosophical Performances of Racial and Sexual Freedom* (Durham: Duke University Press, 2014).
Césaire, Aimé, "La forêt vierge," in Jean-Paul Césaire (ed.), *Oeuvres complètes: Poèmes* (Fort de France, Martinique: Éditions Désormeaux,1976), 110.
Cahier d'un retour au pays natal (Paris: Présence Africaine, 1956).

"Les chiens se taisaient," in *Les armes miraculeuses* (Paris: Gallimard, 1970), 56.

Chakrabarty, Dipesh, "The Climate of History: Four Theses," *Critical Inquiry* 35:2 (Winter 2009), 197–222.

Chapman, Dasha, Durban-Albrecht, Erin L. and LaMothe, Mario, Introduction to "*Nou Mache Ansanm* (We Walk Together): Queer Haitian Performance and Affiliation," *Women & Performance* 27:2 (2017), 143–59.

Child, Lydia Maria, "Letter XI, April 7, 1844," in *Letters from New York*, 11th ed. (New York: C.S. Francis, 1850).

Chesnutt, Charles W., *Paul Marchand, F.M.C.* (Oxford: University of Mississippi Press, 1998).

Clarke, Vèvè A., "Developing Diaspora Literacy and Marasa Consciousness," *Theatre Survey* 50:1 (May 2009), 9–18.

Clavin, Matthew, *Toussaint Louverture and the American Civil War: The Promise and Peril of a Second Haitian Revolution* (Philadelphia: University of Pennsylvania Press, 2012).

Cole, Jean Lee, "Theresa and Blake: Mobility and Resistance in Antebellum African American Serialized Fiction," *Callaloo* 34:1 (Winter, 2011), 158–75.

Collins, Patricia Hill, *Fighting Words: Black Women and the Search for Justice* (Minneapolis: University of Minnesota Press, 1998).

Connolly, Brian, and Fuentes, Marisa, "Introduction: From Archives of Slavery to Liberated Futures?," *History of the Present* 6:2 (Fall 2016), 105–16.

Copeland, M. Shawn, *Enfleshing Freedom: Body, Race and Being* (Minneapolis: Fortress, 2008).

"'Wading through Many Sorrows': Toward a Theology of Suffering in a Womanist Perspective," in Charles Curran, Margaret Farley, and Richard McCormick (eds.), *Feminist Ethics and the Catholic Moral Tradition* (Mahwah: Paulist Press, 1996), 136–63.

Cordell, Sigrid Anderson, "'The Case Was Very Black Against Her': Pauline Hopkins and the Politics of Racial Ambiguity at the Colored American Magazine," *American Periodicals: A Journal of History and Criticism* 16:1 (2006), 52–73.

Covey, Herbert C., *African American Slave Medicine: Herbal and Non-Herbal Treatments* (New York: Lexington Books, 2007).

Coviello, Peter, *Tomorrow's Parties: Sex and the Untimely in Nineteenth-Century America* (New York: New York University Press, 2013).

Cowling, Camillia, Machado, Maria Helena Pereira Toledo, Paton, Diana, and West, Emily (eds.), *Motherhood, Childlessness and the Care of Children in Atlantic Slave Societies* (New York: Routledge, 2020).

Crabtree, Adam, *From Mesmer to Freud: Magnetic Sleep and the Roots of Psychological Healing* (New Haven: Yale University Press, 1993).

Crooks, Mark, "On the Psychology of Demon Possession: The Occult Personality," *The Journal of Mind and Behavior* 39:4 (2018), 257–344.

Crosby, Sara L., *The Poisonous Muse: The Female Poisoner and the Framing of Popular Authorship in Jacksonian America* (Iowa City: University of Iowa Press, 2016).

Dagget, Cara New, *The Birth of Energy* (Durham: Duke University Press, 2019).

Dalmas, Antoine, *Histoire de la révolution de Saint-Domingue* (Paris: Chez Mame Frères, 1814).

Daniels, Jason "Recovering the Fugitive History of Marronage," *Journal of Caribbean History* 46:2 (2012), 121–53.

Danticat, Edwidge, "We Are Ugly But We Are Here," *The Caribbean Writer* 10 (1996) www2.webster.edu/~corbetre/haiti/literature/danticat-ugly.htm [accessed October23, 2021].

Darnton, Robert, *Mesmerism and the End of the Enlightenment in France* (Cambridge, MA: Harvard University Press, 2009).

Dash, J. Michael, *Culture and Customs of Haiti* (New York: Greenwood, 2000).

Culture and Customs of Haiti (Westport, CT: Greenwood Press, 2001), 70.

Haiti and the United States: National Stereotypes and the Literary Imagination, 2nd ed. (New York: Palgrave Macmillan, 2016).

Daut, Marlene, "'Alpha and Omega' of Haitian Literature: Baron de Vastey and the U.S. Audience of Haitian Political Writing," *Comparative Literature* 64:1 (Winter 2012), 49–72.

Baron de Vastey and the Origins of Black Atlantic Humanism (New York: Palgrave Macmillan, 2017).

"Before Harlem: The Franco-Haitian Grammar of Transnational African American Writing" *J:19 The Journal of Nineteenth Century Americanists* 3:2 (2015), 385–92.

Tropics of Haiti: Race and the Literary History of the Haitian Revolution in the Atlantic World, 1789–1865 (Liverpool: Liverpool University Press, 2015).

Davidson, Marc, "Parallels in Reactionary Argumentation in the US Congressional Debates on the Abolition of Slavery and the Kyoto Protocol," *Climate Change* 86 (2008), 67–82.

Davis, Angela, "Racism, Birth Control, and Reproductive Rights," in Reina Lewis and Sara Mills (eds.), *Feminist Postcolonial Theory: A Reader* (New York: Routledge, 2003), 353–55.

Davies, Thomas, "New York's Black Line: A Note on the Growing Slave Population," *Afro-Americans in New York Life and History* (January 1978).

Davis, Ralph, *The Rise of Atlantic Economies* (Ithaca: Cornell University Press, 1973).

Dayan, Colin, *Haiti, History, and the Gods* (Berkeley: University of California Press, 1998).

Debien, Gabriel, *Les esclaves aux Antilles français aux 17e et 18e siecles* (Basse Terre: Société d'histoire de la Guadeloupe, 1974).

"Marronage in the French Caribbean," in Richard Price (ed.), *Maroon Societies: Rebel Slave Communities in the Americas* (Baltimore: Johns Hopkins University Press, 1996), 107–34.

"Marrons autour du Cap," *Bulletin de l'institut français d'Afrique noir* 27: Série B (1965), 755–99.

Debien, Gabriel and Fouchard, Jean, "Aspects de l'esclavage aux Antilles françaises: le petit marronage à Saint Domingue autour du Cap

(1790–1791)," *Cahiers des Amèriques latines, scène sciences de l'homme* 3 (1969), 31–67.

Delbourgo, James, *A Most Amazing Scene of Wonders: Electricity and Enlightenment in Early America* (Cambridge, MA: Havard University Press, 2006).

Delle, James A., *The Limits of Tyranny* (Nashville: University of Tennessee Press, 2015).

DeLombard, Jeannine Marie, *Slavery on Trial: Law, Abolitionism, and Print Culture* (Chapel Hill: University of North Carolina Press, 2009).

Demangles, Leslie, "The Faces of the Gods," in Philip W. Scher (ed.), *Perspectives on the Caribbean: A Reader in Culture, History, and Representation* (New York: Wiley, 2010), 185–206.

Dewey, Loring Daniel, *Correspondence Relative to the Emigration to Hayti, of the Free People of Colour, in the United States: Together with the Instructions to the Agent Sent Out by President Boyer* (New York: M. Day, Antislavery Pamphlet Collection, UMass Amherst Libraries, 1824).

Dewulf, Jeroen, "The Many Languages of American Literature: Interpreting Sojourner Truth's Narrative (1850) as Dutch-American Contact Literature," *Dutch Crossing: Journal of Low Countries Studies* 38:3 (2014), 220–34.

"Pinkster: An Atlantic Creole Festival in a Dutch-American Context," *The Journal of American Folklore* 126:501 (Summer 2013): 245–71.

"'A Strong Barbaric Accent': America's Dutch-Speaking Black Community from Seventeenth-Century New Netherland to Nineteenth Century New York and New Jersey," *American Speech* 90:2 (2015), 131–53.

The Pinkster King and the King of Kongo: The Forgotten History of America's Dutch-Owned Slaves (Jackson: University of Mississippi Press, 2016).

Diamanti, Jeff, and Bellamy, Brent Ryan (eds.), special "Energy Humanities" issue of *Reviews in Cultural Theory* 6:3 (2016).

Dick, Bruce, and Reed, Ishmael, "A Conversation with Ishmael Reed," in Bruce Dick (ed.), *Conversations with Ishmael Reed* (Westport, CT: Greenwood Press, 1999), 228–50.

Dillon, Catherine, "Voodoo" Unpublished manuscript, Louisiana Writers' Project (1940). Folders 118, 317, 319, Watson Memorial Library, Cammie G. Henry Research Center, Northwestern State University, Natchitoches, Louisiana.

Dillon, Elizabeth Maddock, *New World Drama: The Performative Commons in the Atlantic World, 1649–1849* (Durham: Duke University Press, 2014, 187–201.

Dillon, Elizabeth Maddock, and Drexler, Michael (eds.), *The Haitian Revolution and the Early United States: Histories, Textualities, Geographies* (Philadelphia: University of Pennsylvania Press, 2016).

Diouf, Sylviane A., *Slavery's Exiles: The Story of the American Maroons* (New York: New York University Press, 2014).

Dixon, Chris, *African America and Haiti: Emigration and Black Nationalism in the Nineteenth Century* (Austin: University of Texas Press, 2000).

"Nineteenth-Century African-American Emigrationism: The Failure of the Haitian Alternative," *Western Journal of Black Studies*, 18:2 (1994), 77–92.

Dodson, Jualynne E., *Engendering Church: Women, Power, and the AME Church* (New York: Rowman & Littlefield, 2002).

Dombrowski, Daniel A., and Deltete, Robert John, *A Brief, Liberal, Catholic Defense of Abortion* (Champaign: University of Illinois Press, 2000).

Donaldson, Thomas C., *Walt Whitman: The Man* (New York: Frances P. Harper, 1896).

Dormon, James H., "Louisiana's 'Creoles of Color': Ethnicity, Marginality, and Identity," *Social Science Quarterly* 73 (1992), 615–26.

Doyle, William, *Old Regime France: 1648–1788* (Oxford: Oxford University Press, 2001).

Drake, Kimberly, "Rewriting the American Self: Race, Gender, and Identity in the Autobiographies of Frederick Douglass and Harriet Jacobs," *MELUS* 22:4 (1997), 91–108.

Drew, Kimberly, and Wortham, Jenna (eds.), *Black Futures* (New York: Random House, 2021).

Drexler, Michael J., and White, Ed, "The Constitution of Toussaint: Another Origin of African-American Literature," in Gene Andrew Jarrett (ed.), *Companion to African American Literature* (Chichester, U.K: Wiley-Blackwell, 2010), 59–74.

Dubois, Laurent, *Avengers of the New World: The Story of the Haitian Revolution* (Cambridge, MA: Harvard University Press, 2005).

"The Haitian Revolution and the Sale of Louisiana," *Southern Quarterly* 44:3 (Spring 2007), 18–41.

Dubois, Laurent, and Josué, Erol, "Afro-Atlantic Music as Archive," unpublished paper, *Africa N'Ko: La bibliothèque coloniale en débat.*

"Le vodou, miroir de l'histoire: Dialogue," *Tabou: Revue du Musée d'Ethnologie de Genève* 5 (2007), 325–40.

Dumesle, Hérard, *Voyage dans le Nord d'Hayti* (Les Cayes: Imprimerie du Gouvernement, 1824).

Dun, James Alexander, *Dangerous Neighbors: Making the Haitian Revolution in Early America* (Philadelphia: University of Pennsylvania Press, 2016).

Dworkin, Ira (ed.), *Daughter of the Revolution: The Major Nonfiction Works of Pauline E. Hopkins* (New Brunswick, NJ: Rutgers University Press, 2007).

Edelman, Lee, *No Future: Queer Theory and the Death Drive* (Durham: Duke University Press, 2004).

Eddins, Crystal, "'Rejoice! Your Wombs Will Not Beget Slaves!' Marronnage as Reproductive Justice in Colonial Haiti," *Gender & History* 23:3 (October 2020), 562–80.

Edwards, Brent, *The Practice of Diaspora: Literature, Translation, and the Rise of Black Internationalism* (Cambridge, MA: Harvard University Press, 2003).

Ellenberger, Henri, *The Discovery of the Unconscious: The History and Evolution of Dynamic Psychiatry* (New York: Basic Books, 1973).

Ernest, John, "The Floating Icon and the Fluid Text: Rereading the Narrative of Sojourner Truth," *American Literature* 78:3 (2006), 459–486.

Faber, Eberhard L., *Building the Land of Dreams: New Orleans and the Transformation of Early America* (Princeton: Princeton University Press, 2018).

Fandrich, Ina Johanna. "Defiant African Sisterhoods: The Voodoo Arrests of the 1850s and 1860s in New Orleans," in Patrick Bellegarde-Smith (ed.), *Fragments of Bone: Neo-African Religions in a New World* (Urbana: University of Illinois Press, 2005), 187–207.

The Mysterious Voodoo Queen, Marie Laveaux: A Study of Powerful Female Leadership in Nineteenth-Century New Orleans (New York: Routledge, 2005).

Fanning, Sara, *Caribbean Crossing: African Americans and the Haitian Emigration Movement* (New York: New York University Press, 2015).

Fanon, Frantz, *Peau noire, masques blancs* (Paris: Éditions du Seuil, 1952).

Farclough, Mary, *Literature, Electricity and Politics 1740–1840: 'Electrick Communication Every Where'* (London: Palgrave Macmillan, 2017).

Fett, Sharla M., *Working Cures: Healing, Health, and Power on Southern Slave Plantations* (Chapel Hill, NC: University of North Carolina Press, 2002).

Fick, Carolyn, *The Making of Haiti: The Saint Domingue Revolution from Below* (Nashville: University of Tennessee Press, 1990).

Field, Corinne C., *The Struggle for Equal Adulthood: Gender, Race, Age, and the Fight for Citizenship in Antebellum America* (Chapel Hill: University of North Carolina Press, 2014).

Fischer, Sibylle, "Bolivar in Haiti: Republicanism the Revolutionary Atlantic," in Clevis Headley, Carla Calarge, Raphael Dalleo, and Luis Duno-Gottberg (eds.), *Haiti in the Americas* (Jackson: University Press of Mississippi, 2013), 25–54.

Modernity Disavowed: Haiti and Culture of Slavery in the Age of Revolution (Durham: Duke University Press, 2004).

Fleurant, Gerdès, *Dancing Spirits: Rhythms and Rituals of Haitian Vodun, the Rada Rite* (Westport, CT and London: Greenwood Press, 1996).

Foote, Thelma Wills, *Black and White Manhattan: The History of Racial Formation in Colonial New York City* (New York: Oxford University Press, 2004), 133–38.

Foreman, P. Gabrielle, *Activist Sentiments: Reading Black Women in the Nineteenth Century* (Urbana: University of Illinois Press, 2009).

Foster, Frances Smith, "Forgotten Manuscripts: How Do You Solve a Problem Like Theresa?" *African American Review* 40:4 (2006), 631–45.

Fouchard, Jean, *Les marrons de la liberté, in Regards sur le temps passé, Tome III* (Paris: Éditions de l'École, 1972).

Frailing, Kelly, and Harper, Dee Wood, Jr., "The Social Construction of Deviance, Conflict and the Criminalization of Midwives, New Orleans: 1940s and 1950s," *Deviant Behavior* 31:8 (2010), 729–55.

Freeman, Elizabeth, *Time Binds: Queer Temporalities, Queer Histories* (Durham: Duke University Press, 2010).

Fuentes, Marisa J., *Dispossessed Lives: Enslaved Women, Violence, and the Archive* (Philadelphia: University of Pennsylvania, 2016).

Gaffield, Julia, "Complexities of Imagining Haiti: A Study of National Constitutions, 1801–1807," *Journal of Social History* 41:1 (Fall 2007), 81–103.

Garber, Marjorie B., *Vested Interests: Cross Dressing & Cultural Anxiety* (London: Routledge, 1992).

Garraway, Doris, "Race, Reproduction and Family Romance in Moreau de Saint-Méry's 'Description ... de la partie francaise de l'isle Saint Domingue,'" *Eighteenth-Century Studies* 38:2 (2005), 227–46.

Tree of Liberty: Cultural Legacies of the Haitian Revolution in the Atlantic World (Charlottesville: University of Virginia Press, 2008).

Garrigus, David P., and Burnard, Trevor, *The Plantation Machine: Atlantic Capitalism in French Saint-Domingue and British Jamaica* (Philadelphia: University of Pennsylvania Press, 2016).

Gaspar, David Barr, and Geggus, David Patrick (eds.), *A Turbulent Time: The French Revolution and the Greater Caribbean* (Bloomington: Indiana University Press, 1997).

Gation, Jean-Frantz, *Un Pays Oubli: Scènes De Vie à Port-Au-Prince* (Bloomington IN: AuthorHouse, 2014).

Gautier, Arlette, "Les esclaves femmes aux Antilles françaises, 1635–1848," *Historical Reflections/Réflexions Historiques* 10:3 (1983), 409–33.

Les sœurs de solitude: La condition féminine dans l'esclavage aux Antilles du 17e et 19e siècle (Paris: Éditions Caribéennes, 1985).

Geggus, David P., "The Bois Caïman Ceremony," *The Journal of Caribbean History* 25:1 (1991), 41–57.

Haitian Revolutionary Studies (Bloomington: Indiana University Press, 2012).

"Slave Rebellion During the Age of Revolution," in Geert Oostindie and Wim Klooster (eds.), *Curaçao in the Age of Revolutions, 1795–1800* (Leiden, Netherlands: Brill, 2011), 23–56.

"On the Eve of the Haitian Revolution: Slave runaways in Saint Domingue in the year 1790," in Gad Heumann (ed.), *Out of the House of Bondage: Runaways, Resistance and Marronage in Africa and the New World* (London: Cass, 1986), 112–28.

Gehman, Mary, and Dennis, Lloyd, *The Free People of Color of New Orleans, An Introduction* (New Orleans: Dville Press, 1994).

Gehman, Mary, and Reis, Nancy, *Women and New Orleans: A History* (New Orleans, 1988).

Genovese, Elizabeth Fox, *Within the Plantation Household: Black and White Women of the Old South* (Chapel Hill: University of North Carolina Press, 1988).

Ghachem, Malick, *The Old Regime and the Haitian Revolution* (Cambridge: Cambridge University Press, 2012).

Ghosh, Amitav, *The Great Derangement: Climate Change and the Unthinkable*, Randy L. and Melvin R. Berlin Family Lectures (Chicago: University of Chicago Press, 2016).

Giles, Paul, *Transatlantic Insurrections: British Culture and the Formation of American Literature* (Philadelphia, University of Pennsylvania Press, 2014).
Gillman, Susan, "Pauline Hopkins and the Occult: African-American Revisions of Nineteenth-Century Sciences," *American Literary History* 8:1 (Spring 1996), 57–82.
Gilroy, Paul, *The Black Atlantic: Modernity and Double-Consciousness* (Cambridge, MA: Harvard University Press, 1995).
Girard, Philippe, "Rebelles with a Cause: Women in the Haitian War of Independence, 1802–1804," *Gender & History* 21:1 (2009), 60–85.
Glaude, Eddie, *Exodus! Religion, Race and Early Nineteenth Century Black America* (Chicago: University of Chicago Press, 2000).
Glave, Thomas (ed.), *Our Caribbean: A Gathering of Lesbian and Gay Writing from the Antilles* (Durham: Duke University Press, 2008).
Glissant, Édouard, "Avertissement" *Monsieur Toussaint* (version scénique) (Paris: Seuil, 1986).
La case du commandeur (Paris: Editions du Seuil, 1981).
Le discours antillais (Paris: Seuil, 1981).
Le quatrième siècle (Paris: Editions du Seuil, 1964).
Glover, Kaiama L., *Haiti Unbound: A Spiralist Challenge to the Postcolonial Canon* (Liverpool: Liverpool University Press).
"New Narratives of Haiti; or, How to Empathize with a Zombie," *Small Axe* 16, 3:39 (2012), 199–207.
Gomez, Michael, *Black Crescent: The Experience and Legacy of African Muslims in the Americas* (New York: Cambridge University Press, 2005).
Gonzalez, Johnhenry, "Defiant Haiti: Free-Soil Runaways, Ship Seizures and the Politics of Diplomatic Non-Recognition in the Early Nineteenth Century," *Slavery & Abolition* 36:1 (2015) 124–135.
Maroon Nation: A History of Revolutionary Haiti (New Haven: Yale University Press, 2019).
Goodfriend, Joyce D., "Burghers and Blacks: The Evolution of a Slave Society at New Amsterdam," *New York History* 59:2 (1978), 125–44.
"The Souls of New Amsterdam's African American Children," in Albert M. Rosenblatt and Julia C. Rosenblatt (eds.), *Opening Statements: Law, Jurisprudence, and the Legacy of Dutch New York* (Albany: SUNY Press, 2013), 27–35.
Who Should Rule at Home? Confronting the Elite in British New York City (Ithaca: Cornell University Press, 2017).
Gordon, Michelle Y., ""Midnight Scenes and Orgies": Public Narratives of Voodoo in New Orleans and Nineteenth-Century Discourses of White Supremacy," *American Quarterly* 64:4 (December 2012), 767–786.
Gottlieb, Karla, *The Mother of Us All: A History of Queen Nanny, Leader of the Windward Jamaican Maroons* (Trenton: Africa World Press, 2000).
Gould, Virginia (ed.), *Chained to the Rock of Adversity: To Be Free, Black, and Female in the Old South* (Athens: University of Georgia Press, 1998).

Goyal, Yogita, *Romance, Diaspora, and Black Atlantic Literature* (Cambridge: Cambridge University Press, 2010).

Gronniosaw, James Albert Ukawsaw, *A Narrative of the Most Remarkable Particulars in the Life of James Albert Ukawsaw Gronniosaw, an African Prince, as Related by Himself* (Bath: S. Southwick, 1774).

Groth, Michael E., *Slavery and Freedom in the Mid-Hudson Valley* (Albany: SUNY Press, 2017).

Gumbs, Alexis Pauline, "M/other Ourselves: A Black Queer Feminist Genealogy for Radical Mothering" in Alexis Pauline Gumbs, China Martens, and Mai'a Williams (eds.), *Revolutionary Mothering: Love on the Front Lines* (Toronto: PM Press, 2016).

"We Can Learn to Mother Ourselves: The Queer Survival of Black Feminism 1968–1996," unpublished Ph.D. dissertation, Duke University (2010).

Hahn, Steven, *The Political Worlds of Slavery and Freedom* (Cambridge, MA: Harvard University Press, 2009).

Halberstam, J., *In a Queer Time and Place: Transgender Bodies, Subcultural Lives* (New York: New York University Press, 2005).

Hall, Gwendolyn Midlo, *Africans in Colonial Louisiana: The Development of Afro-Creole Culture in the Eighteenth Century* (Baton Rouge: Louisiana State University Press, 1992).

Hammond, Charlotte, *Entangled Otherness: Cross-gender Fabrications in the Francophone Caribbean* (Liverpool: Liverpool University Press, 2019).

Haraway, Donna, "Ecce Homo, Ain't (Ar'n't) I a Woman, and Inappropriate/d Others: The Human in a Post-Humanist Landscape," in Judith Butler and Joan Scott (eds.), *Feminists Theorize the Political* (New York: Routledge, 1992), 86–100.

Harris, Leslie, *In the Shadow of Slavery: African Americans in New York City, 1626–1863* (Chicago: University of Chicago Press, 2004).

Harrison, Carol, *Rethinking Augustine's Early Theology: An Argument for Continuity* (New York: Oxford University Press, 2006).

Hartman, Saidiya, "The Belly of the World: A Note on Black Women's Labors," *Souls* 18:1 (2016), 166–173.

Scenes of Subjection: Terror, Slavery, and Self-Making in Nineteenth-Century America (New York: Oxford University Press, 1997).

"Venus in Two Acts," *Small Axe* 12:2 (2008), 1–14.

Wayward Lives, Beautiful Experiments: Intimate Histories of Riotous Black Girls, Troublesome Women and Queer Radicals (New York: Norton, 2019).

Hay, John, *Postapocalyptic Fantasies in Antebellum American Literature* (New York: Cambridge University Press, 2017).

Hayley, Sarah, *No Mercy Here: Gender, Punishment, and the Making of Jim Crow Modernity* (Chapel Hill: University of North Carolina Press, 2016).

Haynes, April R., *Riotous Flesh: Women, Physiology, and the Solitary Vice in Nineteenth-Century America* (Chicago: University of Chicago Press, 2015).

Hazzard-Donald, Katrina, *Mojo Workin': The Old African American Hoodoo System* (Urbana/Champaign: University of Illinois Press, 2012).

Hedrick, Joan D., *Harriet Beecher Stowe: A Life* (New York: Oxford University Press, 1995).

"'Peaceable Fruits': The Ministry of Harriet Beecher Stowe," *American Quarterly* 40:3 (1988), 307–32.

Hendler, Glenn, *Public Sentiments: Structures of Feeling in Nineteenth-Century American Literature* (Chapel Hill: University of North Carolina Press, 2001).

Heywood, Linda M., and Thornton, John K., *Central Africans, Atlantic Creoles, and the Foundation of the Americas, 1585–1600* (New York: Cambridge University Press, 2007).

The Portuguese, Kongo, and Ndongo and the Origins of Atlantic Creole Culture to 1607 (New York: Cambridge University Press, 2007).

Higginbotham, A. Leon, *In the Matter of Color: Race and the American Legal Process: The Colonial Period* (New York: Oxford University Press, 1980).

Higginbotham, Evelyn Brooks, *Righteous Discontent: The Women's Movement in the Black Baptist Church, 1880–1920* (Cambridge, MA: Harvard University Press, 2004).

Hine, Darlene C., and Wittenstein, Kate, "Female Slave Resistance: The Economics of Sex," *Western Journal of Black Studies* 3 (1979), 123–27.

Hinks, Peter, "'Perfectly Proper and Conciliating': Jean-Pierre Boyer, Freemasonry, and the Revolutionary Atlantic in Eastern Connecticut, 1800–1801," *Atlantic Studies* 16:3 (2019), 364–85.

Hodges, Graham Russell Gao, *Root and Branch: African Americans in New York and East Jersey, 1613–1863* (Durham: University of North Carolina Press, 2005).

Hodgson, Kate, "'*Pays-là chaviré*': Revolutionary Politics in Nineteenth-Century Haitian Creole Popular Music," *Small Axe* 20:1 (2016), 18–36.

Hoffman, Léon-François, "Histoire, mythe et idéologie: La cérémonie du Bois-Caïman," *Études créoles* 13 (1990), 9–34.

Homans, Margaret, "'Women of Color' Writers and Feminist Theory," *New Literary History* 25:1 (1994), 73–94.

Hoogbergen, Wim, "Marronage and Slave Rebellion in Surinamin Wolfgang Binder (ed.), *Slavery in the Americas* (Würzburg: Königshausen & Neumann, 1993), 165–95.

Horvitz, Deborah, "Hysteria and Trauma in Pauline Hopkins's *Of One Blood*; or, the Hidden Self," *African American Review* 33:2 (Summer 1999), 245–60.

Houlberg, Marilyn, "Ritual Cosmos of the Twins," in Patrick Bellegarde-Smith (ed.), *Fragments of Bone: Neo-African Religions in a New World* (Urbana: University of Illinois Press, 2005), 13–31.

Hudson, Peter James, *Bankers and Empire: How Wall Street Colonized the Caribbean* (Chicago: University of Chicago Press, 2017).

Hughes, David McDermott, *Energy without Conscience: Oil, Climate Change, and Complicity* (Durham: Duke University Press, 2017).

Humez, Jean H. (ed.), *Gifts of Power: The Writings of Rebecca Cox Jackson, Black Visionary, Skaker Eldress* (Amherst: University of Massachusett Press, 1981).

'Reading the Narrative of Sojourner Truth as a Collaborative Text," *Frontiers: A Journal of Women's Studies* 16 :1 (1996), 29–52.

Hoogbergen, Wim, "Maronnage and Slave Rebellion in Surinam," in Wolfgang Binder (ed.), *Slavery in the Americas* (Würzburg: Königshausen & Neumann, 1993), 165–95.

Hopkins, Pauline, "The Dark Races of the Twentieth Century," *Voice of the Negro*, February–July 1905.

"Frederick Douglass," *The Colored American*, December 1900, 131.

Of One Blood, in Henry Louis Gates (ed.), *The Magazine Novels of Pauline Hopkins*. (New York: Oxford University Press, The Schomburg Library of Nineteenth-Century Black Women Writers, 1988) 441–621.

"Toussaint Louverture," *The Colored American*, November 1900, 9–24.

Winona: A Tale of Negro Life in the South and Southwest, in Henry Louis Gates (ed.), *The Magazine Novels of Pauline Hopkins*. (New York: Oxford University Press, The Schomburg Library of Nineteenth-Century Black Women Writers, 1988).

Hugo, Victor, *Les Misérables*, Tome I (Chez Bombarda V) (Paris: Bibliothèque de la Pléiade, 1951).

Hunt, Alfred J., *Haiti's Influence on Antebellum America: Slumbering Volcano in the Caribbean* (Baton Rouge: Louisiana State University, 2006).

Hurston, Zora Neale, "Hoodoo in America," *Journal of American Folklore* 44 (1931), 318–417.

to Langston Hughes August 6, 1928; cited in Carla Kaplan, *Zora Neale Hurston: A Life in Letters* (New York: Anchor, 2003), 18.

Mules and Men (New York: Harper Collins, 2008). Reprint 1935.

"Reviewed Work: Voodoo in New Orleans by Robert Tallant," *The Journal of American Folklore* 60:238 (1947), 436–38.

Tell My Horse: Voodoo and Life in Haiti and Jamaica (New York: Harper Modern Classics, 2008).

Jackson, Zakiyyah Iman, "'Theorizing in a Void': Sublimity, Matter, and Physics in Black Feminist Poetics," *South Atlantic Quarterly* 117:3 (2018), 617–48.

Jacobs, Jaap, *The Colony of New Netherland: A Dutch Settlement in Seventeenth-Century America* (Ithaca: Cornell University Press, 2009).

Jacobs, Harriet (Linda Brent), *Incidents in the Life of a Slave Girl, Written by Herself*, ed. Lydia Maria Child 1861; ed. Jean Fagan Yellin (Cambridge, MA: Harvard University Press, 1987).

Jacqui, Alexander M., *Pedagogies of Crossing: Meditations on Feminism, Sexual Politics, Memory, and the Sacred* (Durham, NC: Duke University Press, 2005).

James, C.L.R *The Black Jacobins: Toussaint L'Ouverture and the San Domingo Revolution* (New York: Random House) Second edition, revised. 1989. Reprint 1963.

Jemisin, N. K., "The Effluent Engine," in *How Long 'til Black Future Month?* (London: Orbit Books, 2018), 75–112.

Jenson, Deborah, "The Writing of Disaster in Haiti: Signifying Cataclysm from Slave Revolution to Earthquake," in Martin Munro (ed.), *Haiti Rising: Haitian History, Culture and the Earthquake of 2010* (Liverpool: Liverpool University Press, 2010), 103–12.

Johnson, Bob, *Carbon Nation: Fossil Fuels in the Making of American Culture* (Culture America) (Lawrence: University Press of Kansas, 2014).

Mineral Rites: An Archaeology of the Fossil Economy (Baltimore: Johns Hopkins University Press, 2019).

Johnson, Jessica Marie, *Wicked Flesh: Black Women, Intimacy, and Freedom in the Atlantic World* (Philadelphia: University of Pennsylvania Press, 2019).

Johnson, Walter, *Soul by Soul* (Cambridge, MA: Harvard University Press, 1999).

Jones, Christopher F., "Petromyopia: Oil and the Energy Humanities," *Humanities* 5:2 (2016), 1–10.

Jones, Jamie L., "Beyond Oil: The Emergence of the Energy Humanities," *Resilience: A Journal of the Environmental Humanities* 6:2–3 (2019), 155–63.

Joseph, Celucien L., *Thinking in Public Faith, Secular Humanism, and Development in Jacques Roumain* (London: Pickwick Publications, 2017).

Joseph, Celucien L., and Cleophat, Nixon S., eds., *Vodou in the Haitian Experience: A Black Atlantic Perspective* (New York: Lexington, 2016).

Kammen, Michael, *Colonial New York: A History* (New York: Oxford University Press, 1996).

Kaplan, Carla, *Zora Neale Hurston: A Life in Letters* (New York: Anchor, 2003).

Kassanoff, Jennie, "'Fate Has Linked Us Together': Blood, Gender, and the Politics of Representation in Pauline *Hopkins's Of One Blood,"* in John Cullen Gruesser (ed.), *The Unruly Voice: Rediscovering Pauline Elizabeth Hopkins* (Champaign: University of Illinois Press, 1996), 158–81.

Kastor, Peter J., *The Nation's Crucible: The Louisiana Purchase and the Creation of America* (New Haven: Yale University Press, 2004).

Kastor, Peter J. and Weil, Francois (eds.), *Empires of the Imagination : Transatlantic Histories of the Louisiana Purchase* (Charlottesville: University of Virginia Press, 2009).

Keeling, Kara, *Queer Times, Black Futures* (Durham: Duke University Press, 2019).

Kimball, Chase Patterson, "A Case of Pseudocyesis Paused by 'Roots,'" *American Journal of Obstetrics and Gynecology* 107:5 (1970), 801–3.

King, Stewart, *Blue Coat or Powdered Wig: Free People of Color in Pre-Revolutionary Saint Domingue* (Athens: University of Georgia Press, 2007).

Kingsbury, Kate, and Chestnut, R. Andrew, "In Her Own Image: Slave Women and the Re-imagining of the Polish Black Madonna as Ezili Dantò, the Fierce Female Law of Haitian Vodou," *International Journal of Latin American Religions* 3 (2019), 212–32.

Klepp, Susan, *Revolutionary Conceptions: Women, Fertility and Family Limitation in America 1760–1820* (Williamsburg, VA: Omohundro Institute and University of North Carolina Press, 2009).

Klooster, Wim, *The Dutch Moment: War, Trade, and Settlement in the Seventeenth-Century Atlantic World* (Ithaca: Cornell University Press, 2016).

"Manumission in an Entrepôt: The Case for Curaçao" in Rosemary Brana-Shute and Randy J. Sparks (eds.), *Paths to Freedom: Manumission in the Atlantic World* (Columbia: University of South Carolina Press, 2009), 161–74.

Knight, Alisha R., "Furnace Blasts for the Tuskegee Wizard: Revisiting Pauline Elizabeth Hopkins, Booker T. Washington and the Colored American Magazine," *American Periodicals: A Journal of History and Criticism* 17:1 (2007), 41–64.

Kobayashi, Kazuo, "Indian Cotton Textiles in the Eighteenth Century Atlantic Economy," *Why India – Africa Relations Matter* (blog), Firoz Lalji Centre for Africa Online Series London School of Economics, June 2013.

Kopytoff, Barbara Klamon, "The Early Political Development of Jamaican Maroon Societies," *William and Mary Quarterly* 25 (1978), 287–307.

Lacoste, Mary, "'Quadroon Ball' Myths are Debunked by Historian," *Louisiana Weekly*, February 27, 2006.

Landers, Jane, *Black Society in Spanish Florida* (Urbana: University of Illinois Press, 1999).

Laplace, Pierre-Simon, *Essai philosophique sur les probabilités*, in *Théorie Analytique des Probabilités* (Paris: V Courcier, 1820). Translated by F.W. Truscott and F.L. Emory as *A Philosophical Essay on Probabilities* (New York: Dover, 1951).

Lazarus, Neil, *Nationalism and Cultural Practice in the Postcolonial World* (Cambridge: Cambridge University Press, 1999).

LeMenager, Stephanie, *Living Oil: Petroleum Culture in the American Century* (New York: Oxford University Press, 2014).

Lepore, Jill, *New York Burning: Liberty, Slavery, and Conspiracy in Eighteenth-Century Manhattan* (Doubleday: New York, 2007).

Levine, Robert S., *Dislocating Race and Nation: Episodes in Nineteenth-Century Literary Nationalism* (Chapel Hill: University of North Carolina Press, 2009).

Lewis, Adam, "A Traitor to His Brethren? John Brown Russwurm and the 'Liberia Herald,'" Special Issue: Black Periodical Studies, *American Periodicals* 25:2 (2015), 112–23.

Linthicum, Kent, Relford, Mikaela, and Johnson, Julia C., "Defining Energy in Nineteenth-Century Native American Literature," *Environmental Humanities* 1, 13:2 (November 2021), 372–90.

Livre, Eugène Aubin, *En Haïti: Planteurs d'autrefois, nègres d'aujourd'hui* (Paris: Librairie Armand Colin, 1910).

Locke, John, *An Essay Concerning Human Understanding*. Ed. P. Nidditch (Oxford: Clarendon Press, 1975).

Lockley, Timothy (ed.), *Maroon Communities in South Carolina: A Documentary Record* (Columbia, SC: University of South Carolina Press, 2009).

Lokken, Paul, "A Maroon Moment: Rebel Slaves in Early Seventeenth-Century Guatemala," *Slavery & Abolition* 25:3 (2004), 44–58.

Long, Carolyn Morrow, *A New Orleans Voudou Priestess: The Legend and Reality of Marie Laveau* (Gainesville: University of Florida Press, 2007).

Lopez, C. A., "Franklin and Mesmer: An Encounter," *Yale Journal of Biology and Medicine* 66:4 (1993), 325–31.

Lorde, Audre, "Black Women, Hatred and Anger," *Essence*, October 1983, 90–58.

"Eye to Eye," in *Sister Outsider* (Berkeley: Crossing Press, 2007), 145–75.

Luciano, Dana, "Passing Shadows: Melancholy Nationality and Black Publicity in Pauline E. Hopkins's *Of One Blood*," in David Eng and David Kazanjian (eds.), *Loss: The Psychic and Social Contexts of Melancholia* (Berkeley: University of California Press, 2003), 148–81.

Malm, Andreas, *Fossil Capital: The Rise of Steam Power and the Roots of Global Warming* (New York: Verso Books, 2016).

Malone, Christopher, *Between Freedom and Bondage: Race, Party, and Voting Rights in the Antebellum North* (New York: Routledge, 2012).

Mandziuk, Roseann M., and Fitch, Suzanne Pullon, "The Rhetorical Construction of Sojourner Truth," *Southern Communication Journal* 66.2 (2001), 120–38.

Manning, Susan, "Watching Dunham's Dances 1937–1945," in V. Clark and S. E. Johnson (eds.), *KAISO! Writings By and About Katherine Dunham* (University of Wisconsin Press, 2005), 256–266.

Maris-Wolf, Ted, "Hidden in Plain Sight: Maroon Life and Labor in Virginia's Dismal Swamp," *Slavery & Abolition: A Journal of Slave and Post-Slave Studies* 34:3 (2013), 446–64.

Martin, Joan M., "*Plaçage* and the Louisiana *Gens de Couleur Libre*: How Race and Sex Defined the Lifestyles of Free Women of Color," in Sybil Klein (ed.), *Creole: The History and Legacy of Louisiana's Free People of Color* (Baton Rouge: Louisiana State University Press, 2000), 57–70.

McAlister, Elizabeth M., "The Madonna of 115th Street Revisited: Vodou and Haitian Catholicism in the Age of Transnationalism," in R. Stephen Warner and Judith G. Witne (eds.), *Gatherings in Diaspora: Religious Communities and the New Imagination* (Philadelphia: Temple University Press, 1998), 123–60.

Rara! Vodou, Power, and Performance in Haiti and Its Diaspora (Berkeley: University of California Press, 2002).

McCarthy Brown, Karen, *Mama Lola: A Vodou Priestess in Brooklyn* (Berkeley: University of California Press, 2010).

"Afro-Caribbean Spirituality: A Haitian Case Study," in Claudine Michel and Patrick Bellegarde-Smith (eds.), *Vodou in Haitian Life and Culture: Invisible Powers* (New York: Palgrave Macmillan, 2006), 1–26.

McClellan, James, *Colonialism and Science: Saint Domingue and the Old Regime* (Chicago: University of Chicago Press, 1992).

McClellan, Michael E., "Counterrevolution in Concert: Music and Political Dissent in Revolutionary France," *The Music Quarterly* 80:1 (Spring 1996), 31–57.

McDowell, Deborah, "Recycling: Race, Gender and the Practice of Theory," in Robyn R. Warhol and Diane Price Herndl (eds.), *Feminisms: An Anthology of Literary Theory and Criticism* (New Brunswick: Rutgers University Press, 1997), 234–47.

McKittrick, Katherine, *Demonic Grounds: Black Women and Cartographies of Struggle* (Minneapolis: University of Minnesota Press, 2006).

"Mathematics Black Life," *The Black Scholar: Journal of Black Studies and Research* 44:2 (2014), 16–28.

McManus, Edgar J., *A History of Negro Slavery in New York* (Syracuse: Syracuse University Press, 1966).

McMichael, Francis Andrew, *Atlantic Loyalties: Americans in Spanish West Florida, 1785–1810* (Athens: University of Georgia Press, 2008).

McQueeney, Kenneth, "The City That Care Forgot: Apartheid Health Care, Racial Health Disparity, and Black Health Activism in New Orleans, 1718–2018," unpublished Ph.D. dissertation, Georgetown University (2020).

Médéric-Louis, Elie, "The Border Maroons of Saint Domingue: Le Maniel," in Richard Price (ed.), *Maroon Societies: Rebel Slave Communities in the Americas* (Baltimore: Johns Hopkins University Press, 1976), 135–42.

Merrill, Lisa, "'May She Read Liberty in Your Eyes?' Beecher, Boucicault and the Representation and Display of Antebellum Women's Racially Indeterminate Bodies," *Journal of Dramatic Theory and Criticism* 26:2 (2012), 127–44.

Mesmer, Franz Antoine, *Mémoire sur la découverte du magnétisme animale* (Geneva and Paris: Chez P. Fr. Didot le jeune, libraire-imprimeur de Monsieur, quai des Augustins, 1779).

Metral, Antoine, *Histoire de l'expédition des français, à Saint-Domingue, sous le consulat de Napoléon Bonaparte* (Paris: Imprime Chez Paul Renouard, 1825),

Michel, Claudine, "Vodou in Haiti: Way of Life and Mode of Survival," in Patrick Bellegarde-Smith and Claudine Michel (eds.), *Vodou in Haitian Life and Culture: Invisible Powers* (New York: Palgrave Macmillan, 2006), 98–110.

Michelle, Y. Gordon, "'Midnight Scenes and Orgies': Public Narratives of Voodoo in New Orleans and Nineteenth-Century Discourses of White Supremacy," *American Quarterly* 64:4 (December 2012): 767–86.

Miller, Paul B., "Boukman in Books: Tracing a Legendary Genealogy," in Hanétha Vété-Congolo (ed.), *The Caribbean Oral Tradition: Literature, Performance, and Practice* (London: Palgrave Macmillan, 2016): 167–91.

Milnel, Lorna, "Sex, Gender and the Right to Write: Patrick Chamoiseau and the Erotics of Colonialism," *Paragraph* 24:3 (November 2001), 59–75.

Mintz, Sidney W., "The Question of Caribbean Peasantries," *Caribbean Studies* 1 (1961), 31–4.

"Was the Plantation Slave a Proletarian?", *Review*, 2:1 (Summer 1978), 81–98.
Mintz, Sidney, and Hall, Douglas, "The Origins of the Jamaican Internal Marketing System," in Verene A. Shepherd and Hilary Beckles (eds.), *Caribbean Slavery in the Atlantic World: A Student Reader* (Kingston: University of West Indies Press, 2000), 758–73.
Mintz, Sidney, and Trouillot, Michel-Rolph, "The Social History of Haitian Vodou," in Donald J. Cosentino (ed.), *Sacred Arts of Haitian Vodou* (Los Angeles, 1995), 123–47.
Mitchell, Timothy, *Carbon Democracy: Political Power in the Age of Oil* (London: Verso, 2013).
Mohr, James C., "*Patterns of Abortion and the Response of American Physicians, 1790–1930*," in Judith Walzer Leavitt (ed.), *Women and Health in America* (Madison: University of Wisconsin Press, 1994).
Moody, Jocelyn, *Sentimental Confessions: Spiritual Narratives of Nineteenth-Century African American Women* (Athens: University of Georgia Press, 2003).
Morazon, Ronald, "Quadroon Balls in the Spanish Period," *Louisiana History* 14 (1973), 310–15.
Moreau de Saint-Méry, Louis-Élie, *Description topographique, physique, civile, politique et historique de la partie française de l'isle Saint-Domingue* (Philadelphia: Chez l'auteur, 1797).
Morgan, Jennifer L., *Laboring Women: Reproduction and Gender in New World Slavery* (Philadelphia: University of Pennsylvania Press, 2004).
Reckoning with Slavery: Gender, Kinship, and Capitalism in the Early Black Atlantic (Durham: Duke University Press, 2021).
Morgan, Winifred, "Gender-Related Difference in the Slave Narratives of Harriet Jacobs and Frederick Douglass," *American Studies* 35:2 (Fall 1994), 73–94.
Morh, J. C., "Patterns of Abortion and the Response of American Physicians, 1790–1930," in J. W. Leavitt (ed.), *Women and Health in America* (Madison: University of Wisconsin Press, 1994).
Morrow, Carolyn Long, *A New Orleans Voudou Priestess: The Legend and Reality of Marie Laveau* (Gainesville: University Press of Florida, 2006).
Mouhot, Jean-François, *Des esclaves énergétiques. Réflexions sur le changement climatique* (Seyssel: Champ Vallon, 2011).
"Past Connections and Present Similarities in Slave Ownership and Fossil Fuel Usage," in Dominic Boyer and Imre Szemann (eds.), *Energy Humanities: An Anthology* (Baltimore: Johns Hopkins University Press, 2017), 205–19.
Muñoz, José Esteban, *Cruising Utopia: The Then and There of Queer Futurity* (New York: New York University Press, 2009).
Munro, Martin, *Tropical Apocalypse: Haiti and the Caribbean End Times* (Charlottesville: University of Virginia Press, 2015).
Murphy, Kieran, "Magic and Mesmerism in Saint-Domingue" *Paroles gelées* 24:1 (2008), 31–48.
"The Occult Atlantic: Franklin, Mesmer, and the Haitian Roots of Modernity," in Elizabeth Maddock Dillon and Michael Drexler (eds.), *The Haitian*

Revolution and the Early United States: Histories, Textualities, Geographies (Philadelphia: University of Pennsylvania Press, 2016), 145–61.

Nantucket Historical Association, MS 15 box 8, folder 205.

Narcisse, Jasmine, *Mémoire de femmes* (Port-au-Prince: UNICEF, 1997).

Nesbitt, Nick, *Universal Emancipation: The Haitian Revolution and the Radical Enlightenment* (Charlottesville: University of Virginia Press, 2008).

Nevius, Marcus P., *City of Refuge: Slavery and* Petit Marronage *in the Great Dismal Swamp, 1763–1856* (Athens: University of Georgia Press, 2020).

Newman, Richard S., *Freedom's Prophet: Bishop Richard Allen, the AME Church, and the Black Founding Fathers* (New York: New York University Press, 2008).

Newton, Isaac, *Scholium Generale*, in *Philosophiae Naturalis Principia Mathematica* (London, 1687; Cambridge, 1713).

Nora, Pierre, and Kritzman, Lawrence D. (eds.), *Realms of Memory: The Construction of the French Past* (New York: Columbia University Press, 1998).

Nott, G. William, "Marie Laveau, Long High Priestess of Voudouism in New Orleans," *Times Picayune*, November 19, 1922, rpt. in Lyle Saxon, *Fabulous New Orleans* (Gretna: Pelican, 2004), 244–6.

Nwokocha, Eziaku, "The 'Queerness' of Ceremony," *Journal of Haitian Studies* 25:3 (Fall 2019), 71–91.

O'Brien, Colleen, 'Blacks in All Quarters of the Globe': Anti-Imperialism, Insurgent Cosmopolitanism, and International Labor in Pauline Hopkins's Literary Journalism," *American Quarterly* 26:2 (June 2009), 244–70.

Ogden, Emily, *Credulity: A Cultural History of U.S. Mesmerism* (Chicago: University of Chicago Press, 2018).

O'Rourke, Stephanie, *Art, Science, and the Body in Early Romanticism* (Cambridge: Cambridge University Press, 2021).

Osbey, Brenda Marie, "Why We Can't Talk to You about Voodoo," *Southern Literary Journal* 43:2 (2011), 1–11.

Otten, Thomas J., "Pauline Hopkins and the Hidden Self of Race," *ELH* 59 (1992): 227–56.

Owens, Deirdre Cooper, *Medical Bondage: Race, Gender, and the Origins of American Gynecology* (Athens: University of Georgia Press, 2017).

Painter, Nell Irvin, *Sojourner Truth: A Life, a Symbol* (Norton: New York, 1997).

"Sojourner Truth's Religion in Her Moment of Pentecostalism and Witchcraft," in Elizabeth Reis (ed.), *Spellbound: Women and Witchcraft in America* (New York: Rowman & Littlefield, 1998), 145–55.

Palmer, Vernon Valentine, "The Origins and Authors of the Code Noir," *Louisiana Law Review* LVI (1996), 363–40.

Parisi, David, *Archaeologies of Touch* (Minneapolis: University of Minnesota Press, 2018).

Paton, Diana, "Maternal Struggles and the Politics of Childlessness under Pronatalist Caribbean Slavery," *Slavery & Abolition* 38:2 (2017), 251–68.

"Witchcraft, Poison, Law, and Atlantic Slavery," *The William and Mary Quarterly* 69:2 (April 2012), 235–64.

Patterson, Martha, "Remaking the Minstrel: Pauline Hopkins's Peculiar Sam and the Post-Reconstruction Black Subject," in Carol P. Marsh-Lockett (ed.), *Black Women Playwrights: Visions on the American Stage* (New York and London: Garland Publications, 1999), 13–24.

Pavletich. JoAnn, "Pauline Hopkins and the Death of the Tragic Mulatta," *Callaloo* 38:3 (Summer 2015), 647–63.

Peabody, Sue, *There Are No Slaves in France: The Political Culture of Race and Slavery in the* Ancien Régime (Oxford: Oxford University Press, 2002).

Penningroth, Dylan C., *The Claims of Kinfolk: African American Property and Community in the Nineteenth-Century South* (Chapel Hill: University of North Carolina Press, 2003).

Pérez, Elizabeth, *Religion in the Kitchen: Cooking, Talking, and the Making of Black Atlantic Traditions* (New York: New York University Press, 2016).

Peterson, Carla L., *"Doers of the Word": African-American Women Speakers and Writers in the North (1830–1880)* (New Brunswick: Rutgers, 1998).

"Eccentric Bodies," in Michael Bennett and Vanessa D. Dickerson (eds.), *Recovering the Black Female Body: Self-Representation by African American Women* (New Brunswick: Rutgers University Press, 2001), ix–xvi.

"Unsettled Frontiers: Race, History, and Romance in Pauline Hopkins's 'Contending Forces,'" in Alison Booth (ed.), *Famous Last Words: Changes in Gender and Narrative Closure* (Charlottesville: University of Virginia Press, 1993), 177–99.

Phillips, Rasheedah, *Black Quantum Futurism: Theory and Practice* (Philadelphia: Afrofuturist Affair/House of Future Sciences Books, 2015).

Space-Time Collapse II: Community Futurisms, Vol. 1 (Philadelphia: Afrofuturist Affair/House of Future Sciences Books, 2020).

Pierce, Yolanda, *Hell without Fires: Slavery, Christianity, and the Antebellum Spiritual Narrative* (Gainesville: University Press of Florida, 2005).

Pierre, Nora, and Kritzman, Lawrence D. (eds.), *Realms of Memory: The Construction of the French Past* (New York: Columbia University Press, 1998).

Pierrot, Grégory, *The Black Avenger in Atlantic Culture* (Athens: University of Georgia Press, 2019).

Pinto, Samantha, *Difficult Diasporas: The Transnational Feminist Aesthetic of the Black Atlantic* (New York: New York University Press, 2013).

Polgar, Paul J., *Standard-Bearers of Equality: America's First Abolition Movement* (Chapel Hill: University of North Carolina Press, 2019).

Power-Greene, Ousmane K., *Against Wind and Tide: The African American Struggle against the Colonization Movement* (New York: New York University Press, 2014).

Prescod-Weinstein, Chanda, *The Disordered Cosmos* (New York: Boldtype Books, 2021).

Pressley-Sanon, Toni, "One Plus One Equals Three: Marasa Consciousness, the Lwa, and Three Stories," *Research in African Literatures* 44:3 (Fall 2013), 118–37.

Price, Hannibal, *De la réhabilitation de la race noire par la République d'Haïti* (Port-au-Prince: J. Verrollot, 1900).
Price, Richard, *The Guiana Maroons: A Historical and Biographical Introduction* (Baltimore: Johns Hopkins University Press, 1976).
Prose, Francine, *Marie Laveau* (New York: Berkley Books, 1977).
Racine, Karen, "Britannia's Bold Brother: British Cultural Influence in Haiti During the Reign of Henry Christophe (1811–1820)," *Journal of Caribbean History* 33:1–2 (1999), 125–45.
Ramsey, Kate, *The Spirits and the Law: Vodou and Power in Haiti* (Chicago: University of Chicago Press, 2014), 42–4.
Rapport des commissaires chargés par le Roi de l'examen du magnétisme animal (Imprimé par ordre du Roi: Paris, 1784).
Rauh Bethel, Elizabeth, "Images of Hayti: The Construction of an Afro-American *Lieu de Mémoire*" *Callaloo* 15:3 (Summer 1992), 827–41.
Rawick, George P., *The American Slave: A Composite Autobiography* (Westport, CT: Greenwood Press, 1972).
Reed, Ishmael, *The Last Days of Louisiana Red* (London and Funks Grove, Illinois: Dalkey Archive Press, 2000. Reprint 1974.
Mumbo-Jumbo (New York: Scribner, 1996). Reprint 1972.
Reinhardt, Mark, *Who Speaks for Margaret Garner?* (Minneapolis: University of Minnesota Press, 2010).
Rey, Terry, *The Priest and the Prophetess: Abbé Ouvière, Romaine Rivière, and the Revolutionary Atlantic World* (New York: Oxford University Press, 2017).
Rhodes, Barbara C., and Ramsey, Allen, "An Interview with Jewell Parker Rhodes," *African American Review* 29:4 (1995), 593–603.
Riello, Giorgio, and Parthasarathi, Prasannan (eds.), *The Spinning World: A Global History of Cotton Textiles, 1200–1850* (Oxford: Oxford University Press/Pasold Research Fund, Oxford, 2011).
Rigaud, Milo, *Secrets of Vodou* (San Francisco: City Lights Books, 1969).
Secrets of Voodoo, Robert B. Cross, trans. (San Francisco: City Lights Publisher, 2001).
Rigaud, Milo, Cross, Robert B., and Mennesson-Rigaud, Odette (eds.), *Secrets of Vodou* (New York: City Lights Publish, 1985).
Rink, Oliver A., *Holland on the Hudson: An Economic and Social History of Dutch New York* (Ithaca and London: Cornell University Press, 1986).
Roberts, Dorothy, *Killing the Black Body: Race, Reproduction, and the Meaning of Liberty* (New York: Knopf, 1997).
Roberts, Neil, *Freedom as Marronage* (Chicago: Chicago University Press, 2015).
Romney, Susanah Shaw, *New Netherland Connections: Intimate Networks and Atlantic Ties in Seventeenth-century America* (Chapel Hill: University of North Carolina Press, 2014).
Rothberg, Michael "Small Acts, Global Acts: Paul Gilroy's Transnationalism," *Found Object* 4 (Fall 1994), 17–26.

Rothman, Adam, *Slave Country: American Expansion and the Origins of the Deep South* (Cambridge, MA: Harvard University Press, 2005).

Rupert, Linda M., *Creolization and Contraband: Curaçao in the Early Modern Atlantic World* (Atlanta: University of Georgia Press, 2012).

Sala-Molins, Louis, *Dark Side of the Light: Slavery and the French Enlightenment* (Minneapolis: University of Minnesota Press, 2006).

Salt, Karen, "Haitian Soil for the Citizens' Soul," in Joni Adamson and Kimberly N. Ruffin (eds.), *American Studies, Ecocriticism, and Citizenship: Thinking and Acting in the Local and Global Commons* (New York: Routledge, 2013), 37–50.

Sánchez-Eppler, Karen, *Touching Liberty: Abolition, Feminism and the Politics of the Body* (Berkeley: University of California Press, 1993).

Saxon, Lyle, *Fabulous New Orleans* (Gretna: Pelican, 2004).

Sayers, Daniel O., *A Desolate Place for a Defiant People: The Archaeology of Maroons, Indigenous Americans, and Enslaved Laborers in the Great Dismal Swamp* (Gainesville: University of Florida Press, 2014).

Schindler, Melissa, "Home, or the Limits of the Black Atlantic," *Research in African Literatures* 45:3 (2014), 72–90.

Schneider-Mayerson, Matthew, *Peak Oil: Apocalyptic Environmentalism and Libertarian Political Culture* (Chicago: University of Chicago Press, 2015).

Schrager, Cynthia D., "Pauline Hopkins and William James: New Psychology and the Politics of Race," in Elizabeth Abel, Barbara Christian, and Helene Moglen (eds.), *Female Subjects in Black and White: Race, Psychoanalysis, Empiricism* (Berkeley: University of California Press, 1997), 307–29.

Schwartz, Marie Jenkins, *Birthing a Slave: Motherhood and Medicine in the Antebellum South* (Cambridge, MA: Harvard University Press, 2006).

Schwartz, Stuart B., "The 'Mocambo': Slave Resistance in Colonial Bahia," *Journal of Social History* 3:4 (1970), 313–33.

Slaves, Peasants, and Rebels Reconsidering Brazilian Slavery (Urbana: University of Illinois Press, 1995).

Scott, David, *Conscripts of Modernity: The Tragedy of Colonial Enlightenment* (Durham: Duke University Press, 2004).

Sepinwall, Alyssa Goldstein, *Haitian History, New Perspectives* (New York: Routledge, 2013).

Sharpe, Christina, *In the Wake: On Blackness and Being* (Durham, NC: Duke University Press, 2016).

Sheffer, Jolie A., *The Romance of Race: Incest, Miscegenation, and Multiculturalism in the United States, 1880–1930* (New Brunswick: Rutgers University Press, 2013).

Shilliam, Robbie, *The Black Pacific: Anti-Colonial Struggles and Oceanic Connections* (London: Bloomsbury, 2015).

Singer, Merrill, and Baer, Hans (eds.), *Critical Medical Anthropology*, 2nd ed. (New York: Routledge, 2018).

Smallwood, Stephanie E., *Saltwater Slavery: A Middle Passage from Africa to American Diaspora* (Cambridge, MA: Harvard University Press, 2008).

Smith, Valerie, *Not Just Race, Not Just Gender: Black Feminist Readings* (New York: Routledge University Press, 2013).

Snorton, C. Riley, *Black on Both Sides: A Racial History of Trans Identity* (Minneapolis: University of Minnesota Press, 2017).

Souffrant, Kantara, "Vodou Aesthetics, Feminism, and Queer Art in the Second-Generation Haitian Dyaspora," in Claudine Michel and Patrick Bellegarde-Smith (eds.), *Vodou in Haitian Life and Culture: Invisible Powers* (New York: Palgrave Macmillan, 2006), 35–65.

Southern, Eileen (ed.), *Nineteenth-Century American Musical Theater* (New York and London: Garland Publications, 1994).

Spector, Rachel E., *Cultural Diversity in Health and Illness,* 9th ed. (New York: Pearson, 2017).

Spillers, Hortense J., "Mama's Baby, Papa's Maybe: An American Grammar Book," in *Black, White and in Color: Essays on American Literature and Culture* (Chicago: University of Chicago Press, 2003), 203–229.

Spillers, Hortense J., Hartman, Saidiya, Griffin, Farah Jasmine, Eversley, Shelly, and Morgan, Jennifer L., "Whatcha Gonna Do?": Revisiting "Mama's Baby, Papa's Maybe: An American Grammar Book," *Women's Studies Quarterly* 35:1/2 (Spring–Summer, 2007), 299–309.

Stagenborg, Suzanne, and Skoczylas, Marie B., "Battles over Abortion and Reproductive Rights: Movement, Mobilization and Strategy," in Holly J. McCammon, Jo Reger, Rachel L. Einwohner, and Verta A. Taylor (eds.), *The Oxford Handbook of U.S. Women's Social Movement Activism* (New York: Oxford University Press, 2017), 214–31.

Stewart, Maria W., "An Address Delivered before the African-American Female Intelligence Society of America," in Marilyn Richardson (ed.), *Maria W. Stewart, America's First Black Woman Political Writer: Essays and Speeches* (Bloomington: Indiana University Press, 1987).

"An Address: Delivered before the African-American Female Intelligence Society of Boston," *Liberator* 2:17 (1832).

"Meditations: From the Pen of Mrs. Maria W. Stewart," *Black Self-Publishing*, accessed Oct. 23, 2021, https://www.americanantiquarian.org/blackpublishing/items/show/10732

Stoler, Ann Laura, *Along the Archival Grain: Epistemic Anxieties and Colonial Common Sense* (Princeton: Princeton University Press, 2008).

"Colonial Archives and the Arts of Governance," *Archival Science* 2:1 (March 2001), 87–109.

Stowe, Harriet Beecher, "The Libyan Sibyl," *Atlantic Monthly* XI:66 (April 1863), 473–81.

Uncle Tom's Cabin or Life Among the Lowly, ed. Kathryn Kish Sklar (New York: Library of America, 1982).

Strongman, Roberto, "The Afro-Diasporic Body in Haitian Vodou and the Transcending of Gendered Cartesian Corporeality," *Kunapipi* 30:2 (2008), 11–29.

Queering Black Atlantic Religions: Transcorporeality in Candomblé, Santería, and Vodou (Durham: Duke University Press, 2019).

Stuckey, Sterling, *Going through the Storm: The Influence of African American Art in History* (Oxford: Oxford University Press, 1994).

Sweeney, Shauna J., "Market Marronage: Fugitive Women and the Internal Marketing System in Jamaica 1781–1834," *William and Mary Quarterly* 76:2 (2019), 197–222.

Sweet, James H., "The Hidden Histories of African Lisbon," in Jorge Cañizares-Esguerra, Matt D. Childs, and James Sidbur (eds.), *The Black Urban Atlantic in the Age of the Slave Trade* (Philadelphia: University of Pennsylvania Press, 2016), 147–62.

Szeman, Imre and Boyer, Dominic (eds.), *Energy Humanities: An Anthology* (Baltimore: Johns Hopkins University Press, 2017).

"The Rise of Energy Humanities," *University Affairs* (March 2014).

Taketani, Etsuko, *The Black Pacific Narrative: Geographic Imaginings of Race and Empire between the World Wars* (Hanover: Dartmouth College Press, 2014).

Tallant, Robert, *The Voodoo Queen of New Orleans* (New Orleans: Pelican Publishing, 1984).

Tanaka, Shouhei, "Fossil Fuel Fiction and the Geologies of Race," *PMLA* 137:1 (2022), 36–51.

Tann, Jennifer "Steam and Sugar: The Diffusion of the Stationary Steam Engine to the Caribbean Sugar Industry 1770–1840," *History of Technology* 19 (1997), 63–84.

Tate, Claudia, *Domestic Allegories of Political Desire: The Black Heroine's Text at the Turn of the Century* (New York: Oxford University Press, 1992).

Psychoanalysis and Black Novels: Desire and Protocols of Race (New York: Oxford University Press, 1998).

Thompson, Alvin O., *Flight to Freedom: African Runaways and Maroons in the Americas* (Kingston: University of the West Indies Press, 2006).

"Gender and Marronage in the Caribbean," *Journal of Caribbean History* 39:2 (2005), 262–89.

Thompson, Joyce, and Varney Burst, Helen, *A History of Midwifery in the United States: The Midwife Said Fear Not* (New York: Springer Publishing, 2015).

Tinker, Keith, *The African Diaspora to the Bahamas* (Victoria, BC: Friesen Press, 2013).

Tinsley, Omise'eke Natasha, "Black Atlantic, Queer Atlantic: Queer Imaginings of the Middle Passage" *GLQ* 14:2–3 (2008), 191–215.

Ezili's Mirrors: Imagining Black Queer Genders (Durham: Duke University Press, 2018).

"Songs for Ezili: Vodou Epistemologies of (Trans) gender," *Feminist Studies*, 37:2 (2011), 417–36.

Thiefing Sugar: Eroticism between Women in Caribbean Literature (Durham: Duke University Press, 2010).

Tippet, Krista and Bellegarde-Smith, Patrick, "Speaking of Faith: Living Vodou," *Journal of Haitian Studies* 14:2 (Fall 2008), 144–56.

Trafton, Scott, *Egypt Land: Race and Nineteenth Century American Egyptomania* (Durham: Duke University Press, 2004).

Trouillot, Michel-Rolph, *Haiti: State against Nation* (New York: New York University Press, 1990).

Silencing the Past: Power and the Production of History (Boston: Beacon Press, 1995).

Turner, Mary, *Chattel Slaves to Wage Slaves: The Dynamics of Labour Bargaining in the Americas* (Bloomington: University of Indiana Press, 1995).

Turner, Sasha, "The Nameless and the Forgotten: Maternal Grief, Sacred Protection, and the Archive of Slavery, *Slavery & Abolition* 38:2 (2017), 232–250.

Ulysse, Gina Athena, *Why Haiti Needs New Narratives: A Post-Quake Chronicle* (Middletown, CT: Wesleyan University Press, 2015).

de Vaissière, Pierre, *Saint-Domingue (1629–1789): La société et la vie créoles sous l'ancien régime* (Paris: Perrin, 1909).

Van Zandt, Cynthia. *Brothers among Nations: The Pursuit of Intercultural Alliances in Early America, 1580–1660* (New York: Oxford University Press, 2008).

Verter, Bradford, "Interracial Festivity and Power in Antebellum New York: The Case of Pinkster," *Journal of Urban History* 28:4 (May 2002), 398–428.

Vivaldi, Jean-Marie, "Kant and Trouillot on the Unthinkability of the Haitian Revolution," *Souls: A Critical Journal of Black Politics, Culture, and Society* 15:3 (2013), 241–257.

Walcott, Derek, *Marie Laveau* (Bordeaux: Presses Universitaires de Bordeaux, 2019).

Ward, Martha, *Voodoo Queen: The Spirited Lives of Marie Laveau* (Jackson: University Press of Mississippi, 2004).

Washington, Margaret, "'From Motives of Delicacy': Sexuality and Morality in the Narratives of Sojourner Truth and Harriet Jacobs," *The Journal of African American History* 92:1 (2007).

Sojourner Truth's America (Champaign: University of Illinois Press, 2011).

Walcott, Derek, *Marie Laveau* (Bordeaux: Presses universitaires de Bordeaux, 2019).

John Watts to John Riddell. 17 November 1762, New York, in *Letter Book of John Watts: Merchant and Coucillor of New York: January 1, 1762–December 22, 1765* (New York Historical Society, 1928), 97.

Weaver, Jace, *The Red Atlantic: American Indigenes and the Making of the Modern World, 1000–1927* (Chapel Hill: University of North Carolina Press, 2014).

Weaver, Karol K., *Medical Revolutionaries: The Enslaved Healers of Eighteenth-Century Saint Domingue* (Champaign: University of Illinois Press, 2006).

"'She Crushed the Child's Fragile Skull': Disease, Infanticide, and Enslaved Women in Eighteenth-Century Saint-Domingue," *French Colonial History* 5 (2004), 93–109.

Weber, David J., *The Spanish Frontier in North America* (New Haven: Yale University Press, 1992).

Weheliye, Alexander G., Habeas Viscus: *Racializing Assemblages, Biopolitics, and Black Feminist Theories of the Human* (Durham: Duke University Press, 2014).

Wenzel, Jennifer "Taking Stock of Energy Humanities," *Reviews in Cultural Theory* 6:3 (2016), 30–33.

Wenzel, Jennifer, and Yaeger, Patricia (eds.), *Fueling Culture: 101 Words for Energy and Environment* (New York: Fordham University Press, 2017).

Wesner, Samantha, "Revolutionary Electricity in 1790: Shock, Consensus, and the Birth of a Political Metaphor," *British Journal for the History of Science* 54:3 (2021): 257–275.

West, Elizabeth, *African Spirituality in Black Women's Fiction: Threaded Visions of Memory, Community, Nature and Being* (New York: Lexington Books, 2011).

White, Ashli, *Encountering Revolution: Haiti and the Making of the Early Republic* (Baltimore: Johns Hopkins University Press, 2012).

White, Deborah Gray, *Ar'n't I a Woman?: Female Slaves in the South* (New York: Norton, 1999).

Gray Ar'n't I a Woman? (New York: Norton, 1999).

White, Shane, "Pinkster in Albany, 1803: A Contemporary Description," *New York History* 70 (1989), 191–9.

Somewhat More Independent: The End of Slavery in New York City, 1770–1810 (Athens: University of Georgia Press, 1995).

Wilder, Steven, *Ebony and Ivy* (London: Bloomsbury, 2013).

Wilder, Gary, *Freedom Time: Negritude, Decolonization, and the Future of the World* (Durham: Duke University Press, 2015).

Wilkie, Laurie, *The Archaeology of Mothering: An African-American Midwife's Tale* (New York: Routledge, 2003).

"Expelling Frogs and Binding Babies: Conception, Gestation and Birth in Nineteenth-Century African-American Midwifery," *World Archaeology* 45:2 (2013), 272–84.

Williams, Linda F., *Playing the Race Card: Melodramas of Black and White from Uncle Tom to O. J. Simpson* (Princeton: Princeton University Press, 2001).

Willson, Nicole, "Unmaking the tricolore: Catherine Flon, Material Testimony and Occluded Narratives of Female-Led Resistance in Haiti and the Haitian Dyaspora," *Slavery and Abolition* 41:1 (2020), 131–48.

Fanm Rebel, Levehulme Truste and the Institute for Black Atlantic Research at the University of Central Lancashire. http://famnrebel.com.

Wilson, Sheena, Carlson, Adam, and Szeman, Imre (eds.), *Petrocultures: Oil, Politics, Culture* (Montreal: McGill Queen's University Press, 2017).

Winch, Julie, *A Gentleman of Color: The Life of James Forten* (New York: Oxford University Press, 2003).

Wright, Nazera Sadiq, *Black Girlhood in the Nineteenth Century* (Champaign: University of Illinois Press, 2016).

Wynter, Sylvia, "Beyond Miranda's Meanings: Un/Silencing the 'Demonic Ground' of Caliban's 'Woman,'" in Carole Boyce Davies (ed.), *Out of the Kumbla: Caribbean Women and Literature* (Chicago: Africa World Press, 1990), 355–72.

"Unsettling the Coloniality of Being/Power/Truth/Freedom: Towards the Human, After Man, Its Overrepresentation – An Argument," *CR: The New Centennial Review* 3:3 (2003), 257–337.

Yaeger, Patricia "Editor's Column: Literature in the Ages of Wood, Tallow, Coal, Whale Oil, Gasoline, Atomic Power, and Other Energy Sources," *PMLA* 126:2 (2011), 305–10.

Ze Winters, Lisa, *The Mulatta Concubine: Terror, Intimacy, Freedom, and Desire in the Black Transatlantic* (Athens: Georgia University Press, 2016).

Index

Recent books in this series *(continued from page ii)*

185. ALEXANDER MENRISKY
Wild Abandon: American Literature and the Identity Politics of Ecology
184. HEIKE SCHAEFER
American Literature and Immediacy: Literary Innovation and the Emergence of Photography, Film, and Television
183. DALE M. BAUER
Nineteenth-Century American Women's Serial Novels
182. MARIANNE NOBLE
Rethinking Sympathy and Human Contact in Nineteenth-Century American Literature
181. ROB TURNER
Counterfeit Culture
180. KATE STANLEY
Practices of Surprise in American Literature after Emerson
179. JOHANNES VOELZ
The Poetics of Insecurity
178. JOHN HAY
Postapocalyptic Fantasies in Antebellum American Literature
177. PAUL JAUSSEN
Writing in Real Time
176. CINDY WEINSTEIN
Time, Tense, and American Literature
175. CODY MARS
Nineteenth-Century American Literature and the Long Civil War
174. STACEY MARGOLIS
Fictions of Mass Democracy in Nineteenth-Century America
173. PAUL DOWNES
Hobbes, Sovereignty, and Early American Literature
172. DAVID BERGMAN
Poetry of Disturbance
171. MARK NOBLE
American Poetic Materialism from Whitman to Stevens
170. JOANNA FREER
Thomas Pynchon and American Counterculture
169. DOMINIC MASTROIANNI
Politics and Skepticism in Antebellum American Literature
168. GAVIN JONES
Failure and the American Writer
167. LENA HILL
Visualizing Blackness and the Creation of the African American Literary Tradition
166. MICHAEL ZISER
Environmental Practice and Early American Literature

165. ANDREW HEBARD
The Poetics of Sovereignty in American Literature, 1885–1910

164. CHRISTOPHER FREEBURG
Melville and the Idea of Blackness

163. TIM ARMSTRONG
The Logic of Slavery

162. JUSTINE MURISON
The Politics of Anxiety in Nineteenth-Century American Literature

161. HSUAN L. HSU
Geography and the Production of Space in Nineteenth-Century American Literature

160. DORRI BEAM
Style, Gender, and Fantasy in Nineteenth Century American Women's Writing

159. YOGITA GOYAL
Romance, Diaspora, and Black Atlantic Literature

158. MICHAEL CLUNE
American Literature and the Free Market, 1945–2000

157. KERRY LARSON
Imagining Equality in Nineteenth-Century American Literature

156. LAWRENCE ROSENWALD
Multilingual America: Language and the Making of American Literature

155. ANITA PATTERSON
Race, American Literature, and Transnational Modernism

154. ELIZABETH RENKER
The Origins of American Literature Studies: An Institutional History

153. THEO DAVIS
Formalism, Experience, and the Making of American Literature in the Nineteenth Century

152. JOAN RICHARDSON
A Natural History of Pragmatism: The Fact of Feeling from Jonathan Edwards to Gertrude Stein

151. EZRA TAWIL
The Making of Racial Sentiment: Slavery and the Birth of the Frontier Romance

150. ARTHUR RISS
Race, Slavery, and Liberalism in Nineteenth-Century American Literature

149. JENNIFER ASHTON
From Modernism to Postmodernism: American Poetry and Theory in the Twentieth Century

148. MAURICE S. LEE
Slavery, Philosophy, and American Literature, 1830–1860

147. CINDY WEINSTEIN *Family, Kinship and Sympathy in Nineteenth-Century American Literature*

Printed in the USA
CPSIA information can be obtained
at www.ICGtesting.com
LVHW091556131223
766171LV00003B/24

9 781009 314244